Rationality Concepts in Environmental Valuation

# Hohenheimer Volkswirtschaftliche Schriften



Band 58

PETER LANG
Frankfurt am Main · Berlin · Bern · Bruxelles · New York · Oxford · Wien

Oliver Frör

# Rationality Concepts in Environmental Valuation

PETER LANG
Frankfurt am Main · Berlin · Bern · Bruxelles · New York · Oxford · Wien

**Bibliographic Information published by the Deutsche Nationalbibliothek**
The Deutsche Nationalbibliothek lists this publication in the Deutsche Nationalbibliografie; detailed bibliographic data is available in the internet at <http://www.d-nb.de>.

Zugl.: Hohenheim, Univ., Diss., 2007

D 100
ISSN 0721-3085
ISBN 978-3-631-57336-5



www.peterlang.de

# Acknowledgments

The work on this dissertation has been a long journey and during its course many people kept me company and have contributed to its completion in one way or many others. Most importantly, I would like to thank my first adviser and academic mentor Prof. Dr. Michael Ahlheim who guided my work in many late-evening discussions and provided invaluable advice and support. I am also indebted to my second adviser Prof. Dr. Dr. h.c. Franz Heidhues for numerous helpful discussions and important comments and suggestions on earlier versions of this dissertation. Special thanks shall be given to my former colleague at the institute Dr. Ulrike Lehr who was never too busy to listen to my unfinished thoughts and who was always available for comments, consultation and consolation, if needed. During the final phase of my work, my colleagues Isabell Benignus and Andreas Zahn took over some of my duties, for which I am very grateful.

I am especially indebted to my family and my parents who never ceased to believe in my ideas and supported my work with a lot of understanding despite the long evenings and weekends I had to take off for this purpose. The completion of this work is certainly as much a relief for them as it is for me.

I would also like to thank the team of the Sonderforschungsbereich 564, both in Germany and in Thailand, whose support in all matters of the research project was of great help. In Thailand, special thanks shall be given to my colleague and fellow researcher Nopasom Sinphurmsukskul, as well as to his assistant Ailada Yathuam. Without their ceaseless help the research project on which my dissertation is based would simply not have been possible. Finally, I would like to thank the Deutsche Forschungsgemeinschaft DFG who funded the research project and provided for this particularly rich and interesting time.

# Table of content

# i List of Figures

# ii List of Tables

# iii List of Abbreviations

| | |
|---|---|
| ABM | Averting Behavior Method |
| ABCM | Attribute Choice Modelling |
| cdf | cumulative (probability) distribution function |
| CEST | Cognitive-Experiential-Self Theory |
| CRT | Cognitive Reflection Test |
| CV | Hicksian Compensating Variation |
| CVM | Contingent Valuation Method |
| DBDC | Double-Bounded Dichotomous Choice |
| DC | Dichotomous Choice |
| EBA | Elimination By Aspects heuristic |
| EEG | Electro Encephalography |
| ELM | Elaboration Likelihood Model |
| EV | Hicksian Equivalent Variation |
| FI | Faith-in-Intuition |
| fMRI | functional Magnet Resonance Imaging |
| FtF | Face-to-Face |
| HPM | Hedonic Pricing Method |
| HSM | Heuristic Systematic Model |
| MBDC | Multiple-Bounded Dichotomous Choice |
| MRWW | Mae Rim Water Works |
| MS | Mail Survey |
| NFC | Need-for-Cognition |
| NOAA | National Oceanographic and Atmospheric Administration |
| OE | Open Ended format |
| PC | Payment Card |
| PET | Positron Emission Tomography |
| PVM | Participatory Valuation Method |
| REI | Rational Experiential Inventory |

| | |
|---|---|
| REI1 | *Intuitive-experiential* REI |
| REI2 | *Analytical-rational* REI |
| RUM | Random Utility Model |
| SBDC | Single-Bounded Dichotomous Choice |
| SFB | Collaborative Research Center (Sonderforschungsbereich) |
| TCM | Travel Cost Method |
| TDF | Task Dependent Factor |
| TDF1_DC | *Uncertain* TDF for the DC respondents |
| TDF2_DC | *Analytical* TDF for the DC respondents |
| TDF3_DC | *Elimination* TDF for the DC respondents |
| TDF1_PC | *Uncertain* TDF for the PC respondents |
| TDF2_PC | *Analytical* TDF for the PC respondents |
| TDF3_PC | *Equal* TDF for the PC respondents |
| TDF4_PC | *Elimination* TDF for the PC respondents |
| TIF | Task Independent Factor |
| TIF1 | *Intuitive-experiential* TIF |
| TIF2 | *Analytical-rational* TIF |
| TIF3 | *Cautious* TIF |
| TIF4 | *Cognitive miser* TIF |
| w. r. t. | with respect to |
| WTA | Willingness-to-Accept Compensation |
| WTP | Willingness-to-Pay |

# 1 Introduction

## 1.1 Motivation and scope

The use of economic valuation methods has become a regular instrument for the assessment of the desirability of public investment projects aiming at the improvement or conservation of environmental goods. This tendency reflects the understanding that the existence of environmental goods or amenities on the one hand has a beneficial impact on various functions in society as well as in the economy, however, on the other hand comes at the cost of forgone economic possibilities or at additional public funds to be expended for conservation or rehabilitation efforts. The improvement of urban air quality through a reduction of particle emissions or the conservation of natural areas by preventing industrial development, for example, require considerations regarding the expected benefits from such measures in relation to the costs to be incurred by society as a whole. Especially in times of increasing fiscal constraints it is of particular importance to possess reliable and transparent indicators for changes in society's well-being resulting from such environmental projects for the process of public policy decision making. The special properties of environmental goods, however, pose a number of problems for the measurement of benefits they generate for society.

In principle, environmental goods belong to the so called non-market goods. Examples of such environmental goods are the possibility to breathe clean air or the knowledge of the existence of certain biological plant and animal species. As in the latter example, environmental goods often have the character of pure public goods characterized by non-excludability and non-rivalry in consumption. For non-market goods a number of difficulties with respect to the assessment of the benefits they provide to society are generally encountered. The assessment of such benefits becomes relevant in case projects are carried out that go along with changes in the quality or the quantity of environmental goods provided. As is well known in the case of market commodities for which excludability from consumption holds the minimum benefit an individual derives from the consumption of such a good can easily be inferred from its price. An individual will only consume a commodity if the benefit from consuming it makes up at least for the costs of purchasing it, otherwise he would not be willing to pay the price asked. The absence of market prices for environmental commodities, therefore, constitutes the main difficulty of assessing the benefits derived from their existence or consumption, or, in case of a public project resulting in a change of their quantity or quality, of assessing the change of benefits to society.

The aim of assessing such social benefits from a project producing or conserving an environmental good is the determination of some figure that enables a comparison of derived benefits against incurred costs. Since costs are in general conveniently measured in monetary terms it has proven useful to develop methods that are able to express the economic value of the provision of environmental goods in monetary units, as well. From this perspective it is not surprising that methods for the valuation of environmental goods were developed much in analogy to established methods of market-good valuation where the price of the good serves as the measuring rod of benefits. The most prominent and most widely used method for the assessment of changes in social well-being due to changes in environmental goods is the Contingent Valuation Method (CVM) (see Mitchell and Carson 1989 for a detailed review of the method).

This method constitutes the particular focus of this study. In principle, it aims at the elicitation of households' utility changes from some envisaged or planned environmental project. Its main feature is the creation of a hypothetical market which functions in analogy to a real market in which economic agents are given the possibility to purchase the environmental good under consideration. The CVM is based on surveying a representative sample of a population that is likely to be affected by some proposed environmental change scenario. During these interviews which can be carried out as face-to-face, mail or telephone interviews the selected respondents are confronted with a specific scenario of a change in the level of an environmental good and, e. g. in the common case of an environmental improvement, are then asked a monetary amount they would be willing to pay for this improvement to actually take place. In the case of a proposed environmental deterioration respondents would either be asked their willingness-to-pay (WTP) to prevent the deterioration and stay in the present state or, alternatively, their willingness-to-accept-compensation (WTA) for their loss in well-being if the deterioration actually took place. The WTP (or in the case of a perceived deterioration the WTA) is generally interpreted as the economic agent's Hicksian Compensating Variation (CV), a theoretical measure for individual welfare changes which represents the maximum amount of money which could be extracted from an agent so that he is not worse off after the change than before.

The main advantage of the CVM, however, the simulation of a market for environmental goods where in fact no such market exists, is at the same time the method's weak point. Usually, in a market households reveal their preferences by making a purchase decision and paying for the purchased good in return. As stated above, it can therefore be inferred that the value they attribute to the purchased good is at least what they have paid for it. At the same time, in a market households usually participate actively, i. e. they play an active part in searching for commodities they desire, acquire information regarding their characteristics and also decide about the time when they purchase these goods. It is obvious, therefore, that the decision situation constructed in a CVM interview is quite different from what a respondent is used to when purchasing real commodities. He plays no active role in a CVM interview, rather he is approached by an interviewer at a time he cannot determine and has to make a decision whether or how much to pay for an environmental good that he usually has not much knowledge of. Furthermore, if he feels that he needs more information to make a well-reflected decision he cannot postpone that decision to some later point in time when he will have acquired sufficient information. The only consolation to a respondent in such a situation is that he is not required to give up money right away but that the cost of the project will come from some increased tax, higher prices or mandatory payments into a project-specific fund in the future. A WTP statement in a CVM interview, thus, resembles only moderately the situation of a purchase decision in a real market.

Still, despite these shortcomings of the simulated market of a CVM interview as compared to a real market this method emulates such a market situation as closely as possible. The alternatives to the CVM would be to use only the various existing indirect valuation methods like the travel cost and the hedonic pricing methods that rely on real market actions but can capture only the use values of environmental goods or to revert entirely to expert valuations. As shown in the literature, these alternatives are not attractive. However, the above mentioned distinctions between real and simulated markets need to be addressed when interpreting the WTP statements of CVM respondents as measures of their welfare changes resulting from a change in an environmental good. Certainly, one of the consequences is not to take the rationality of such WTP statements as given but to scrutinize in detail whether this necessary assumption of rationality is sufficiently fulfilled in practical CVM surveys. Numerous theoretical and practical studies regarding the Contingent Valuation Method have revealed that the rationality of respondents is indeed a problem and that reduced rationality leads to systematic distortions or biases of CVM results. Famous biases reflecting problems of reduced rationality are among others the embedding effect, anchoring effects, social desirability effects caused by the presence of an interviewer and framing effects, just to name a few.

In theory, a rational response to a WTP question in a CVM interview requires that the respondent correctly perceives the proposed environmental change scenario including the consequences for his personal life, that he evaluates this scenario in the light of his personal preferences and states a WTP that reflects his evaluation in monetary terms. Ideally, his WTP statement should neither depend on the format of the WTP elicitation question, i. e. whether he himself states an amount or has to accept or reject a proposed amount, nor on the payment vehicle or the interview form. In short, the WTP response should not depend on the specific question format or interview procedure, i. e. it should be procedure invariant. In practice, however, it was often demonstrated that such procedural invariance is elusive. So far, a number of explanations for an often perceived irrationality of CVM responses have been proposed. However, it appears that until to date little is known about the thought processes that actually take place inside a respondent's head when confronted with a WTP question for an environmental change scenario.

One key problem with this task for respondents in a CVM interview appears to be that they are confronted with a decision situation which is unfamiliar to them. Often, two aspects of unfamiliarity are encountered: first, respondents might be unfamiliar with the particular good to be valued, i. e. they might have heard of the good or of the issue but have no or only little personal experience with it. Unlike with market goods, where a respondent could always be given a sample product to try out its features and functionality and gain some initial experience to get an idea of its utility, this is usually not possible with environmental goods. As a consequence, the respondent remains in a state of uncertainty with respect to the utility that he will finally receive from the proposed environmental change. The expected change in utility will, therefore, be just an estimate or vague expectation. Second, respondents might be unfamiliar with the task of assigning a monetary value to something they have never associated with money before because they consider it a public property as is the case with most environmental goods and amenities. Decisions about the provision of environmental goods and trade-offs between environmental quality and other economic amenities are usually taken on a higher political or administrative level.

In practice, CVM respondents face an additional difficulty: in a typical CVM interview situation, at least in a face-to-face or telephone situation, the respondent will initially be given some considerable amount of information and is then expected to state his WTP within a very short period of time, usually on the spot. A typical CVM face-to-face interview usually lasts between 20 and 40 minutes, and during this little time the respondent needs to assimilate the given information, assess it in the light of his own personal context, generate an expectation of what this new proposed situation would feel like, put this in relation to the loss of possible market consumption resulting from the required payment and, finally, answer a number of personal questions. Typically, the time span between the point at which the respondent first realizes that most likely the interview will require him to make a monetary consideration and the point where he is actually asked to state his WTP is very short. Thus, little time is available to process rather large amounts of new information and to assess the consequences of an environmental change scenario in monetary terms. The cognitive burden in a CVM interview may be quite large and prevent the respondent from fully processing the given information, a situation which is expected to put bounds on the respondent's rationality of decision making.

In a world of perfect rationality where individuals are perceived as rather abstract utility maximizers with unlimited cognitive abilities these cognitive burdens play no role since once the scenario information is given the individual should be able to state a WTP conforming to his personal preferences. In the real world, however, CVM respondents will be limited by their personal cognitive capacities and capabilities and will, thus, find the task of evaluating the scenario information and stating a WTP rather stressful. Moreover, they perceive that the decision cannot be postponed, there will be no second chance to express their valuation for the proposed project. Respondents will search for ways of how to best deal with the complex decision situation in which they are required to consider and process large amounts of new and often unfamiliar information in a short period of time. Are respondents willing and able to consider all information provided thoroughly or will they rather try to find ways to avoid the employment of too many cognitive resources? What are respondents' strategies to cope with such situations?

Recent research on human information processing and reasoning conducted in the field of cognitive psychology suggests that while people certainly aim at making good and rational decisions they try to make these decisions using as little cognitive effort as possible. Some tasks and decisions require the use of analytical information processing characterized by sequential and logical reasoning, i. e. on conscious thought. For many other tasks, however, the individual has learned that good or at least satisfactory outcomes can be achieved also by limited information processing, e. g. by relying on analogies to previous situations or habits or by focusing only on parts of the available information and thereby neglecting information considered to be less important for the task at hand. Often, key words or "heuristic cues" contained in the formulation of the task or the information provided lead to an activation of a particular strategy to save cognitive resources. Such strategies are often termed "heuristics", i. e. rules of thumb using simplified information processing in order to circumvent cognitively effortful analytical thinking. For the individual, the importance of the task as well as the structure of the information provided decide on the cognitive processes to be employed to solve the task using the least amount of cognitive resources. Such behavior characterized by economizing on cognitive resources can, therefore, be characterized as "economy of cognition". Since this behavior will rarely achieve optimal outcomes the rationality concept underlying such limited information processing resulting in suboptimal decisions is termed "bounded rationality", contrasting the idealized world of perfect rationality.

Consequently, in the real world respondents in a CVM survey must be expected to often deviate from the perfectly rational response behavior mentioned above and to employ strategies of information processing to economize on their scarce cognitive resources, instead. Therefore, it appears necessary to perceive respondents as boundedly rational information processors and decision makers. This new perspective on the rationality of respondents allows to analyze and explain the often inconsistent results in CVM surveys. The focus on information processing opens a whole new toolbox for analyzing respondents' use of cognitive resources and, thus, may shed light on ways respondents become victims of their own reasoning and thinking. Biases in the CVM may be the result of respondents' strategies to cope with a complex decision situation by finding appropriate ways to limit the amount of cognitive resources to be invested into decision making. Respondents may use their real-world experience that it is often sufficient for achieving a satisfactory outcome to focus their attention on the most prominent features of a problem or to avoid particularly unwanted outcomes etc. It is reasonable to expect that people's ways of information processing and decision making in a CVM interview are influenced by those experiences of what usually works well. For the analysis of CVM responses, however, this perspective has not yet been adopted.

Furthermore, it is to be expected that people differ in their ways to process complex information and make decisions. Some respondents may be more capable to analyze large amounts of information and evaluate a complex environmental change scenario while others are struggling with such a task and feel overloaded. Such respondents will be more likely to employ strategies that make the decision problem simpler and, thus, may be more susceptible to exhibit the kinds of inconsistent response behavior often found in empirical CVM studies. Recent research in the field of cognitive psychology supports this expectation that individual differences exist in the kinds of information processing generally used. Therefore, the concept of bounded rationality to be adopted here is quite multi-faceted in contrast to the usual assumption of perfect rationality. It incorporates a continuum of people's information processing strategies when facing complex tasks ranging from rather analytical to various kinds of spontaneous and simplified reasoning. The adoption of the perspective of boundedly rational respondents in CVM surveys, therefore, promises an explanation of different kinds of response behavior that allows new insights into the problems of this method, i. e. where systematically distorted responses might be rooted. Such insights may help to improve the performance of the CVM.

The objective of this study, therefore, is to scrutinize respondents' rationality in CVM surveys by contrasting the concept of bounded rationality as the main paradigm of behavioral economics and cognitive psychology against the concept of perfect rationality. The particular interest of this scrutiny is to analyze the explanatory power of this alternative rationality concept for often found inconsistent response patterns in CVM surveys. Furthermore, it shall be attempted to derive recommendations of how the design and the administration of CVM surveys could be improved so that the decisions taken in the simulated market for environmental goods better resemble decisions taken in the real world.

## 1.2 Further outline of this study

The further outline of this study is organized as follows: After this introduction, chapter 2 will first present the theory of environmental economic valuation and the variety of empirical methods for measuring the value of environmental changes found in the literature. This chapter forms the basis of the study since it describes in detail how the assumption of perfect rationality in environmental valuation is implemented both in theory and in the empirical practice. The second part of chapter 2 will address the violations of perfect rationality and review the literature regarding the main empirical findings concerning the various procedural biases of the CVM. Some behavioral explanations for the occurrence of these biases and inconsistent response patterns will be discussed, as well. The last part of chapter 2 will focus on the open debate on preference uncertainty of respondents mentioned above. Various approaches of dealing with preference uncertainty and correcting benefit estimates for this uncertainty will be presented and discussed. In summary, chapter 2 presents the state-of-the-art of environmental valuation research.

The third chapter deals with the emergence of the concept of rationality in economics and offers a classification of alternative rationality concepts that have been developed more recently. First, the history of the rationality postulate starting from Adam Smith via Alfred Marshall will be briefly reviewed and the three rationality axioms forming the basis of the concept of instrumental or perfect rationality in neoclassical economics will be introduced. Subsequently, the behavioral norm of optimization forming the core of perfect rationality will be criticized in the light of experimental and empirical counter-evidence. Furthermore, extensions of the concept of perfect rationality leading to the overarching concept of bounded rationality will be explored. Some typical examples of decisions made under bounded rationality in contrast to perfect rationality will be highlighted, among others the famous conjunction fallacy first formulated by Daniel Kahneman and Amos Tversky and the phenomenon of preference reversals.

Since bounded rationality draws heavily on psychological insights on human information processing and decision making the main concepts of cognitive psychology will be addressed in so far as they are related to information processing in environmental valuation. Finally, specific models of dual processes of reasoning reflecting the concept of an "economy of cognition" will be discussed and their relation to information processing in environmental valuation will be highlighted. These models assume information processing as a problem of allocating scarce cognitive resources to a variety of competing tasks. According to the theories underlying the dual-process models, during the evolution of the human brain two fundamental types of information processing have emerged, one fast and effortless suited for routine and repetitive tasks and one slow and more effortful but particularly suited to deal with novel situations. It is assumed that in a situation of scarce cognitive resources the human brain allocates each of these two types of processing to the competing tasks at hand. These cognitive psychological models shall form the conceptual basis for the development of an empirical survey instrument for the analysis of bounded rationality in environmental economic valuation surveys in chapter 4.

Chapter 4 will then build on this literature review and the connection established between psychological models of reasoning and response behavior in CVM surveys in order to gain a more realistic perspective of the way respondents process complex information in CVM interviews where both time and the available information are limited in principle. As described in the preceding section, two aspects are of particular importance in this respect and shall be analyzed more thoroughly in this study: (1) how respondents deal with preference uncertainty, and (2) whether and to what extent respondents make use of an "economy of cognition" and, consequently, base their decisions in CVM interviews on simplifying heuristics instead of thorough analytical reasoning.

In the first part of chapter 4 these two aspects will first be considered from a theoretical point of view. Regarding preference uncertainty, a modification of the traditional neoclassical model of preference orderings, fuzzy preferences, shall be taken up. This concept will be used to describe the uncertainty over preferences regarding environmental goods. Unfortunately, the practicability of this approach will turn out to be rather limited since it is technically not possible to derive proper value functions for environmental goods like e. g. the Hicksian Compensating Variation necessary for a quantitative representation of environmental values. Therefore, preference uncertainty will have to be analyzed in a more indirect way. Subsequently, information processing in CVM interviews will be addressed specifically from the perspective of bounded rationality and the limitation of respondents' cognitive capacities in the real world. From this discussion a specific set of research questions for the following empirical example shall be developed. The research approach for analyzing the occurrence and the consequences of boundedly rational information processing in CVM surveys is based on the dual-process models of reasoning developed by Epstein et al. (1996). On the basis of their Rational Experiential Inventory (REI) two empirical instruments for detecting, classifying and measuring the use of various types of information processing will be developed to be employed in an empirical CVM study in northern Thailand.

In the second part of chapter 4 these instruments will then be used in an empirical CVM study regarding the social benefits of an improvement of household tap water quality in northern Thailand. The purpose of this empirical application is to test the usefulness of the developed instruments for the analysis of boundedly rational information processing and for the development of recommendations for an improvement of CVM survey designs. The empirical study underlying this test was conducted as part of a subproject within the international collaborative research group (SFB 564) funded by the German Science Foundation (DFG).

Chapter 5 concludes the study with a summary and discussion of the possibilities and limitations of the concept of bounded rationality for a better and deeper understanding of CVM response behavior and for an improvement of CVM studies as a method for the economic valuation of environmental changes.

# 2 Environmental valuation

## 2.1 Theory and practice of environmental valuation: state-of-the-art

### 2.1.1 Environmental valuation - why?

Every economist who has ever mentioned his interest in the valuation of environmental goods to "normal" people has certainly been confronted one time or another with a notion ranging from disgust to simple lack of sympathy in return. The very concept of putting a value, let alone a monetary one, on the environment runs against the basic feelings of a considerable part of the population and is commonly directly associated with the well-known cold-bloodedness of the economist profession. Often, however, some common ground can be found after heated discussions and the view toward economists' character might have been sustainably altered. In reality, it turns out that the valuation of the environment occurs quite often and naturally most of the time without the majority of the population taking serious offense. When roads are built, nature reserves are established, forestry and agricultural management is regulated or simply consumption decisions are made the associated consequences to nature and the environment are implicitly or sometimes explicitly taken into account and are, more or less, considered in relation to the decision to be made. Thus, valuation of the environment is a normal component of private and public decision making. It is not the task and interest of economists to downgrade the importance of nature but to make such valuations more explicit and transparent. This chapter will describe in detail the theoretical background of environmental valuation and will lay out how such a task can be performed in practice.

As just mentioned, the environment enters decisions in many aspects of private and public life. For example, public projects carried out by government authorities are often explicitly or implicitly associated with consequences for the environment. Such consequences can be desired and positive, e. g. when a nature preserve is established or a wetland area is rehabilitated, or they may be negative as in the case of new highway construction cutting through an environmentally sensitive area. In a democratic society it is government's constitutional task to allocate scarce public funds to those activities that enhance the well-being of society so that only those activities should be undertaken for which public benefits at least outweigh the costs (cf. Hanusch 1994: 3). Thus, whenever beneficial effects for the environment are to be achieved by such projects it needs to be determined whether the resulting increase in society's well-being is worth the investment of public money. Similarly, whenever negative environmental consequences are to be expected from some improvement of infrastructure, for instance, it needs to be determined whether the associated loss in well-being does not outweigh the convenience created by the project. Such benefit-cost considerations call for the use of compatible units of measurement in order to allow direct comparisons of created benefits versus incurred costs. The translation of generated utility into monetary units is, therefore, one of the tasks of economic valuation of environmental changes.

The considerations in the preceding paragraph highlight the anthropocentric view of value that is inherent in the benefit-cost approach of economic valuation. Commodities or environmental amenities derive their value to society from the value they create for human beings. This anthropocentric view precludes the concept of an intrinsic value of nature as often propagated by environmentalists according to which nature in itself has a value regardless of the value human beings attribute to it (cf. Madariaga and McConnell 1987: 938). However, it is obvious that intrinsic value is just as well that: a value attributed to nature by human beings so it fits quite well into the anthropocentric framework of economics and a classification of values exists that incorporates all these notions of value in a consistent and operational way. It is obvious that the term "value" cannot be reduced to the value of direct consumption or the value of nature as a resource, e. g. wood in a forest, in production. Certainly, environmental goods carry value for human beings because they can directly consume them, e. g. breathing air, relaxing in natural outdoor activities or watching animals and plants in their natural environments. Additionally, many environmental goods like e. g. natural forests or wetlands contribute indirectly to human well-being through the environmental functions they perform. Forest ecosystems regulate the regional climate, absorb and transform pollutants, regulate the water cycle etc. In mountainous regions forests stabilize the mountain slopes which is a prerequisite for (permanent) human settlements in the valley bottoms. Wetlands regulate the water flow of rivers and can buffer periods of high rainfall and drought with all their effects on agriculture and human settlements (cf. Loreau et al. 2002, Matthews et al. 2002, Ramirez et al. 2002, Fromm 2000, Costanza et al. 1998, Barbier 1994).

Apart from these common functions of environmental amenities that enter the utility functions of human beings either through direct consumption or indirectly through ecosystem services provided, human beings were found to care for the environment also for other reasons. Although a particular environmental amenity may not be consumed, e. g. visited, at present, an individual might value the option of doing so in the future giving rise to the concept of option value (cf. Weisbrod 1964). An option, however, whose use in the future remains vague like e. g. the use of a biodiversity hotspot region for the development of pharmaceuticals in the future is commonly distinguished from the described "pure" option value as "quasi" option value (cf. Arrow and Fisher 1974). In addition to this option value, Krutilla (1967) pointed to the existence value describing the utility derived from the pure knowledge of the existence of environmental goods, e. g. certain plant and animal species or entire ecosystems, that an individual will most likely never see himself but nevertheless perceives as important to preserve. Krutilla also introduced the bequest value referring to the utility one derives from leaving an intact environment, or at least a particular amenity, to future generations. Since these additional categories of value are clearly components of the well-being of society they must be considered as elements of the benefit-cost framework mentioned above.

Therefore, in the environmental economics literature it is now common to use the concept of total economic value that considers all kinds of ways in which human beings derive value from an environmental good (cf. Nunes 2002: 4). This concept differentiates on a first level between use values and non-use values. Use values comprise the value derived from direct consumption (direct use values) and from ecosystem functions (indirect use values) as well as the "pure" option value. Non-use values that are also often termed passive use values comprise the existence value and the bequest value described above. Additionally, the "quasi" option value is usually classified as a non-use value, however, it might as well be considered a use value. Since this distinction is of no practical importance it shall not be elaborated on here. It can be argued that within the concept of total economic value the intrinsic values mentioned above are to some extent subsumed in Krutilla's existence value since it comes closest to the environment having a value regardless of its use to man. When, however, intrinsic values imply a complete lack of substitutability between environmental and produced goods such values cannot be dealt with in an economic approach.

**Figure 2-1:** The concept of total economic value

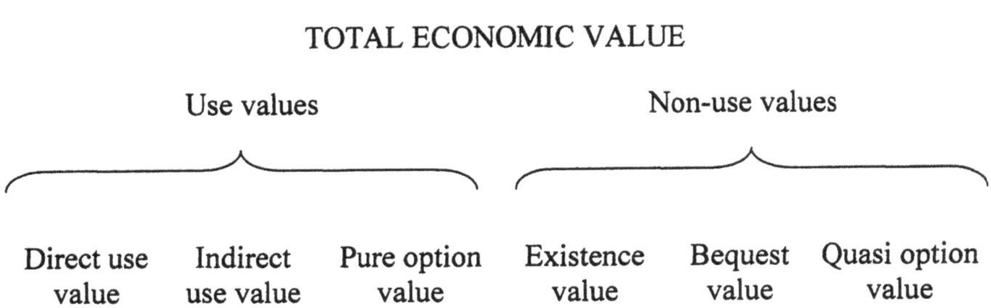


The concept of total economic value with its distinction in use values and non-use values has important implications for the practical methods of environmental valuation. Before the presentation and discussion of these methods, however, the theory of environmental valuation and benefit-cost analysis in neoclassical economics shall be dealt with in the following section in order to derive theoretically consistent measures of value that can then form the reference base for the methods of practical assessment.

### 2.1.2 Environmental valuation and benefit-cost analysis in neoclassical economics

The following section 2.1.2 is largely based on Ahlheim (2003) and Stephan and Ahlheim (1998). For the presentation of the theoretical foundations of environmental valuation let's for simplicity consider a public project aiming at some improvement of the state of the environment. Typically, such a project leads to a number of effects that are important from an economic perspective and, therefore, must be dealt with here since they affect the well-being of the households considered. The desired effect of such a project is the improvement of the environment which is denoted as $z^k$ here, where $k \in \{0, 1\}$. Specifically, $z^0$ stands for the state of the environment before the project, i. e. the initial situation, and $z^1$ refers to the state after the project has been carried out. Since the financing of such a project usually requires government to raise additional funds, e. g. in the form of increased taxes, it is plausible to assume a change in the households' income levels when the project is implemented. Thus, $I_h^k$ denotes household h's income in environmental state k. Additionally, it must be expected that the consumption of market goods $x_h = \{x_{h,1}, x_{h,2}, \ldots, x_{h,N}\}$ changes since the improvement of the environment might lead to more consumption of some goods, e. g. hiking boots, and less of others, e. g. computer games, which has effects on the relative prices of market goods. Let, therefore, $p_n^k$ denote the market price of commodity n in environmental state k.

In cost-benefit analysis we are generally interested in the change of welfare, i. e. well-being, of society resulting from such a public project. We, therefore, aim at finding an indicator from which we can unambiguously tell whether society is better or worse off after the project implementation and financing. In democratic states, to which this theoretical approach refers, society is generally perceived as consisting of individual persons whom economics usually classifies in households since members of one household are for simplicity assumed to make consumption decisions with a joint budget. Thus, social welfare can be expressed formally as

$$W = w\left(U_1, U_2, \ldots, U_H\right), \qquad \text{where } \partial w / \partial U_h \geq 0 \quad \forall h. \tag{2-1}$$

Therefore, the problem of the assessment of the welfare change resulting from the considered project can be divided into a first step of determining the changes in utility of each household in society, the so-called identification problem, and a second step of aggregating all individual household changes in order to determine the overall welfare change, the so-called aggregation problem. Each of these problems will be dealt with in turn.

Let us consider the household's direct utility function that depends on the consumption of market commodities, the vector $x_h$, and the state of the environment z so that

$$U_h = u_h(x_h, z). \tag{2-2}$$

It is assumed that the direct utility function is monotonically increasing in z so that environmental quality is indeed considered as a good. The change in utility of the household due to the implementation of the project can then be defined as the utility difference between the initial situation $k = 0$ and the situation $k = 1$ after the implementation of the project

$$\Delta U_h^{01} = U_h^1 - U_h^0 = u_h(x_h^1, z^1) - u_h(x_h^0, z^0). \tag{2-3}$$

However, as mentioned above, along with an implementation of the environmental project and its financing by government, the consumption of market commodities must be expected to change due to changes in incomes, for instance. Therefore, it is more convenient to employ the indirect utility function, instead, which depends on prices, incomes and the state of the environment. The indirect utility function results from the maximization of the direct utility function subject to a given budget, prices and state of the environment. It symbolizes the maximum level of utility that can be attained given these parameters.

$$v_h(p, z^k, I_h) = \max_x u(x_h, z) \quad \text{s.t.} \quad I_h = p \cdot x_h; \; z = z^k$$

$$\text{i. e.} \quad v_h(p, z^k, I_h) = u(x^*(p, z^k, I_h), z^k). \tag{2-4}$$

The expression $x^*(p, z^k, I_h)$ represents the Marshallian demand functions resulting from the described utility maximization problem of the household, i. e. the optimal consumption quantities of x given p, $z^k$ and $I_h$. With this definition of the indirect utility function the utility difference stated in 2-3 can now be written as

$$\Delta U_h^{01} = v_h(p^1, z^1, I_h^1) - v_h(p^0, z^0, I_h^0). \tag{2-5}$$

However, it is well known that neither the direct nor the indirect utility functions are observable due to their ordinal nature. It is, therefore, necessary to define a measure of individual welfare $\Delta_h$ that is based on the theoretical expression in 2-5 and that is in principle accessible to observation and can be computed using econometric techniques. In general, such a welfare measure needs to satisfy the so-called indicator condition according to which the measure must be able to unambiguously indicate whether an individual household is better or worse off after a change from situations k = 0 to k = 1, i. e.

$$\Delta_h^{01} = \omega_h\left(U_h^0, U_h^1\right) \overset{>}{\underset{<}{=}} 0 \quad \Leftrightarrow \quad U_h^1 \overset{>}{\underset{<}{=}} U_h^0 . \tag{2-6}$$

In order to derive a welfare measure both satisfying the indicator condition and being observable in principle the concept of the expenditure function will be employed. Taking into account the existence of environmental goods the expenditure function defines the minimum expenditure that is necessary for a household to attain a given utility level U when prices p and the environmental state z are given, i. e.

$$e\left(p, z, U\right) = \min_{x \in \mathrm{U}(U)} p \cdot x, \qquad \mathrm{U}(U) = \left\{x \,|\, u(x,z) \geq U\right\}. \tag{2-7}$$

As desired, the expenditure function is strictly monotonically increasing in the utility level U since when prices and the state of the environment are given any increase in U is necessarily accompanied by an increase in expenditure for market goods creating this utility. Due to this strict association of money and utility level the expenditure function is termed "money-metric utility function". Since we are interested in measuring utility changes the expenditure function can be used to define utility differences in monetary terms as the difference between two expenditures necessary to attain two different and predefined levels of utility when prices and environmental state are kept constant. These utility difference measures are based on John Hicks (cf. Hicks 1939, 1942). In the literature two such measures feature very prominently differing only in the chosen level of prices and environmental state to be kept constant (cf. Stephan and Ahlheim 1996: 172f). In the situation under consideration where there is an initial state, i. e. before the project, and a final state, i. e. after project implementation, it is plausible to either choose the prices and environmental state at the initial situation or at the final situations as reference levels of the expenditure functions for the welfare measure. Choosing the initial level as reference gives rise to a welfare measure called Hicksian Equivalent Variation defined as

$$EV_h^{01} = e_h\left(p^0, z^0, U_h^1\right) - e_h\left(p^0, z^0, U_h^0\right)$$
$$= e_h\left(p^0, z^0, U_h^1\right) - I_h^0 , \qquad (2\text{-}8)$$

since the expenditure necessary to attain $U_h^0$ at prices $p^0$ and environmental state $z^0$ equals just the income of household h in the initial situation $I_h^0$. As a monetary expression for the difference in utility between an initial situation and a final situation $EV_h^{01}$ can be interpreted in two directions. On the one hand $EV_h^{01}$ denotes the minimum amount of money that must be given to household h for his utility to remain unchanged if he were to forego an environmental project that would increase his level of utility from $U_h^0$ to $U_h^1$. In this case $EV_h^{01}$ is commonly interpreted as willingness to accept compensation (WTA). On the other hand $EV_h^{01}$ denotes the maximum amount of money that could be extracted from household h if the implementation of a project that would decrease his level of utility from $U_h^0$ to $U_h^1$ were prevented. In this case $EV_h^{01}$ is commonly interpreted as willingness to pay (WTP). In the first case, an environmental improvement, $EV_h^{01}$ would be positive whereas in the second case, an environmental deterioration, $EV_h^{01}$ would be negative. In case the final situation, i. e. $k = 1$, is chosen as reference level in the expenditure function, the Hicksian Compensating Variation is obtained which can be defined formally as

$$CV_h^{01} = e_h\left(p^1, z^1, U_h^1\right) - e_h\left(p^1, z^1, U_h^0\right)$$
$$= I_h^1 - e_h\left(p^1, z^1, U_h^0\right). \qquad (2\text{-}9)$$

Again, the expenditure necessary to attain utility level $U_h^1$ given $p^1$ and $z^1$, $e_h\left(p^1, z^1, U_h^1\right)$, equals just household h's income in the final situation $I_h^1$. In analogy to the Equivalent Variation, the Compensating Variation can assume two states: in case it assumes a negative value, i. e. $CV_h^{01} < 0$, it denotes the minimum amount of money that must be given to the household to compensate him for a loss in utility from $U_h^0$ to $U_h^1$, commonly interpreted as WTA. In case $CV_h^{01} > 0$, however, the Compensating Variation stands for the maximum amount of money that could be extracted from the household and still leave him as well off as before if the environmental project were to be implemented. This latter case where $CV_h^{01}$ is commonly interpreted as WTP is most frequently used in environmental valuation since it describes the natural situation where a household is asked to give up some monetary equivalent for an environmental improvement to occur. Thus, in the following, only the Compensating Variation will be used as a measure of utility differences resulting from environmental changes.

In its formulation in 2-9 $CV_h^{01}$ can still not be computed since while the household income $I_h^1$ is observable the expenditure term $e_h\left(p^1, z^1, U_h^0\right)$ refers to a hypothetical situation since it denotes expenditure necessary to attain the initial level of utility under the final situation of prices and environmental state. Such an expenditure is entirely abstract and can, therefore, not be elicited from the household. In order to render the expression for $CV_h^{01}$ observable it is necessary to transform it into three separate utility differences by adding zeros to equation 2-9 (cf. Stephan and Ahlheim 1996: 175f) yielding

$$CV_h^{01} = e_h\left(p^1, z^1, U_h^1\right) - e_h\left(p^0, z^0, U_h^0\right) + e_h\left(p^0, z^0, U_h^0\right) - e_h\left(p^1, z^0, U_h^0\right) + e_h\left(p^1, z^0, U_h^0\right) - e_h\left(p^1, z^1, U_h^0\right). \qquad (2\text{-}10)$$

The notation of the augmented expression in 2-10 can be simplified to

$$CV_h^{01} = CVI_h^{01} + CVp_h^{01} + CVz_h^{01}, \qquad (2\text{-}11)$$

i. e. the Compensating Variation for the utility change from $U_h^0$ to $U_h^1$ can be separated into three expressions referring respectively to the change in utility from changes in household incomes, $CVI_h^{01}$, the change in utility from the changes in prices, $CVp_h^{01}$, and the change in utility from the change in the environmental state, $CVz_h^{01}$. The advantage of such a separation into single utility changes is that there exist methods of measurement for each of them. $CVI_h^{01}$ simply refers to the change in the income level of the household, i. e. $I_h^1$ - $I_h^0$. This income change is in principle observable from household census data. For the computation of $CVp_h^{01}$ there exists a well-established procedure of measurement (cf. Vartia 1983) which is based on an approximation procedure aiming at computing an integral over Hicksian demand functions when only the respective Marshallian demand functions are known (cf. Ahlheim and Wagenhals 1988). With this procedure any level of accuracy can be achieved depending only on the effort expended. Finally, the expression $CVz_h^{01}$ is the one being most important for environmental valuation since it represents the utility change that is generated for the household by the change of the state of the environment alone. In theory, this expression represents the integral over the shadow prices for the environment between the initial state (without the project) and the final state (after project implementation). Since, however, these shadow prices are not observable from household data, other methods have been developed for an approximate computation of this measure in practice. These methods aim at the elicitation of individual households' WTP for the project under consideration since, as mentioned above, the CV for a utility increasing project is commonly interpreted as the WTP for that project.

In a next step, the problem of aggregating the individual welfare changes needs to be addressed since it is the aim to derive a valid measure for changes in social welfare. An environmental economic policy maker would hardly be able to recommend the implementation of a public project on the basis of countless figures of individual WTP. The aggregation of individual welfare measures, however, poses a fundamental theoretical problem in economics since it involves interpersonal comparisons of utility which is not compatible with ordinal utility theory. In addition, it was demonstrated by Arrow's Impossibility Theorem (cf. Arrow 1950) that no social preference ordering can be constructed on the basis of individual preferences that fulfills certain desirable conditions. Therefore, it is necessary to revert to weaker forms of aggregation for practical purposes. In reality, a policy maker would like to base the decision concerning some publicly funded project on the assessment of whether society as a whole will be better or worse off after the implementation of the project. Such an assessment can at least be approximated by determining whether it is possible for the winners of such a project to compensate the losers and still not be worse off than without the project. This criterion for preference aggregation is known as the Hicks-Kaldor potential Pareto criterion (cf. Cullis and Jones 1998: 29). Despite its theoretical shortcomings it has been widely accepted as one possible and transparent way of deriving a social benefit-cost measure from measures of individual welfare change. Using the derived measure of individual welfare changes on the basis of the Hicksian Compensating Variation above yields the following expression for the Hicks-Kaldor criterion in our case:

$$\sum_{h=1}^{H} CV_h^{01} = \sum_{h=1}^{H} CVI_h^{01} + \sum_{h=1}^{H} CVp_h^{01} + \sum_{h=1}^{H} CVz_h^{01} \;\; \begin{matrix} > \\ = \\ < \end{matrix} \;\; 0 \;\; \Rightarrow \;\; W^1 \;\; \begin{matrix} > \\ = \\ < \end{matrix} \;\; W^0 \qquad (2\text{-}12)$$

where $W^k$, $k \in \{0, 1\}$ denotes social welfare at situation k. Separability of the three components of the individual welfare measure $CV_h^{01}$ implies that the aggregated CV can simply be obtained by summing the individual components over all households. For further discussion of the Hicks-Kaldor criterion in the literature see e. g. Johansson (1994).

In practical applications, however, it will not be viable to apply the Hicks-Kaldor criterion fully as specified above. In order to compute a numerical value for the social value of an environmental project it would, thus, be necessary to know the income changes of all households, to estimate the entire demand system of society and the utility changes resulting from the environmental improvement using suitable empirical methods. Therefore, in practice, a simpler approach is usually chosen that relies on a comparison of the costs necessary to implement the project versus the aggregated individual benefits from the intended environmental improvement yielding the following benefit-cost expression

$$BC^{01} = \sum_{h=1}^{H} CVz_h^{01} - q^1 \cdot y, \qquad (2\text{-}13)$$

where y denotes the vector of the quantities of input factors necessary for the implementation of the project and $q^1$ denotes the vector of the respective factor prices. If $BC^{01}$ is positive the implementation of the project under consideration is recommended, if it turns out to be negative the proposed project should be scrapped. For the conditions under which this approximation of the benefit-cost measure is reasonable see Hanusch (1994: 57) and Ahlheim (2003: 27ff). Therefore, the focus of empirical methods of environmental valuation is directed on the assessment of the term $\sum_{h=1}^{H} CVz_h^{01}$, i. e. on the assessment of household's WTP for the project under consideration as a common interpretation of the Compensating Variation in practice. The methods currently available for this task shall be described and discussed in the following section.

### 2.1.3 Methods of environmental valuation

Since the theoretically correct assessment of the individual welfare change $CVz_h^{01}$ by computing the integral over the compensated shadow price function of environmental states is not possible in practice it is necessary to employ empirical methods that allow to deduce the value that households attribute to a particular environmental change from data that are observable from these households. As mentioned above, willingness to pay for an environmental improvement or for preventing an environmental deterioration is usually considered as a suitable proxy for the associated utility change of the household due to the economic trade-off involved in the decision of how much money, i. e. market consumption, should be sacrificed in return for an environmental good.

This consideration gives rise to two fundamentally different approaches for the elicitation of WTP. The first approach makes use of the weak complementarity between some market goods and environmental goods and bases WTP elicitation on households' observed consumption behavior of these goods. This implies that the value of the environmental good is assessed indirectly through the consumption of its complementary market goods. Therefore, the methods relying on observed market behavior of such goods are usually called indirect methods of environmental valuation. Alternatively, since they require the households to reveal their preferences for environmental goods through the consumption of market goods they are often called *revealed-preference methods*. Weak complementarity between a market good and an environmental good exists whenever consumption of a good is positively associated with an environmental good, i. e. when ceteris paribus the existence, the level or the quality of an environmental good leads to a higher consumption of those market goods or if prices of market goods are positively influenced by the environmental good (cf. Stephan and Ahlheim 1996: 154, Mäler 1974).

However, the indirect methods can only assess that part of the value attributed to the environment which is directly associated with its use since the use of the environment determines the consumption of the market goods that are related to it by weak complementarity. Therefore, the indirect methods are only of limited use for environmental valuation. When it is expected that an environmental good creates considerable non-use values as described in 2.1.1 the so-called direct valuation methods have to be employed. These methods are based on direct questioning of households concerning the value they attribute to some environmental improvement. The idea of the direct methods is to simulate a market situation for environmental goods where the household is given the opportunity to "buy" the environmental good in question. From the household's behavior in this simulated, or hypothetical, market situation his willingness to pay for the environmental good in question can be inferred. Since these methods rely on households' direct statements of value in a hypothetical situation rather than on true market behavior, they are often called *stated-preference methods*. Since the research in this study focuses on stated-preference methods they will be discussed in greater detail in 2.1.3.2. For completeness sake, however, a brief overview of the most prominent revealed-preference, or indirect, methods shall be given here.

#### 2.1.3.1 Indirect methods

The three most prominent indirect valuation methods are the travel cost method, the hedonic-pricing method and the averting behavior method. The *travel cost method* (TCM) dating back to Clawson (1959) is usually applied if the use value of some recreational site, e. g. a natural park or a lake, is to be valued. Its basic premise is that this value can be inferred from the expenditures on consumption goods related to the use of the recreation site and the time invested for using it. Certain market goods like e. g. transportation, hiking equipment, bathing suits, barbecue equipment etc. are necessary for and closely associated with the use of the site under consideration for recreation. The minimum value of the site for a specific household would then equal the expenditures for the associated market goods plus the valuation of the time spent for travel and recreation. However, in practice it proves to be difficult to determine the share of the expenditure on market goods that is exclusively related to the use of the specific site, e. g. bathing suits can also be used at other sites. Equally, the value of time is not so straightforward since in most cases the opportunity cost of time in people's free-time cannot simply be equated to foregone earnings in their jobs. Most people do not work on weekends and on holidays anyway, so that it seems impossible to value time in monetary terms in this case. Nevertheless, the travel cost method is still often used due to its computational simplicity, sometimes even in conjunction with direct valuation methods.

The main idea underlying the *hedonic-pricing method* (HPM) dating back to Ridker (1967) is the assumption that the price of a market commodity that is weakly complementary to an environmental good contains as a part the value the consumer attributes to this environmental good. In other words, the consumer is willing to pay a higher price for a certain market commodity if it is positively associated with an environmental good. The standard example is the supposed influence of environmental amenities like e. g. a scenic view or a natural recreation area on property values or rents in the housing market (cf. Rosen 1974, Bartlik and Smith 1987, Freeman 1993, Palmquist 2004 for detailed reviews of theory and practical applications of the hedonic-pricing method). The same, but opposite, influence on property values can be observed for environmental disamenities like e. g. the proximity to environmentally hazardous sites (cf. Kohlhase 1991, Cameron 2006 for the influence of Superfund sites in the USA on regional property values). From the variation of property values of houses with the same characteristics differing only in the environmental attribute (scenic view, distance to hazardous sites etc.) the share of the commodity's price pertaining to the environmental attribute can be determined and, under certain conditions, a WTP for an environmental change can be computed (cf. Horowitz 1984). However, there exist a number of theoretical concerns that question the validity of WTP estimates derived from the hedonic-pricing method (cf. Freeman 1993: 680f, Palmquist 1991).

While, in principle, it is argued that indirect methods can only assess direct use values, the hedonic-pricing method could also, in special cases, elicit indirect use values and even non-use values like the existence value. The indirect use value of ecosystem services, for example the protection of settlements from landslides in mountainous regions by natural forest ecosystems, should be reflected in the variation of property values in areas endangered by such catastrophic events. Furthermore, it is reasonable to assume that the existence value of dolphins might, at least to some part, be contained in the higher price that some consumers are willing to pay for canned tuna where the tuna fish were caught with dolphin-friendly nets as opposed to regular nets harmful to dolphins. Clearly, these represent only special cases since such market commodities as in the dolphin-tuna case will hardly be found to exist for many environmental goods.

Finally, valuation of environmental goods on the basis of the *averting behavior method* (ABM) makes use of the costs incurred and expended for preventing a negative influence of an environmental good on the well-being of a household. The value of a change of the state of an environmental good from its actual state of being harmful to a state in which no harm for households would be felt can, therefore, be approximated by the costs that households incur to prevent this harmful influence. A typical example where such averting behavior is comparatively easy to assess is the valuation of an improvement of water quality, especially in developing or emerging countries where household tap water is often of minor quality. Households can prevent catching water-borne diseases from buying bottled water, drilling wells or installing filters all of which are associated with an increase of household expenditure for drinking water (cf. Abdalla et al. 1992, Um et al. 2002). It can, however, be argued that these costs simply measure people's valuations of their health, i. e. of not catching such diseases, so that other aspects associated with an improvement of water quality are not taken into account.

Due to the obvious shortcomings of the indirect valuation methods in the context of environmental goods, especially since they are unable to consistently assess indirect use and non-use values, direct methods of measurement have become the preferred alternative for this task. These methods will be described and discussed in greater detail in the following section since the most prominent of them, the Contingent Valuation Method, forms the basis of the present research approach.

#### 2.1.3.2 Direct methods

The aim of direct methods for an economic valuation of environmental goods is to gain access to a direct statement of households concerning the value of the specific environmental good under consideration. The advantage of such a direct approach is that the characteristics of the environmental good to be valued can be exactly specified so that use values as well as non-use values can be conveniently assessed. The underlying idea of these methods is to treat an environmental good (which is usually not traded in markets) in analogy to a market commodity by creating the illusion of a market where households are given the opportunity to purchase the environmental good and thus express, i. e. directly state, the value they attribute to it. From these purchase decisions in the hypothetical market the WTP of the population for the good in question can then be estimated. Naturally, such an "experiment" will in practice not be conducted with all households of a population affected by a particular environmental project. Rather, a representative sample of the population is selected which is subjected to this hypothetical market and from whose hypothetical purchase decisions the value pertaining to the entire population is inferred. Thus, the direct methods rely on household surveys. In these hypothetical market situations the interviewed respondent is led to believe that the environmental good will only be made available if the households within the population make a contribution to the financing of the good. Therefore, the crucial aspect of any direct valuation method is the credibility of the market situation, otherwise the respondents, being aware that their responses will have no effect in reality anyway, have no incentive to give truthful value statements.

In the literature three types of direct valuation methods can be found where the most widely used method is the Contingent Valuation Method (CVM). A variant of the CVM is the Participatory Valuation Method which, unlike the CVM, is based on group interactions in conjunction with a hypothetical market situation. A third type, the so-called Attribute Based Choice Modelling (ABCM), breaks down full environmental change scenarios as employed in the CVM into its single components in order to assess values for every single element of such a change scenario. The three methods will be dealt with in turn.

*The Contingent Valuation Method (CVM)*

The Contingent Valuation Method (CVM) is the most basic of the direct valuation methods. It has been widely applied in practice so that considerable experience has been gained w. r. t. its performance and validity. As mentioned already in chapter 1, a number of open issues still exist in this respect to the resolution of which the present study wants to contribute. The basic idea of the CVM was first proposed by Ciriacy-Wantrup (1947: 1189) in a theoretical paper on the collective value of soil-conservation practices: "How then can demand schedules for collective extra-market goods be obtained? Individuals of a sample or of a social group as a whole may be asked how much money they are willing to pay for successive additional quantities of a collective extra-market good." Since Ciriacy-Wantrup's basic idea the CVM was employed for the assessment of the value of many such "extra-market goods", especially environmental goods like the preservation of species, the establishment of nature preserves, national parks or recreational areas, the preservation or rehabilitation of whole ecosystems (e. g. wetlands, tropical rainforests) etc. (cf. Bateman and Willis 2001 and Ahlheim and Frör 2003 for reviews of empirical CVM studies).

In general, the CVM is based on interviews with a representative sample of households from a population considered to be affected by some environmental project. The interviews are based on a standardized questionnaire which assures that the course of the interview is identical for all respondents and that comparable responses will be obtained for subsequent statistical analysis. A typical CVM interview follows a number of steps where the main aim is the elicitation of the respondent's WTP for the project in question. In principle, it is also possible to use the willingness to accept compensation (WTA) in CVM studies e. g. in order to value an environmental damage or deterioration. However, WTA was found to be less suitable in practice than WTP (cf. Ahlheim and Buchholz 2000, Kolstad and Guzman 1999, Morrison 1997, Shogren et al. 1994 for discussions of WTP vs. WTA). In a first step the basic idea of the survey is introduced so that the respondent knows what the interview will be about. A number of warm-up questions will be asked in which the respondent gets acquainted with the interview situation and relaxes from the suddenness of the task. Subsequently, questions are asked concerning the relation the respondent has with the environmental good that is to be valued, e. g. prior experience with the good, problems that are associated with the present state of the environment and worries w. r. t. the future state of the particular environmental good. These questions set the stage for the description of the valuation scenario that follows in the second step.

The presentation of the scenario to be valued is a crucial element of the CVM procedure. Here, the respondent is provided with the information on the basis of which he is supposed to give his direct value statement. Usually, the scenario starts with a description of the actual state of an environmental good, the status quo forming the reference point for the change of the state of the environmental good. In an environmental improvement scenario the respondent is then told that it is intended to change the state of the environment leading to an improvement. It should be described in detail what this improved state will look like, what it entails, which measures are undertaken to achieve it and who is in charge and responsible for its implementation. The scenario presentation necessarily contains a lot of information since some respondents might have more prior information on the good than others so that it should be tried to create some common level of information for all households. However, the description should not be too long in order not to overload the limited capabilities of respondents to perceive and process information. Ideally, the scenario presentation should be based on various media: spoken language by the interviewer, written text and graphical material for illustration.

Following the scenario presentation the next step sets the stage for the contingent market, i. e. the payment scheme is explained. Respondents are told that if the environmental project were to be implemented contributions of the individual households would be required for financing it and that otherwise, i. e.

if the WTP of the population falls short of the amount required for the project implementation, the project will not be put in place (*implementation rule*). The choice of the payment vehicle is of high importance for the behavior of respondents. Many CVM studies employ the increase of some tax as payment vehicle since it conveys to the respondents that every household will actually contribute to the financing of the project. However, it has to be verified in pretests prior to the main survey that no aversion toward taxes exists in the population which might lead the respondents to reject the project simply because they are skeptical toward government and object any tax increase in general regardless of its purpose. Such behavior would seriously distort estimated WTP and, indeed, this payment vehicle bias was found in many studies early on (cf. Brookshire et al. 1980, Daubert and Young 1981). Alternative payment vehicles consist of mandatory contributions to publicly managed funds or direct increases of amenity-related costs like entrance fees to recreation areas, water prices etc. Aversions toward these alternative vehicles might exist as well so that careful investigations in pretests are paramount. It is crucial, however, that respondents not be given any incentives to strategically misreport their WTP as might be the case for voluntary contributions. Here, respondents would see no harm in overstating their WTP if they are not forced to commit themselves to this payment. Therefore, it must be specified precisely in the *payment rule* how the contribution to the project that the household will subsequently state will actually be collected in case the project is implemented as a result of the CVM study.

The next, and most important, step is the WTP elicitation question itself. A number of different question formats have been proposed in the literature and tried in empirical CVM studies. The controversy of which question format is most suited, i. e. produces as little undesired biases of WTP estimates as possible, is still on-going since every idea of improving an existing and problematic question format was found to solve some problems and create others. In early studies an open-ended (OE) format was used where respondents were simply asked which amount of money they would at maximum be willing to pay if the project were implemented as described. This format, however, turned out to be rather difficult to answer and the results achieved with this format were largely unsatisfactory (cf. Mitchell and Carson 1989: 97f). Since respondents are to the most part both unfamiliar with the environmental good in question and, usually, not accustomed to put a monetary value on the environment they seem to have problems to express the envisaged utility increase from the proposed project in a money figure. This uncertainty seems to result in many responses of zero as is commonly found in studies using the open-ended question (cf. Smith et al. 1983).

An improvement of the open-ended question format was seen in the so-called payment card (PC) format which consists of a list of payment intervals ranging from zero to some cut-off value at the upper end of the payment card. Respondents are asked to select the interval of proposed payment amounts (bids) that contains their individual WTP for the project. While this format is open-ended in principle (the respondent can actively select intervals containing any amount from zero to infinity) the given monetary figures and the upper cut-off value were thought to help respondents to express their felt utility change in a monetary figure. The interval structure of the payment card also allows some uncertainty since the naming of precise figures of WTP is avoided. Additionally, the cut-off value serves as an indication to respondents where, from the perspective of the project organizers, an "absurd" WTP begins. The main controversy with respect to the PC format concerns the existence of a range bias and a centering bias induced by the choice of particular cut-off values on the payment card. A range bias occurs if the WTP estimate is found to depend significantly on the cut-off value whereas the centering bias describes the phenomenon that the center of the payment card, i. e. between zero and the cut-off value "attracts" the respondents so that those intervals are chosen significantly more often. Since the center of the payment card depends on the cut-off value these two biases are closely related. While Arrow et al. (1993) argue that significant range bias and centering bias are expected to occur in studies employing the PC format, Ryan et al. (2004) and Rowe et al. (1996) detect no such biases. It is shown in the latter study, however, that WTP estimates are significantly distorted downward if the cut-off value is chosen too low, i. e. when a considerable share of respondents have a higher WTP than the cut-off on the payment card. In the CVM survey underlying the research of this study no significant range and centering biases were detected in the PC data (see chapter 4).

A fundamental change of WTP elicitation formats was achieved by introducing closed-ended question formats (cf. Bishop and Heberlein 1979). The basic idea of this dichotomous choice (DC) format is to intensify the analogy to market commodities where a consumer in a store (usually) is confronted with the simple choice to buy the commodity at the offered price or leave it in the store and spend his money on other commodities. Under the DC format in a CVM setting, then, respondents are confronted with a "price" (bid) for the proposed environmental project which they can either accept in case their true WTP is larger or equal to this price or reject in case their true WTP is smaller than the offered bid. In comparison to the OE and the PC format the information content obtained from the answer of one single respondent is much lower in the DC format since it is only known whether the respondent's true WTP lies above or below the proposed bid. In practice different subsamples of respondents receive different bids which allows an econometric estimation of WTP on the basis of observed acceptance rates of different bids (see 2.1.4 for details). Therefore, the sample sizes for the DC format must be larger than for the OE or

PC formats. Furthermore, the econometric models for an estimation of WTP are more complicated and rest to a larger extent on distributional assumptions of WTP in the population. The econometric procedures for the estimation of WTP from DC and PC data will be described in section 2.1.4.

In order to improve the statistical efficiency of the DC format the double-bounded dichotomous choice format was developed (cf. Hanemann et al. 1991, Kanninen 1993) that extracts more information out of each respondent. In contrast to the single-bounded DC format (SBDC) described in the previous paragraph, in the double-bounded version (DBDC) a follow-up question depending on the response to the first bid offered to the respondent is added. In case the respondent accepts the first bid the respondent will be asked an even higher bid which he can either accept or reject. In case the first bid was rejected the second bid of the follow-up question will be lower. Thus, the intervals of the respondent's WTP are narrowed down which increases both the complexity of the statistical model (see 2.1.4) and the efficiency of the welfare estimate. However, a number of procedural problems are associated with the DC elicitation format. Empirical studies have revealed the existence of a starting point bias, i. e. a systematic influence of the amount of the (first) bid on the WTP estimate (cf. Desvousges et al. 1993, McFadden and Leonard 1993, Cooper and Loomis 1992, 1993, Kanninen and Kriström 1993, Boyle et al. 1998: 74). The findings of these studies suggest that in a situation where respondents are rather unfamiliar with the good as well as the valuation task to be performed they search for a hint of what the good might "reasonably" be worth and, thus, interpret the proposed bid as a "reasonable" cost estimate which makes the project seem acceptable (cf. Frykblom and Shogren 2000), especially when they are rather uncertain about the value such a project has for them.

A second explanation of the widely observed starting point bias is the so-called "yea"-saying phenomenon according to which respondents say "yes" in general to any bid level regardless of the true value they attribute to the project. Such "yea"-saying was found in the SBDC format by Boyle et al. (1998) and in the DBDC format by Kanninen (1995) and Holmes and Kramer (1995), Herriges and Shogren (1996), Alberini et al. (1997), Blamey et al. (1999) and many others. Whereas "yea"-saying alone would result in an upward bias of WTP the counter-acting effect of anchoring on the first bid was found to be strong resulting in a downward bias of the DBDC format in comparison to the SBDC format (cf. DeShazo 2002). Respondents who had already accepted the first bid presented to them were found to reject the second, higher bid much more often than respondents who were, in a different questionnaire version, confronted with this higher bid as their first bid. Thus, respondents perceive the follow-up bid as an attempt of the interviewer to bargain over a deal already accepted in the first bid and, as a result, feel reluctant to accept again. The analogous effect when the first bid was rejected, i. e. showing a higher tendency to accept the lower follow-up bid than when this lower bid is the first bid, was not found to be as strong. DeShazo (2002) explains this asymmetric anchoring effect with prospect theory (cf. Kahneman and Tversky 1979) according to which people are loss averse, i. e. inclined to reject a higher follow-up bid perceived as a loss in comparison to the first bid, and risk seeking, i. e. trying their luck even further when offered the lower follow-up bid. Due to these consistent shortcomings of the DBDC format DeShazo (2002) developed a DC format where the respondent is asked a follow-up bid only in case he has already rejected the first bid. It was shown, and could be replicated in the empirical example underlying this study (see chapter 4), that this DeShazo format yields WTP estimates practically identical to those of the SBDC format while being statistically more efficient due to the larger amount of information extracted per respondent as a result of the lower follow-up bid.

Cooper et al. (2002) attribute the anchoring effects found in DeShazo (2002) to the surprise that respondents feel when a follow-up bid, especially a higher one, is presented to them. The authors propose to modify the DBDC format by announcing to the respondent prior to the WTP question a range in which the project costs will most likely lie. Respondents are then either asked a bid at the upper end of that range and asked a follow-up bid, the amount of the lower bound of the announced range, whenever the first bid was rejected. Or, alternatively, the lower amount is asked first, followed by the upper bound of the range in case the first bid was accepted. Cooper et al. (2002) call this format the one-and-one-half-bounded DC (OOH). However, it was shown by Bateman et al. (2004b) that this approach is itself highly vulnerable to the specific range presented to the respondents so that strong anchoring effects cannot be avoided by this format, either. Thus, at the moment the DeShazo format seems to be the most desirable format out of the set of possible DC formats.

In empirical comparisons between WTP results obtained from open-ended formats like the OE or the PC format with those from the DC formats many studies report systematic differences (cf. Ready et al. 1996, Herriges and Shogren 1996, Boyle et al. 1996, Frew et al. 2003, Ryan et al. 2004, Champ and Bishop 2006). The WTP estimates from open-ended formats are consistently below those from dichotomous choice formats. While the controversy w. r. t. the "correct" question format cannot be settled by such a comparison due to the lack of a valid reference point on which the performance of the formats can be compared the consistent findings of starting point bias and anchoring effects in the DC format and only few proofs of statistically significant range biases (cf. Whynes et al. 2004) in the PC format put considerable doubt on recommendations to use the DC format in order to make use of its direct analogy to the purchase of market goods. In case the DC format is chosen for a study, the literature suggests that it is very advisable, however, to avoid bids in the upper tail of the expected WTP distribution. The bid design, i. e. the choice of the different bid values should be based on pretests using open-ended formats in order to avoid bid designs that are already biased upwards (cf. Kanninen 1993, Boyle et al. 1998).

After the WTP elicitation question the interview proceeds to the final step where a number of attitudinal, socio-economic and demographic questions are asked. The purpose of the elicitation of this kind of information is threefold: first, the socio-economic and demographic information about the sample can be used to check whether the WTP estimates are gained from a representative selection out of the entire population and, thus, forms a suitable basis for the computation of an aggregated welfare estimate. Second, these variables can be used in econometric models as explanatory variables, i. e. as variables that are systematically associated with the observed WTP. This analysis can serve as a plausibility test of the WTP responses obtained in the survey since there exist a number of a priori expectations w. r. t. the association of some of these variables with WTP. For example, it is reasonable to expect that WTP increases systematically with the level of household income, often also with education and the level of worry w. r. t. the environmental good under consideration. If these prior expectations are verified in the dataset the credibility of the validity of the WTP is reinforced. Third, the found systematic relationships between socio-economic and demographic variables and WTP represent an important information for policy makers who will be able to assess which group of the population would benefit most from the planned project and which group(s) might be expected to lose. These considerations are very important for practical environmental policy.

Apart from personal interviews at a household's home, a number of alternative interview forms have been proposed for CVM interviews like mail surveys, telephone interviews or mall-stop interviews in large shopping malls or streets. Mall-stop and telephone interviews are usually regarded less reliable than personal and mail surveys. Mall-stop samples are hardly representative in the first place and there is usually very little time available for the interview so that a thorough consideration of the proposed scenario cannot be expected. While it is easier to obtain a representative sample in telephone interviews the possibilities for a detailed presentation of the valuation scenario are scarce since neither written nor graphical material can be employed. Thus, currently only face-to-face and mail interviews are judged to lead to fairly reliable WTP estimates. Nevertheless, CVM studies using mail surveys (MS) are often considered less reliable than studies using face-to-face interviews (FtF) due to low return rates associated with self-selection of respondents returning the questionnaires (cf. Whitehead et al. 1993), limited possibilities to convey a complex valuation scenario to the respondent and less possibilities to force respondents to strictly follow the standardized order of questions in the questionnaire (cf. Cameron et al. 1999, Ethier et al. 2000). On the other hand, however, MS have a number of advantages that make their employment attractive: respondents are much more likely to respond truthfully to personal questions so that the problem of social desirability and interviewer biases, a well known problem of FtF surveys, can be avoided (cf. Krysan 1994). Also, respondents can take as much time as they need to think about the proposed scenario and their answer to the WTP elicitation question (cf. Dillman 1978). Last but not least, mail surveys are generally considerably less expensive than FtF surveys. As a result of the described procedural shortcomings of both interview forms widely divergent estimates of project benefits for FtF surveys as compared to MS are reported in the literature where FtF surveys are usually regarded as the interview form leading to more reliable results (cf. NOAA 1994). Recent findings of the comparison of the performance of face-to-face versus mail surveys are reported for a CVM study in Thailand of which the empirical research of this study is a part (cf. Ahlheim et al. 2007).

After this detailed description of the general CVM procedure and the discussion of its main practical problems two further direct methods of environmental valuation shall be briefly described in the following sections.

*The Participatory Valuation Method (PVM)*

One of the main criticisms of the CVM often voiced in the literature is that respondents in the traditional face-to-face CVM setting have little time to perceive and process the information of the valuation scenario, have no possibility to acquire additional information if they feel it is necessary and lack the chance to discuss their views with other people in order to reflect on the task at hand more thoroughly. This criticism is based on the view that in most CVM studies respondents will not have clearly defined preferences for the environmental good to be valued that they are able to readily express in monetary terms. Rather, it is sometimes argued that preferences for more or less unfamiliar goods or goods that are usually not perceived to have value in monetary terms need to be constructed by the respondent during the valuation task (cf. Payne and Schkade 1999, Bettman et al. 1998, Payne et al. 1992). This view contrasts the prevailing notion in the valuation literature that well-defined preferences for environmental goods exist which simply need to be unveiled by a suitable valuation method. If preferences are not so readily available and the construction of preferences is initiated only when respondents are confronted with a specific valuation task great care must be laid into this construction process in order to avoid manipulation of the respondents into one direction or another. Several authors have proposed valuation techniques based on the interaction of respondents in group meetings, so-called participatory valuation techniques (cf. Macmillan et al. 2002, Philip and Macmillan 2005).

Usually, this Participatory Valuation Method (PVM) is based on the CVM (see, however, Alvarez-Farizo and Hanley 2006 and Powe et al. 2005 for participatory valuation techniques in the ABCM setting presented below). Unlike the traditional individual-based interviews groups of respondents, e. g. 10 to 15 people, are formed that meet for two or more moderated sessions. The purpose of these sessions is to provide respondents with the opportunity to actively learn more about the valuation scenario, to ask questions and obtain more information on the issue at hand if they wish and to enable them to share their opinions and views on the project so that they can reflect and deliberate on the proposed environmental project as deeply as possible. In this process, expert information should be presented, ideally from different sources and angles in order to avoid undue manipulation of the participants. At the end of the sessions, participants are given a CVM questionnaire containing the WTP elicitation question that they can fill out in private and anonymously.

While this approach to environmental valuation seems very promising since it enables respondents to invest great effort into the detection of their "true" WTP for the project a number of critical issues need to be addressed briefly. From a practical point of view this method requires a lot of effort for the organization and moderation of the group meetings. The overall sample size will necessarily remain limited so that the WTP estimates are rather inefficient from a statistical point of view. Furthermore, it is doubtful whether the preferences toward the specific environmental project will really represent the preferences of the general population should the project be implemented since the general population will hardly ever attain the level of information on the project that the participants of the group meetings had when stating their WTP (cf. Ahlheim and Frör 2003). Thus, the PVM is clearly not sufficient as a stand-alone technique for assessing environmental values but it appears to be a promising tool for complementing the traditional survey methods based on representative samples of respondents.

*Attribute Based Choice Modelling (ABCM)*

Unlike in the CVM the respondents in a survey employing Attribute Based Choice Modelling (ABCM) are not simply confronted with the task of valuing a project scenario in relation to some status quo but can make choices among various alternative combinations of valuation scenarios. The ABCM which is closely related to Conjoint Analysis commonly employed in marketing research is based on Lancaster's (1966) characteristics theory of value according to which the value of a commodity is determined by the specific combination of the characterics, i. e. the attributes, which in conjunction define that commodity. An environmental good, therefore, is seen to consist of a number of attributes, e. g. area of a nature preserve, endangered plant and animal species, water quality of the rivers etc. Combining these attributes with different levels yields a set of possible environmental goods to be valued. The aim of the ABCM is the valuation of the aggregate environmental goods in relation to the status quo as well as of the single attributes of which the good consists. In practice, respondents are successively presented a number of choice sets consisting usually of two alternative combinations of attributes as well as the status quo. Each of the two alternatives contains a cost attribute which states the monetary amount that the respondent would have to pay if that particular alternative were implemented. The respondent is then asked to select between the three combinations presented, i. e. the two project alternatives and the status quo. From the successive choices among different such choice sets both a WTP estimate for every possible combination of attributes as well as for discrete changes of the levels of the attributes can be obtained.

The ABCM has already been applied in many empirical valuation studies (cf. Stevens et al. 1997, Garrod and Willis 1997, Adamowicz et al. 1998, Foster and Mourato 2000, Haefele and Loomis 2001, Hanley et al. 2001). The ABCM approach is certainly a valuable extension of the CVM technique whenever it is possible to create meaningful environmental goods by combinations of different attribute values. The advantage of this method is the simultaneous valuation of a number of alternative project scenarios which allows a policy maker who is not already committed to some fixed and unchangeable environmental project to determine among an entire set of possible projects the one that exhibits the most favorable ratio of social benefits to costs of the project. Thus, the ABCM, whenever applicable, seems a powerful tool for environmental policy making.

Summarizing the discussion of practical methods of environmental valuation it becomes obvious that rationality plays quite a different role for direct methods in comparison to indirect methods. Since indirect valuation methods are based on people's observed market choices where money is actually expended for environmental goods the assumption of rational, i. e. utility maximizing, behavior is already implied. In neoclassical economics it is generally presumed that people can be trusted when it comes to deciding which goods will generate the highest utility for the available budget.[1] At the same time it must be assumed that before purchasing a good people have gathered information about the good they consider sufficient for making that purchase decision. In simulated markets as generally used in the context of direct valuation methods, however, the situation is different. First, economic choices of respondents are not real, i. e. people do not sign a binding contract to purchase an environmental good for money. However realistically a payment scenario may be crafted, statements of WTP will merely remain announcements of what respondents would pay for an environmental good in case they would have to do so in the future. Second,

---

1 Sometimes, however, this assumption is questioned as will be discussed in chapter 3.

respondents cannot search actively for the information they require to make a good WTP statement, they are left with what is provided to them in the course of the interview. These two distinctions show that it cannot be taken for granted that choices made in the course of a CVM, PVM or ABCM interview are perfectly rational since the very context of the interview, i. e. degree of realism, elicitation question format, type and quality of provided information etc., bears the potential to influence stated WTP. Such biases of WTP as already briefly discussed in the preceding section shall be addressed in more detail in 2.1.5 below.

### 2.1.4 Statistical estimation models for the CVM

The aim of this section is to provide a brief overview of the statistical estimation approaches commonly used for the analysis of CVM response data. These comprise models for the estimation of WTP as the main objective of the CVM and for the estimation of the determinants of WTP used for plausibility tests and as information for policy makers. This overview is based mainly on Haab and McConnell (2002) with some useful modifications in notation as well as on Hanemann (1984) and Hanemann et al. (1991) where further details w. r. t. the estimation of dichotomous choice models can be found.

For the open-ended question format the estimation of WTP is very simple since direct and precise figures of WTP are obtained from each respondent. From these responses mean WTP can be computed as the arithmetic mean over all individually stated WTP figures. Mean WTP serves as the basis for an aggregation of WTP to the whole population affected by the project under consideration by simply multiplying this estimate by the number of households affected. For the mean WTP 95%-confidence intervals as a measure for the estimation error can be computed using the standard textbook procedures (cf. Griffiths et al. 1993: 143). Similarly, the median WTP can be directly obtained from the open-ended responses indicating the WTP stated by at least 50% of the households. Median WTP indicates the amount for which exactly 50% of the households would have voted in a referendum on the proposed project and would, therefore, serve as a useful figure for environmental policy makers in case households were obliged to pay this amount as a result of project implementation. In general, median WTP was found to be considerably lower than mean WTP for open-ended data since, as mentioned above, the answers are not symmetrically distributed and exhibit a spike of responses at "zero". In addition, very high WTP statements contribute to the tendency of higher means. Due to the regularly observed mass of "zero" responses regression models using ordinary least squares (OLS) estimation for the analysis of determinants of WTP would yield biased parameter estimates of the explanatory variables (cf.

Maddala 1983). Thus, censored regression models like the tobit model are commonly used for an analysis of WTP determinants (cf. Tobin 1958, Halstead et al. 1991).

The estimation of WTP from dichotomous choice and payment card responses, however, is more complicated since responses are given only in the form of intervals of WTP. Since these responses are to be interpreted as the result of a rational, i. e. utility maximizing, choice it is necessary to derive a suitable statistical model from an economic model of utility maximization. Therefore, the derivation of the model starts with the following consideration. If a utility maximizing respondent h agrees to pay a monetary amount A in return for an environmental project proposed in a CVM interview the following weak inequality must hold

$$v_h\left(z^0, I_h, s_h\right) \leq v_h\left(z^1, I_h - A_h, s_h\right) \tag{2-14}$$

where $v_h(\cdot)$ denotes the household's indirect utility function when market prices are held constant and $s_h$ denotes the vector of the household's socio-economic and demographic characteristics as well as personal attitudinal variables. Thus, the household will only agree to pay $A_h$ if he is at least as well off with the project as without it but not having to pay $A_h$. Since $v_h(\cdot)$ is not observable and its true functional form is unknown this expression has to be separated into a deterministic term $\bar{v}_h(\cdot)$ that represents the researcher's model of household h's preferences and a stochastic term $\varepsilon_h^k$:

$$v_h\left(z^k, I_h^k, s_h\right) = \bar{v}_h\left(z^k, I_h^k, s_h\right) + \varepsilon_h^k. \tag{2-15}$$

The deterministic part of $v_h(\cdot)$ is based on the observable characteristics of the household, including his income $I_h^k$, the particular environmental state $z^k$ and the household's behavior w. r. t. the WTP question, i. e. whether he accepts or rejects the proposed bid. The error term $\varepsilon_h^k$ represents all unobservable characteristics of the household, e. g. personal and only privately known situational factors or preference uncertainty (see below). For the observer $v_h(\cdot)$ is, therefore, a random variable so that utility as specified here belongs to the so-called Random Utility Models (RUM) for which a well-developed framework of statistical analysis exists (cf. McFadden 1974). For the analysis of CVM interval data it is useful to derive an expression for the probability to accept the proposed bid, i. e. to say "yes" to the WTP question, using the above random utility specification:

$$\Pr\{yes_h\} = \Pr\left\{v_h\left(z^1, I_h - A_h, s_h\right) \geq v_h\left(z^0, I_h, s_h\right)\right\}$$

$$= \Pr\left\{\bar{v}_h\left(z^1, I_h - A_h, s_h\right) + \varepsilon_h^1 \geq \bar{v}_h\left(z^0, I_h, s_h\right) + \varepsilon_h^0\right\}$$

$$= \Pr\left\{\bar{v}_h\left(z^1, I_h - A_h, s_h\right) - \bar{v}_h\left(z^0, I_h, s_h\right) \geq \varepsilon_h^0 - \varepsilon_h^1\right\} \quad (2\text{-}16)$$

Thus, in other words, the probability that household h experiences no loss in utility if he has to pay $A_h$ for the environmental project is simply the probability that the difference of the observable utility change is at least as great as the difference of the unobservable error terms. 2-16 shows the necessary rationality assumption inherent in this formulation of the statistical model. A respondent's "yes"-response implies that he is able to perfectly observe whether he will be at least as well of with the project as without it. Whenever a rational response is not guaranteed, however, i. e. whenever the response is not in congruence with the respondent's "true" utility difference, the statistical model will necessarily fail to estimate this "true" WTP.

Defining the utility difference $\Delta\bar{v}_h = \bar{v}_h\left(z^1, I_h - A_h, s_h\right) - \bar{v}_h\left(z^0, I_h, s_h\right)$, $\eta = \varepsilon_h^0 - \varepsilon_h^1$ and $F_\eta(\cdot)$ as the cumulative distribution function (cdf) of $\eta$ the probability to accept the bid can be written as

$$\Pr\{\text{yes}_h\} = \Pr\{\eta \leq \Delta\bar{v}_h\} = F_\eta(\Delta\bar{v}_h), \quad (2\text{-}17)$$

i. e. the larger the deterministic utility difference $\Delta\bar{v}_h$ the larger the probability that this difference exceeds the error term $\eta$ and the larger the probability to accept the proposed bid A. In order to operationalize this expression for an estimation model of WTP both the deterministic component $\Delta\bar{v}_h$ and the stochastic component $F_\eta(\cdot)$, i. e. the distribution of the error term $\eta$, must be specified. A simple and commonly employed specification of the utility difference $\Delta\bar{v}_h$ is the linear utility model

$$\Delta\bar{v}_h = \bar{v}_h^1 - \bar{v}_h^0 = \left(\alpha^1 + \beta\left(I_h - A_h\right)\right) - \left(\alpha^0 + \beta I_h\right) \quad (2\text{-}18)$$

$$= \alpha - \beta A_h \quad (2\text{-}19)$$

where $\alpha = \alpha^1 - \alpha^0$ subsumes the observable characteristics $s_h$. A more detailed explanatory model will be used below. Alternative specifications for the utility difference where the influence of household income on WTP is modeled more realistically have been proposed (cf. Hanemann and Kanninen 1999), however, in this study the commonly employed simple model specified in 2-19 will be used throughout.

The stochastic specification depends on the assumption of the distribution of the error terms $\varepsilon_h^k$. The assumption of independently and normally distributed errors leads to $F_\eta(\Delta\bar{v}_h) = \Phi(\Delta\bar{v}_h)$ where $\Phi(\cdot)$ denotes the standard normal cumulative distribution function resulting in a probit model for WTP estimation. In the probit model, errors are assumed to be distributed standard normal with a mean of 0 and variance $\sigma^2$ of 1, i. e. $\varepsilon_h^k \sim N(0, 1)$. Since the errors $\varepsilon_h^k$ are $N(0, \sigma^2)$ distributed the parameters $\alpha$ and $\beta$ need to be normalized to $\frac{\alpha}{\sigma}$ and $\frac{\beta}{\sigma}$ for statistical estimation. Thus, in the probit model the probability to say "yes" becomes $\Phi\left(\frac{\alpha}{\sigma} - \frac{\beta}{\sigma}A_h\right)$. The same applies to the commonly used logit model where the assumption of an independent and identical extreme value distribution of errors leads to the logistic distribution $F_\eta(\Delta\bar{v}_h) = (1 - e^{-\Delta\bar{v}_h})^{-1}$. Since the standard normal and the standard logistic distributions differ merely by the latter assuming higher probability density in the tails of the distribution there is only a slight difference between probit and logit models in practice. For further specification of the stochastic part of the model assuming asymmetric distributions and taking account of the fact that WTP should be strictly non-negative see Hanemann and Kanninen (1999).

From the parametric specification in 2-19 a welfare measure based on WTP can be obtained directly by assuming that $\Delta\bar{v}_h = 0$ exactly if $A_h = WTP_h$, thus for the probit and the logit model it must hold that $0 = \alpha - \beta\, WTP_h$ so that

$$WTP_h = \frac{\alpha}{\beta}. \tag{2-20}$$

Due to the symmetry of the standard normal and standard logistic distributions the resulting welfare measure represents both mean and median WTP. Alternative specifications of the stochastic part of utility based on asymmetric probability density distributions lead to different expressions for the welfare estimate where the mean and the median differ.

For the estimation of the parameters $\alpha$ and $\beta$ in expression 2-20 it is convenient to use the Maximum Likelihood technique now commonly available in econometric software packages like LIMDEP (cf. Greene 2002). For the single-bounded dichotomous choice interval data the log-likelihood function using the probit model is specified as

$$\ln L(\alpha, \beta | A_h) = \sum_{h=1}^{H} Yes_h \cdot \ln\left[\Phi\left(\frac{\alpha}{\sigma} - \frac{\beta}{\sigma}A_h\right)\right] + (1 - Yes_h)\cdot \ln\left[1 - \Phi\left(\frac{\alpha}{\sigma} - \frac{\beta}{\sigma}A_h\right)\right] \tag{2-21}$$

where $Yes_h$ indicates whether household h has accepted ($Yes_h = 1$) or rejected ($Yes_h = 0$) the proposed bid $A_h$. For the DeShazo interval data where information on three WTP intervals is obtained the log-likelihood function becomes

$$\ln L(\alpha, \beta | A_h^{first}, A_h^{follow}) = \sum_{h=1}^{H} Yes_h \cdot \ln\left[\Phi\left(\tfrac{\alpha}{\sigma} - \tfrac{\beta}{\sigma} A_h^{first}\right)\right]$$

$$+ \; NoYes_h \cdot \ln\left[\Phi\left(\tfrac{\alpha}{\sigma} - \tfrac{\beta}{\sigma} A_h^{follow}\right) - \Phi\left(\tfrac{\alpha}{\sigma} - \tfrac{\beta}{\sigma} A_h^{first}\right)\right]$$

$$+ \; NoNo_h \cdot \ln\left[1 - \Phi\left(\tfrac{\alpha}{\sigma} - \tfrac{\beta}{\sigma} A_h^{follow}\right)\right] \qquad (2\text{-}22)$$

where $A_h^{first}$ denotes the first bid, $A_h^{follow}$ denotes the (lower) follow-up bid and $NoYes_h$ and $NoNo_h$ indicate the sequence of responses to the first and the follow-up bids. The Log-Likelihood function for the payment card interval data can be specified in a similar way since the selection of a specific bid interval $\left[A_h^{low}, A_h^{up}\right]$ on the payment card implies that the respondent accepts the bid amount of the lower bound of the interval $A_h^{low}$ and (approximately) rejects the upper bound $A_h^{up}$. The log-likelihood function therefore becomes

$$\ln L(\alpha, \beta | A_h^{low}, A_h^{up}) = \sum_{h=1}^{H} \ln\left[\Phi\left(\tfrac{\alpha}{\sigma} - \tfrac{\beta}{\sigma} A_h^{low}\right) - \Phi\left(\tfrac{\alpha}{\sigma} - \tfrac{\beta}{\sigma} A_h^{up}\right)\right]. \qquad (2\text{-}23)$$

The maximization of the respective Log-Likelihood functions yields the parameters $\alpha$ and $\beta$ from which the mean and median WTP can be directly computed according to 2-20. Since the welfare estimate is computed as the ratio between two parameter estimates each of which has its own standard error of estimation the computation of the 95%-confidence interval as a measure for the variance of the WTP estimate is not as straightforward as for the open-ended WTP described above. For CVM interval data a number of simulation approaches for the approximate computation of confidence intervals are available in the literature (cf. Cooper 1994). The present study will employ the approach of Park et al. (1991). In their bootstrap approach a large number, e. g. 1000, of values for WTP are simulated by randomly drawing values of the parameters $\alpha$ and $\beta$ on the basis of their estimated variance-covariance matrix. From these simulated WTP values the 95%-confidence interval can easily be obtained by discarding the lower and upper 2,5% of these values, respectively.

Finally, the determinants of WTP can be analyzed by augmenting the simple utility difference model in 2-19 where the vector $s_{hj}$ , $j = \{1, 2, ..., J\}$, consisting of the households' J socio-economic, demographic and observable attitudinal variables is included in the model so that

$$\Delta \overline{v}_h = \alpha - \beta A_h + \varphi_j s_{hj} \qquad (2\text{-}24)$$

where $\varphi_j$ denotes the parameter (row) vector of the J observed variables of the (column) vector $s_{hj}$. From the signs of $\varphi_j$ and the estimated levels of significance of these parameters the positive or negative associations of the explanatory variables found to be statistically significant can be assessed as the determinants of WTP. In practice, it is necessary to limit the number of explanatory variables in such a regression model in order to obtain efficient estimates of the significant variables. Therefore, the statistical method of factor analysis has proven to be very useful to aggregate the large amount of variables assessed in the course of a CVM interview to a smaller number of factors carrying the information of the single variables. This method of dimension reduction, thus, allows to include most of the ample information on the households contained in $s_{hj}$. A practical example of the employment of the methods described in this section will be given in detail in an empirical example underlying this study in chapter 4.

## 2.2 Rationality problems in environmental valuation

As mentioned briefly earlier it must not be taken for granted that responses to valuation questions in surveys employing direct valuation techniques like the CVM, PVM or ABCM are given on the ground of full rationality of respondents. The formulation of the statistical models for the evaluation of DC and PC elicitation formats in CVM shows that from the perspective of the respondent a rational valuation requires that the response to the WTP question be in congruence with the true difference in utility the respondent expects to experience as a result of the proposed environmental project. However, due to the setting of a simulated market for environmental goods, in practice there are a number of critical issues within direct valuation interviews where the method is prone to produce wrong, i. e. irrational, valuation estimates.

It is the aim of this study to highlight rationality problems that occur in environmental valuation using direct valuation methods, focusing specifically on the CVM, and to add to an explanation of the psychological mechanisms of their occurrence in order to recommend survey designs to mitigate such problems. Therefore, the following section will scrutinize where CVM responses go wrong regarding the postulate that they should reflect full rationality of respondents.

Many of these problems were described and investigated in the literature, where they are commonly known as biases.

### 2.2.1 Biases in Contingent Valuation

Regarding the elicitation question format in CVM biases like the payment vehicle bias, starting point bias and the range bias have already been addressed in detail in the preceding section. These biases reflect problems with respondents' rationality since rational responses would require that respondents are not influenced by these rather technical characteristics of the survey. Apart from these, there are a number of further effects discussed in the literature that are considered to exhibit systematic and distorting influences on WTP in the sense that the rationality of these responses is questionable. Some authors (e. g. Sugden 2005) consider these biases to result from so-called preference anomalies where these are defined as "patterns in responses that are inconsistent with standard economic assumptions about preferences". The existence of such anomalous behavior in CVM has often raised great concern w. r. t. the validity of the method, yet for a number of these effects suitable remedies have not yet been found by CVM researchers, so far.

*Social desirability effects*

Social desirability refers to a systematic effect on stated WTP caused by the presence of an interviewer, whether physical or on the phone. Often the concern is expressed that respondents especially in face-to-face interviews feel that they have to please the interviewer who, as they presume, expects the respondent to support the environmental project and accept the proposed bid or state a high WTP. This effect can be seen in close relation to the "yea"-saying behavior in DC questions mentioned above. Even for telephone surveys Ethier et al. (2000) show the existence of social desirability by comparing the responses to personal questions between telephone and mail survey modes.

In general, it is expected that social desirability would result in an upward bias of WTP (cf. Leggett et al. 2003). The recommendation of the NOAA panel (cf. Arrow et al. 1993: 4611) is to test for such effects by either providing respondents with the possibility to state their WTP anonymously and deposit it in a ballot box or even to mail their WTP from their homes after the personal interview has finished. In chapter 4 results are presented showing a direct comparison of anonymous versus non-anonymous administration of the WTP question in a face-to-face CVM survey.

*Hypothetical bias*

The hypothetical bias describes respondents' tendency to overstate their WTP in situations where they do not have to fully commit to pay the accepted bid or the stated amount (cf. Bohm 1972, Cummings et al. 1986). In CVM interview situations respondents simply state that they would pay the amount, however, they are in general not made to pay that amount during the interview but envisage to incur these costs at some distant time in the future which renders the monetary payment considerably less real.

Hypothetical bias was found in a number of empirical studies comparing stated WTP with real payments, e. g. in the situation of intended and real purchase of private goods (cf. List and Shogren 2002, Blumenschein et al. 1998, Johannesson et al. 1998, Foster et al. 1997). However, the direction of the bias is controversial in the literature. While Harrison and Rutström's (1999) literature review detect positive hypothetical biases ranging from 2% to as much as 2600% Carson et al. (1996a) find the opposite effect in studies comparing valuations from stated and revealed preferences. In practice, there are a number of ways how hypothetical bias can be mitigated or corrected for. First and most important, the payment mechanism must be credible so that respondents believe in the consequences of their statements and that the perceived payment will take place in the immediate future. Respondents must be led to believe that they act in a real market. For example, it was shown by Polome et al. (2006) that respondents' WTP was significantly larger when it was mentioned that the study was actually part of a referendum. Second, it has proven useful to use "cheap talk" (Cummings and Taylor 1999, Menges et al. 2005), i. e. telling respondents about the problem of strategic responses and free riding and asking them not to do it in the valuation task at hand. Finally, as already suggested by the NOAA-Panel (cf. NOAA 1994) with its "divide by 2" rule some authors propose to use calibration factors to adjust hypothetical valuations based on the experience gained with real valuations (cf. Fox et al. 1998, Macmillan et al. 2002). Since these valuation differences, however, seem to depend crucially on the kind of good to be valued it is elusive to detect generalizeable rules (cf. Hanley and Shogren 2005).

*Embedding and warm-glow-of-giving*

Perhaps the most contested bias in the environmental economics literature is the phenomenon known as *embedding*, *scope sensitivity*, *part-whole bias* or, under a slightly different perspective, *warm-glow-of-giving*. All these terms refer to the common suspicion among CVM critics (cf. Hausman 1993) that respondents' stated WTPs do not actually refer to the specific environmental improvement proposed in the scenario of the CVM interview but to some symbolic meaning that respondents personally associate with the scenario. For example, it was found in a classic study by Desvousges et al. (1993) that WTP to save 2000, 20000 or 200000 migratory birds from dying in oil holding ponds was roughly identical where differences were not significant (cf. Diamond et al. 1993 for similar examples, Schkade and Payne 1994 for a replication of the Desvousges et al. 1993 study). It would have been expected that WTP increases significantly with the number of birds saved since more birds saved should create a larger change in utility than less birds saved, especially when those differ by orders of magnitude.

On a slightly different line of research using part-whole scenarios, it was found that the sequence in which two different improvement levels, where one, the "part", was a subset of the other, the "whole", were presented for valuation to the respondent had an influence on the WTP stated for these improvements (cf. Bateman et al. 2004a). WTP for the "part" was significantly higher when it was valued first than when it was second in a sequence and the "whole" was valued first. Thus, it was concluded that the obvious insensitivity to scope found in Desvousges et al. (1993) and the significant sequencing effects must be due to respondents substituting the specific scenario with some environmental good on a "higher level" like e. g. "supporting the environment in general" where the specific quantitative scope (or scale) of the scenario is not explicitly the basis for their valuations. In such cases WTP estimates obtained from CVM surveys are widely considered to be meaningless unless one aims at the assessment of this "general" environmental sentiment.

Other studies, however, were able to confirm the theoretically expected sensitivity to scope (cf. Carson 1997, Veisten et al. 2004, Barreiro et al. 2005, Bateman et al. 2005, Alberini and Chiabai 2005) so that the question of why insensitivity to scope occurs sometimes and sometimes not needs to be addressed. Heberlein et al. (2005) take a new perspective on this old dispute by suggesting to consider two additional types of scope, the *affective scope* and the *cognitive scope*, when characterizing the respondent's perception of the whole and the part. Affective scope exists if the respondent likes the whole more than the part, cognitive scope exists when the respondent knows more about the whole than about the part. Both of these statements are not necessarily true and depend, as is shown in their study, on the character of the good to be valued. Thus, when a respondent likes the part more than the whole or knows more about the part than about the whole one would expect either no sensitivity to scope or even a negative one. Heberlein et al. (2005) showed that this was the case in a CVM assessing the value of either 300 or 800 wolves in a region, where respondents clearly liked the part more than the whole (nevertheless a positive WTP was elicited for the preservation of wolves). Similar results were obtained for an environmental good like biodiversity where the part, i. e. local plant and animal species, are often better known and more cared for than the whole that often remains rather abstract. The authors conclude to put less emphasis on scope sensitivity and suggest not to perform it as a standard validity test since it is both expensive and often misleading.

Similarly to embedding, the *warm-glow-of-giving* effect (cf. Andreoni 1989, 1990), also termed impure altruism, refers to the motive of a good feeling from having contributed to some good cause, e. g. the improvement of a public good like the environment. Kahneman and Knetsch (1992) criticize that due to impure altruism CVM studies often do not provide valuations of the specific public good but that they rather indicate the "purchase of moral satisfaction". Some authors like e. g. Nunes and Schokkaert (2003) even try to correct CVM datasets for this effect by separating "true" value statements specifically referring to the environmental good in question from the warm-glow valuations. While CVM critics generally argue that WTP statements based on the warm-glow-of-giving do not reflect their true values for the environmental goods and, therefore, should not be counted as benefits of that good, other authors (cf. Randall and Hoehn 1996, Harrison 1992) hold the view that warm-glow-of-giving must be counted as a part of the utility generated from the specific scenario since those respondents who feel this "glow" by contributing to the project will experience an increase in utility nonetheless. Thus, no final conclusion has been reached in the literature so far as to whether a warm-glow response can be considered a rational response or not.

*Budget constraint bias*

Furthermore, concern has been raised in the literature as to the role of households' budget constraints for stated WTP. Critics argued that households often fail to consider that their WTP statement would reduce their budget available for the consumption of market goods. WTP, therefore, reflects only a valid economic tradeoff if the effect of the WTP statement on the available budget is taken into account. Not considering one's available budget should, thus, clearly violate the rationality assumption. Therefore, one of the important recommendations of the NOAA-Panel was to explicitly remind respondents of their available household budget (cf. Arrow et al. 1993). It is argued, however, by Ahlheim (1998: 211) that the budget constraint should only be taken into account by respondents in those situations where the households would actually have to pay for the environmental projects. In most cases in reality it would not be feasible to increase taxes for an environmental project so that financing would rather be achieved by reallocation of presently available funds. In these cases household budgets would not be reduced so that the budget constraint reminder in CVM interviews would distort households' value assessments.

The budget constraint, however, actually seems to play a crucial role in households' considerations of WTP and might even lead to systematic underestimations of WTP. It has been found in many empirical studies that household WTP tends to decrease with household size whereas it would be expected that the utility change from some environmental improvement project increases with the number of people living in a household. However, it is obvious that the household budget is relatively tighter for larger households since the free disposable income usually decreases with the number of people living in one household. It is shown in Ahlheim and Lehr (2001) that in such a case the principle "a dollar is a dollar" which is generally applied in cost-benefit analysis for the aggregation of single household benefit estimates leads to a systematic underestimation of aggregate WTP since ceteris paribus the same dollar in a large household refers to a larger absolute sacrifice in the consumption of market goods than in a small household. In order to correct for the ensuing estimation biases the authors propose a method based on household equivalence scales (cf. e. g. Lewbel 1989) taking household sizes into account.

*Biases due to risk and uncertainty*

The literature on environmental valuation knows many empirical studies examining individual valuations of a reduction of risk of harmful consequences due to environmental states. In such studies, respondents are typically asked their WTP for a measure that would reduce their risk of morbidity or mortality from a present state by a specified percentage (cf. Jones-Lee et al. 1993, Baron and Greene 1996, Jones-Lee and Loomes 1997, Beattie et al. 1998, Carthy et al. 1999). In the literature on choice under risk and uncertainty, however, it was shown that people often violate the standard axioms of expected utility theory leading to a variety of anomalous behavior like the famous Allais paradox (cf. Allais 1953) and the Ellsberg paradox (cf. Ellsberg 1961) where people were frequently found to make inconsistent choices between lotteries (cf. Machina 1987, Thaler 1992, Kahneman et al. 1982, Eichenberger 1992 for detailed compilations and discussions of anomalies). This observed behavior puts the assumption of rational responses in decisions made under risk and uncertainty into question and is, therefore, highly relevant for CVM response behavior where environmental outcomes are not certain.

In CVM studies the commonly observed anomalies in decisions under risk and uncertainty have been found to play an important role. Especially in the context of environmental problems it was observed that people's subjective views of environmental and health risks differ substantially from objective risks as assessed by scientific experts or policy makers. People tend to evaluate environmental and health risks which are usually characterized by low probability paired with high severity in case of occurrence in a "bimodal" way: "they either ignore the risk completely or overreact" (cf. Hanley and Shogren 2005: 22). Both of these possible reactions are not in line with the expected utility criterion which requires people to think about the probability of occurrence and the severity of an event simultaneously. As Machina (1987) observed people tend to separate odds and consequences of an event and focus on the element that seems more "attractive" to them. Some focus on the low probability of occurrence and thus ignore the harmful event altogether which would lead to an underprovision of protection against harmful events. Others focus on the consequences of its occurrence and fail to take into account that it is rather unlikely to occur so that they exhibit overly cautious behavior termed "plan for the worst, hope for the best" by Sunstein (2002). A cost-benefit analysis where people exhibit predominantly this latter behavior would lead to biased benefit estimates and thus to an overprovision of protection against harmful events.

Another anomaly widely known as preference reversal occurs frequently when evaluating lotteries (cf. Lichtenstein and Slovic 1973, Sugden 1999). Seidl (2001: 621f) defines preference reversals as "an empirical regularity such that there exists a robust experimental design of lotteries for which substantial fractions of subjects state prices [...] which are opposite to the preferences expressed for or the choices made out of the respective lotteries". In other words, preference reversals represent a violation of the principle of procedure invariance according to which valid methods for preference elicitation should yield the same preference ordering. Preference reversals matter in CVM studies of risk and uncertainty because respondents in a CVM interview might state a monetary value for some risk reduction policy when asked their WTP, however, one cannot be sure that the same result would have been obtained if the respondent had been asked to choose between two uncertain alternatives based on his preferences. As Hanley and Shogren (2005: 24) note such cost-benefit analyses reveal little useful information since the valuation depends strongly upon the context in which the policy is framed. The authors propose a mechanism based on Cherry et al. (2003) for CVM studies inducing respondents to avoid preference reversing behavior in CVM settings, however this mechanism appears rather impractical and time consuming in practice.

The problems associated with valuation of risky and uncertain outcomes using the CVM and the solutions proposed in the literature so far reveal that unresolved methodological issues remain. Respondents have trouble behaving according to the normative rational decision criterion of expected utility so that simple CVM studies not taking these problems into account will necessarily lead to non-optimal outcomes, in most cases to an overvaluation of risk reduction.

### 2.2.2 Rationality problems due to preference uncertainty

In addition to uncertainty over future outcomes or environmental states it was shown in the literature that respondents often face some uncertainty w. r. t. their own preferences between environmental and market goods, especially so when they are asked to think about their personal trade-offs between these goods. Such preference uncertainty might be the source of a number of the procedural biases discussed above since uncertainty over their preferences would make respondents susceptible to answer WTP questions in a systematically distorted way. It is reasonable to expect that in a situation where respondents are uncertain of whether they prefer one situation over another or not their answers could easily be influenced by specific elements of the CVM questionnaire and survey design giving rise to irrational WTP statements thus leading to socially desirable responses and starting point bias etc. The question formats and the methods for analyzing CVM responses described above do not take the existence of preference uncertainty into account. Therefore, this section will briefly analyze existing approaches for dealing with preference uncertainty in CVM studies.

It is hypothesized that one main source of such preference uncertainty is the respondent's unfamiliarity with the environmental good to be valued, i. e. his lack of experience in using it or, in case of an environmental degradation, his lack of experience in being deprived of it and its environmental services. Another important source of preference uncertainty is certainly missing familiarity with the valuation task, i. e. to think in monetary terms about environmental goods (cf. Samnaliev et al. 2006: 508). Although people might acknowledge that in reality there are numerous situations where environmental goods are actually traded off against market goods, these decisions usually occur in the domain of public decision making where the general population is not involved since such decisions are delegated to a higher administrative level. Being all of a sudden put into the situation to personally attribute a monetary value to some environmental improvement is certainly not an everyday and common task.

However, preference uncertainty seems not to be restricted to non-market goods. As Ariely et al. (2003) demonstrate even the valuations of commonly used market goods exhibit a considerable degree of arbitrariness. In their experiments test persons were asked whether they would accept to purchase some common market good, e. g. a cordless trackball, a cordless computer keyboard, bottles of average and rare wines etc, at a price in dollar terms equaling the last two digits of their social security numbers. Subsequently they had to state their maximum WTP for the product. The answers were consequential since the test persons were required to purchase the good if a random device chose that the item would be sold at the stated price. It was demonstrated that although the test persons were made aware of the randomness of this bid amount their valuations were anchored on it so that a significantly positive relation between the amount derived from the social security numbers and the personal valuations of the goods was found. However, within the product categories the test persons exhibited consistent valuations in that cordless trackballs were consistently valued lower than cordless keyboards and average wines lower than rare wines. The authors of this study describe the observed behavior as "coherent arbitrariness" since on the one hand valuations seem coherent due to the expected relations of value within the product categories but on the other hand are significantly influenced by the arbitrary anchor. It is hypothesized, therefore, that consumers in general do not have specific WTP values for products, they rather have some range of values what the item would be worth to them (cf. Ariely et al. 2003: 77). If the price falls below this range they will certainly purchase the item, if it exceeds the range they will decline the purchase. However, it is uncertain how they will decide if the price falls within the range which opens the opportunity for the observed arbitrariness of valuations.

If such uncertainty ranges exist for common market goods that are familiar to people it is only plausible to assume the same in the case of the valuation of environmental goods. Respondents in CVM surveys certainly have a clear idea which bid they would definitely accept in a dichotomous choice format and which bid is clearly beyond being acceptable. Whenever the proposed bid falls between these two values that respondents would clearly accept or, respectively, reject, uncertainty of their true valuation exists. A number of methodological CVM studies have approached the issue of dealing with respondents' uncertainties of their preferences in order to obtain more valid welfare estimates.

The approaches of dealing with respondent uncertainty can be classified into two categories: (1) uncertainty questions in combination with open-ended and dichotomous choice question formats and (2) multiple category (polychotomous choice) valuation questions allowing respondents to express uncertainty. In the first approach respondents are usually in a first step asked their WTP for some environmental project in the standard way. Subsequently, they are asked to rate on a given scale, e. g. between 0% and 100%, how certain they are that they would actually pay the stated amount (cf. Li and Mattsson 1995, Champ et al. 1997, Loomis and Ekstrand 1998, Berrens et al. 2002). Other studies use discrete categories like "definitely sure" and "probably sure" in order to avoid specific probabilistic statements (cf. Blumenschein et al. 1998, Johannesson et al. 1998). The validity of the first approach resulting in a post-decisional certainty measure must be seen very critical. It is highly doubtful that respondents will be able and motivated to reassess their just previously made WTP statement correctly in the light of their preference uncertainty. Such an approach bears the risk that respondents feel like fools when they have to admit that their statement is actually quite doubtful.

Therefore, the second approach of assessing the level of preference uncertainty using a polychotomous choice question format is more promising. In this format respondents are given the possibility to express uncertainty directly when stating their WTP, either in a DC or in a PC format. The simplest form of polychotomous choice which was already recommended by the NOAA-panel in 1993 is to include a "not sure"-option in a DC question format. Carson et al. (1996b) recommend to treat "not sure"-responses conservatively as "no" responses since it must be expected that if those respondents were forced to choose strictly between "yes" and "no" they would reject the bid.

In an alternative, however more complex, polychotomous choice approach respondents can choose from a wide range of feeling uncertain about their "true" WTP while not being forced to contradict themselves. Multiple-bounded discrete choice (MBDC) represents a mixture between the payment card question format and the dichotomous choice format (cf. Ready et al. 1995, Welsh and Poe 1998, Alberini et al. 2003). Like in the PC format respondents are presented a list of bids, however, instead of indicating the highest acceptable amount for the proposed program respondents in the MBDC format are given a polychotomous choice option of rating for each interval on the list how likely they are to vote for the program if they had to pay the specified amount. Thus, for each bid respondents should indicate one of the given categories of likelihood "definitely yes", "probably yes", "not sure", "probably no" and "definitely no". For bid levels below their uncertainty range it is expected that respondents will indicate "definitely yes" whereas for bid levels above that range "definitely no" will be chosen. The uncertainty categories in this format give the respondent the possibility to express uncertainty about the respective bid levels in the three broad verbal categories "probably yes", "not sure" and "probably no", thus in this format respondents consider their certainty about bid levels not in retrospect but simultaneously. In contrast to the post-decisional certainty measures, therefore, expressed uncertainty in the MBDC format directly refers to preference uncertainty and not to the likelihood of having told the truth in the preceding WTP question.

The response data collected in a MBDC format allow to formulate different models for the estimation of WTP based on the desired level of certainty. For example, if absolute certainty of the "yes"-response is desired a "definitely yes"-model can be estimated where the highest amount on the list of bids for which "definitely yes" was indicated is taken as the lower bound of the respondent's WTP interval and the next higher bid level is taken as upper bound. Alternatively, one could generate a "probably yes"-model or a "not sure"-model. A comparison of the "definitely yes"-, the "probably yes"- and the "not sure"-model with WTP responses obtained from regular open-ended (OE), PC and single-bounded DC formats reveals three interesting results: the "definitely yes"-model yields WTP estimates well below those obtained from the regular OE, PC and DC formats, the "probably yes"-model yields estimates close to the OE and PC formats, whereas the DC estimates are nearly identical with the "not sure"-model (cf. Welsh and Poe 1998: 179). These results shed light on the reasons for the differences between the elicitation question formats: in the OE and PC formats respondents behave more cautiously and state as their maximum WTP only those values they feel quite confident with. In contrast, the DC format induces respondents to answer "yes" to the proposed bid although they feel considerably uncertain about whether they are actually willing to pay this amount. Thus, these findings are in line with the observed starting point bias in the DC format.

The rationality of WTP statements made under preference uncertainty is certainly an issue that deserves scrutiny, especially if respondents have no possibility to express this feeling while giving their WTP responses. This issue will, therefore, be taken up again in chapter 4 where a theoretical approach employing fuzzy preferences will be discussed that may prove useful to incorporate the phenomenon of preference uncertainty into environmental valuation methods.

## 2.3 Summary

This chapter gave an overview of the main aspects of the state of the art of environmental valuation with a focus on the Contingent Valuation Method. As a direct method of preference elicitation the CVM has the advantage to allow the assessment of both use and non-use values which play an important role in the context of environmental goods. In 2.2 the Hicksian Compensating Variation was derived as an appropriate individual welfare measure for environmental improvement projects. The Compensating Variation in this case can, as an approximation, be interpreted as the willingness to pay for a proposed improvement of an environmental good and is as such accessible to valuation using the CVM. In order to lay the foundations for further research of the CVM in this study the main approaches of questionnaire design and econometric estimation as well as the main theoretical and procedural concerns addressed in the past and current literature were presented. It was shown, however, that the simulated market settings employed by the direct valuation methods in order to measure also non-use values of environmental changes come at the cost of concerns that respondents often do not behave fully rationally. Such irrational behavior in CVM interviews may, therefore, result in biased benefit estimates.

Therefore, the second section of this chapter discussed in detail what can go wrong in CVM interviews when respondents do not behave fully rationally and approaches found in the literature to mitigate biases resulting from irrational response behavior were presented. Finally, the issue of preference uncertainty was addressed and its effects in CVM surveys were highlighted. Preference uncertainty was identified to be one of the prerequisites for the occurrences of procedural biases since the lack of firm preferences between market and environmental goods may make respondents susceptible to being unduly influenced by specific characteristics of the survey instrument employed.

It is the purpose of this study to build on this previous work in the literature and find new ways of describing unexplained response behavior and make recommendations for an improvement of the CVM design in order to better account for the behavior of real world decision makers.

# 3 Rationality in economics

## 3.1 Outline of the chapter

The assumption of rational economic agents has always played a prominent and very important role in economic theory. Rational action and decision making is seen as the underlying postulate of economic behavior. In fact, it is argued that the rationality postulate is essential for economic models to have a meaning, i. e. to have explanatory value with respect to economic behavior. As Silberberg (1990: 300) puts it, "Anything in the world can be explained on the basis that the participants are stupid [... ].", but no systematic conclusions or refutable hypotheses could be drawn from such an assumption. The challenge and at the same time the value of building economic models is to explain people's observed economic behavior based on the assumption that they make rational decisions, i. e. that they are not stupid. At the same time, over the course of time the rationality assumption has proven to be one of the most controversial and criticized of all the assumptions stated in economic models. This stems from the fact that on the one hand side the definitions or axioms of rationality used in many economic models are often unrealistic in that real economic agents could not be expected to fully act on the basis of these axioms and on the other hand it has been shown that in certain and reproducible circumstances people consistently violate these rationality axioms in their observed economic behavior.

This chapter presents the emergence and further development of rationality concepts in economics. To this end, in section 3.2.1 the history of the rationality postulate starting from Adam Smith via Alfred Marshall is briefly reviewed. The three axioms of rationality which form the basis of the concept of instrumental rationality in neoclassical economics are introduced. Subsequently, the main points of criticism of the central rationality axiom, transitivity, will be highlighted. Specifically, arguments are presented as to why it is not reasonable to expect that economic agents always optimize. Section 3.2.2 will explore extensions of the concept of instrumental rationality leading to the overarching concept of bounded rationality. In section 3.3 the emergence of the bounded rationality concept as well as prominent instances of boundedly rational behavior will be presented. Since bounded rationality draws heavily on psychological insights on human information processing and decision making the main concepts of cognitive psychology shall be addressed in the light of decision making in environmental valuation. Finally, specific models of dual-processes of reasoning reflecting boundedly rational decision making in environmental valuation will be outlined. These models form the conceptual basis for the development of an empirical survey instrument for the analysis of bounded rationality in chapter 4.

## 3.2 Rationality concepts in economics – an overview

### 3.2.1 What is rationality?

Although Adam Smith does not use the term "rationality" explicitly in his work "The Wealth of Nations" first published in 1776, his reflections on human behavior in economic contexts serve as a good starting point for a discussion of what "rationality" means in economics and how the interpretation and operationalization of this term has changed over time. In his famous sentence "It is not from the benevolence of the butcher, the brewer, or the baker, that we expect our dinner, but from their regard to their own interest" (cf. Smith 1993: I.ii, p. 22) he postulates that people enter into mutually beneficial bargains out of their selfishness. Thus, Smith establishes the individual's focus on his self-interest as the fundamental driver of any economic behavior, and any action that an individual undertakes should be in pursuit of this self-interest. In this respect, the major task of human beings as economic agents is "to judge where self-interest lies" (cf. Simon 1997: 6). Without referring to the term "rational" directly Smith clearly provides a description of the appropriate criterion of economic behavior. His view of rationality stems from everyday common sense, with respect to their behavior he simply assumes that people have reasons for what they do, i. e. in Silberberg's words: that they are not stupid.

Smith's common sense view of rationality was soon going to be further specified and adapted to the requirements of the developing economic theory (cf. Simon 1987). Alfred Marshall who developed the marginalist approach to economics uses in his book "Principles of Economics" (cf. Marshall 1890: 6) the formulation "[...] free choice by each individual of that line of conduct which after careful deliberation seems to him the best suited for attaining his ends, [...]" in order to specify how an economic choice should be made. Thus, Marshall proposes that an economic agent who is to make the choice out of a number of alternative economic actions uses active reasoning given the available information about these alternative actions in order to find out which of the given actions represents the best way to satisfy the individual agent's goals and needs. This formulation, therefore, sets the scene for two fundamental assertions of neoclassical economics: (1) reasoning about the utility that is generated by each available alternative and, (2) choosing among the given alternatives so as to maximize the utility that can be achieved from the given alternative economic actions. It must be noted, that Marshall extends Smith's notion of self-interest as the main driver of economic action. He explicitly states that the ends that an economic agent wishes to attain by some economic action might be either selfish or unselfish. With this remark, Marshall already acknowledges that other-regarding behavior, i. e. altruism, can be as much an element from which people derive individual utility as behavior that one might call selfish or egoistic. It can be speculated that Adam Smith used the term "self-interest" in quite the same sense as Marshall without explicitly making the difference between strict selfishness on the one hand and unselfishness on the other.

The view of rationality that was established by Marshall and that is currently the view of rationality in the standard neoclassical economic models is usually termed *full*, *perfect*, *global* or *instrumental* rationality. The terms *perfect* and *global* should indicate that under this rationality concept economic agents are assumed to have full knowledge or information about all possible economic actions and their resulting outcomes and are able to fully compute the (expected) consequences of these actions and outcomes on their utilities in order to be able to make the decisions that maximize their utilities. The term *instrumental* refers to the view that "rational action is defined with respect to a given set of objectives: it is the action which best satisfies those objectives" (cf. Hargreaves Heap 1989: 40), i. e. the action leading to the outcome that best satisfies those objectives is considered the instrument suitable for achieving these. For every achievable outcome there is at least one instrument, one line of action, which yields this outcome.

In neoclassical microeconomic theory full rationality is described by a set of desirable properties of individuals' preference orderings, the three rationality axioms. A preference ordering that is reflexive, complete and transitive is generally perceived as a rational preference ordering since these properties guarantee that an individual will always make consistent choices out of a set of available consumption bundles (cf. Mas-Colell 1995: 6). Among these axioms, transitivity is by the far the most important one. Given completeness, transitivity imposes logical consistency restrictions on the preferences of an individual. If transitivity holds, the existence of preference cycles is ruled out, i. e. it is assured that for instance if coffee is stated to be at least as good as tea and tea at least as good as coke, then coke cannot be preferred to coffee. It is obvious that one would require an individual to exhibit transitivity in his preferences in order to classify him as rational in this example, the preference of coke over coffee in the above example would simply be logically inconsistent with the previous two preference assertions with respect to coffee, tea and coke.

It has been criticized that the concept of instrumental rationality with its three main axioms of rational preference orderings does not adequately capture the rationality inherent in economic decisions of real-world economic agents. It is concerned only with the optimal instrument but not with the possibilities that economic agents actually have to find this instrument in real-world decision environments. There is an abundant literature on the criticism of the neoclassical rationality concept and its operationalization, utility maximization. The most frequently criticized axiom of rational preference orderings in neoclassical economics is transitivity. In general, two lines of criticism are discussed: (1) transitivity and the assumption of stability of preferences over time and (2) unidimensional versus multidimensional consumption bundles. As to issue (1), there is no reason why preferences should not be allowed to change over time, either systematically or unsystematically, and, therefore, exhibit intransitivities among the alternatives available. An example of some systematic, or context dependent, preference change leading to intransitivities is given by Rosenberg (1992, cited in Lagueux, 2004): is it irrational for an individual to prefer regular coffee over milk at breakfast, milk over decaffeinated coffee at lunch, and the latter over regular coffee at dinner? In order to save the stability of preferences of this individual one would have to redefine the commodities like e. g. "milk for breakfast" and "regular coffee for lunch" where "breakfast" and "lunch" represent the different contexts in which the individual beverages need to be evaluated. But even with such a definition stability of preferences and transitivity are not assured. If, on one day, the individual plans a late night out he might well prefer regular coffee to decaf coffee for dinner and thus violate transitivity over time. One could, thus, specify the beverage even further as e. g. "regular coffee for dinner if a late night out is planned". This example could be extended into infinity which would only reveal that preferences can certainly not be assumed to be stable so that the fulfillment of transitivity as a condition for rational choice can reasonably only be expected at any one particular point in time. While under these circumstances it is still possible to represent a commodity choice at that point in time as conforming to the common rationality concept and thus as utility maximizing, the failure of preferences to exhibit transitivity over time makes a generalization of this utility maximizing choice to other similar decision situations impossible.

As to issue (2) it is expected and has generally been found that transitivity is fulfilled in situations of choices among unidimensional or two-dimensional commodities or commodity bundles consisting of only two single commodity quantities. In a set of unidimensional commodities the single commodities differ only in the level of that single attribute that characterizes them, e. g. the face value of a coin. In the situation of choosing from two-dimensional commodity bundles the individual only needs to make trade-offs among the quantities of the underlying commodities, i. e. more of one commodity against less of the other. These situations are usually sufficiently simple for transitivity to prevail. As has been argued and shown already by May (1954) choices from multidimensional commodities or commodity bundles exhibit a substantial potential for intransitivities. May's design of a multidimensional decision problem was the following: three marriage partners were distinguished; each of them was ranked according to three dimensions, namely intelligence, appearance, and wealth. The first partner, call her x, was very intelligent, plain looking, and well-off, the second, y, was intelligent, very good looking, and poor; and the third, z, was fairly intelligent, good looking, and rich. The subjects in this experiment were presented these marriage partners successively in pairs and asked to choose the most preferred, respectively. It turned out that from 62 subjects, 17 exhibited circular preferences of the kind $x \succ y \succ z \succ x$. From these choices it became clear that these individuals seemed to follow a particular decision rule in which they chose that partner that was superior to them in two out of the three criteria. This experiment was later repeated by Tversky (1969) who obtained similar results. Thus, a number of individuals was unable to perform the trade-off among the three relevant characteristics in a consistent way but seemed to rely on a simplifying decision rule that produced intransitive choices. This result indicates that transitivity seems to be a quite strong criterion for rationality that is most likely not always fulfilled in many real-world decision situations (see Rieskamp et al. 2006 for a discussion of theoretical frameworks allowing for intransitive choices, especially in the situation of risk and uncertainty).

Given this short compilation of criticisms of the neoclassical rationality, it is highly questionable that economic agents really should be expected to behave according to the mentioned properties and to apply the maximization of utility fully as their behavioral decision rule. It was shown by numerous empirical and experimental studies that people do not conform to this claim, at least in complex decision situations as are usually encountered in the real world. Thus, while Friedman (1953) correctly argues that optimization theory does not describe the underlying procedures of decision making, it is doubtful that the substance of these decisions, i. e. their outcomes, can be accurately predicted by optimization theory since it relies on the highly formalized and unrealistic axioms of rational choice.

Without doubt the theoretical models relying on the neoclassical rationality axioms have proven extremely useful and have led to a wide variety of insights into economic decision making. However, by focusing on such optimal outcomes the gap between real-world decisions and those explained by the formal economic models has widened and the common sense perspective of Adam Smith's rationality was increasingly forced to take the back seat in economic modeling.

### 3.2.2 Extensions of the neoclassical rationality concept

One way of resolving the conflict between theoretically consistent preferences as described by the transitivity axiom and people's observed violations of such rationality is to distinguish between *normative* and *descriptive* concepts of rationality. The perfect, global and instrumental concept of rationality is in this sense clearly a normative concept since it prescribes how economic agents *should* behave in a perfect model world in order to achieve the outcomes that maximize their utilities. As such, this rationality concept serves as a normative reference against which the descriptive concepts of rationality can be contrasted. Descriptive rationality concepts aim at taking account of real-world rational decisions, i. e. acknowledging cognitive and computational limitations of real economic agents and considering the specific decision environments in which agents are incorporated. As a result of the criticism of instrumental rationality as the appropriate real-world rationality concept a number of descriptive concepts have been developed, some of which have received great attention in the literature.

Herbert Simon was the first to contrast the well-established perspective of instrumental rationality against an alternative perception of rational decision making. His point of view has its roots in the psychological research on human decision making which, quite in contrast to the general view of economics, lays its focus more on how humans make decisions as opposed to how the outcomes of these decisions relate to people's preferences in the end. With this perspective, Simon decidedly takes a step back from the idealized notion of instrumental rationality and orients himself on Adam Smith's common sense view of rationality. He argues that "everything that psychology has learned about the processes of human choice is consistent with the view expressed by Adam Smith" (cf. Simon 1997: 8). And further: "People do have reasons for what they do, but these reasons depend very much on how people frame or represent the situations in which they find themselves, and upon the information they have or obtain about the variables that they take into account." Thus, on the one hand Simon accepts Smith's view of individual self-interest, that people have reasons and, in their actions, follow some intentions in order to achieve explicit or implicit goals. This view is often referred to as the "teleological" assumption of rationality.

On the other hand, and this contrasts the instrumentalists' idealized view, Simon explicitly acknowledges the specific characteristics of the real-world decision environments and the limitations with respect to the information available to the decision makers and to their cognitive abilities to take all relevant variables into account. As a result, Simon's way of looking at economic decisions does not concern as much the substance of the decision as rather the process of decision making, i. e. the way the decision outcome is achieved. Thus, in contrast to an instrumentalist interpretation of rational choice, the focus is shifted onto the process, i. e. the procedure of decision making in which the human decision maker is seen to operate in a social context and is constrained by his cognitive abilities and psychological characteristics. In Simon's words, instrumental rationality "is a theory of decision environments (and utility functions), but not of decision makers." Procedural rationality, in contrast, is interested in "[...] how the decision maker generates alternatives of action and compares them" (cf. Simon 1997: 18). A choice is, thus, procedurally rational if it is the outcome of an explicit rule "regardless of whether or not the choice is optimal" (cf. Pingle and Day 1996: 192).

Consequently, with this focus on cognitive limitations and on the process of decision making, Simon needed to be more explicit about the specific procedures of how economic subjects actually make decisions in complex situations of the real world. In his view, since optimization is not possible under real-world conditions, rules of behavior need to take its place. His procedural action is any action which is guided by a rule, often a rule of thumb, rather than an optimizing calculation. Rules of thumb, or decision heuristics as they are termed in the modern literature, serve as shortcuts, as good (and necessary) alternatives to an unfeasible and, in the case of uncertainty, never ending calculation of optimality. The latter point is known in the literature as the "infinite regress" problem (cf. Conlisk 1996, Lipman 1991, Mongin and Walliser 1988, Winter 1971). An instrumental decision maker, in a complex real world, needs to make a decision whether to choose an alternative or not. In the real world not all of the information needed to take an optimal decision in this respect is available or known *a priori*, it is necessary that the decision maker first acquires this information, i. e. that he searches for it actively. In order to choose one alternative over the others, one must first know all the other alternatives and the benefits associated with these alternatives.

However, in the real world information acquisition is costly, either in terms of time and thus opportunity costs or in actual monetary costs. The decision maker, therefore, is faced with another decision: how much to invest in information search. Instrumentally rational as he is he would continue to invest in additional information until the expected benefit of the last piece of information is just equal to the cost of acquiring this particular piece of information, i. e. until the marginal benefit of information search equals its marginal cost. However, the marginal benefit of this information is unknown until it is acquired so that one would first need to know all the unknown information before making this kind of cost-benefit analysis of optimal information acquisition. But if all the information is known one would not need to determine at which point to optimally stop searching. Thus, what is needed is some rule that tells the decision maker when to stop searching and use the available information about the alternatives to finally make a decision.

With its focus on the process of decision making rather than on the logical consistency of the decision outcomes procedural rationality stands in clear contrast to instrumental rationality. Thus, procedural rationality is clearly a descriptive concept where the outcome of the decision making process is perceived as rational as long as it is in congruence with the limited cognitive and computational capacities of the decision makers. As such, these two concepts seem incompatible so that one is forced to take one position or the other, i. e. insisting that rational decisions must be also logically consistent and everyone who chooses otherwise is simply irrational or surrendering to the sad facts of life and accept that people are simply incapable of knowing what's really good for them.

However, apart from these two extreme world views there are hybrid rationality concepts that draw both on instrumental and procedural rationality at the same time in order to come up with a more adequate and realistic perception of rational decision making: institutional rationality and evolutionary rationality, where both concepts are to some extent related. Both incorporate instrumental rationality as one mode of operation whereas another mode of operation bears close resemblance to rule following as postulated by the concept of procedural rationality. Thus, institutional and evolutionary rationality can be classified as dual-mode rationality concepts. As Redmond (2004: 177) argues, "institutional rationality [...] requires two types of thinking, one which produces rule-following behaviors and one which produces purpose-seeking behaviors". This distinction of modes has its origin in the research on human "cognitive processes which involve a complex and multi-tiered system, one that distinguishes between actions resulting from deliberation on [the] one hand and actions resulting from habit and reflex on the other" (cf. Hodgson 1994, see also section 3.3.3 for details on cognitive psychology). This distinction conforms well to von Hayek's (1973) assertion that "man is as much a rule-following animal as a purpose-seeking one".

In which kinds of situations are these two modes employed for decision making? Purpose-seeking activities can be characterized as situations in which active cognitive reasoning is required, most notably when a novel situation exhibits few parallels to already existing experience or when there is a conflict between various goals of a decision maker. In such situations, the decision maker needs to devise a plan in order to achieve his goals. Rule-following activities, on the other hand, are characterized by little need for cognitive effort since they are backed by personal experiences with the same or similar situations in the past so that a decision maker can simply retrieve from his long-term memory already pre-scripted courses of action. Here, the main task for the decision maker is to classify the respective situation in order to be able to retrieve the appropriate stored rule for behavior.

The underlying logic of this dual mode of operation is to be seen in an economizing on scarce cognitive resources: those situations that can be dealt with by pre-scripted rules that have proven to be useful in the past should not take away scarce cognitive resources from situations in which it is necessary, due to the novelty of the situation, to use active cognitive reasoning in order to devise a plan and find an appropriate course of action that will lead to the individual's goals. Thus, from Redmond's point of view, such a dual system of decision making is rational in the sense that the cognitive limitations, not only in terms of basic computational capabilities but also in terms of competing resources, are best allocated to the multitude of decision tasks that an individual faces every day. This view is highlighted in the following quote by Redmond (2004: 180): "Probability of success is higher when the mind is engaged in fewer tasks. Thus it would confer adaptational value if capacity and attention were conserved in order to be available for those situations of an important, rather than a routine, nature".

However, the borderline between rules, habits or customs and active cognition is hazy but this is precisely the origin of institutions. Institutions, in this case, can be seen as a set of behavioral guidelines for an individual or a group of people. They consist of norms, habits, customs, traditions and laws and as such form the basic behavioral elements of a society. According to Bush (1987) all institutions are the outcome of conscious choices made at some point in time by group members. Persistent institutions have proven to be successful rules for dealing with recurrent problems within a society. Thus, one can observe the development from cognitively effortful problem solving until successful plans are discovered to the establishment of these plans within a group of people so that these plans and courses of action become rules, habits and routines adding to the institutional pool of that group. In this sense, institutional rationality comprises both some form of instrumental rationality in which a problem is solved using cognitive effort, either by groups over an extended period of time or just by one individual, and rule-following based on these culturally or individually learned successful problem solving plans.

The concept of evolutionary rationality[2] is closely related to institutional rationality, however, it makes the evolution of institutions as mentioned above more explicit. It originates from work of Vernon Smith who found systematic deviations from the predictions of instrumental rationality in his experiments. As Smith (2003: 467) noted, hypotheses derived from instrumental, or constructivist rationality as he calls it, were not always confirmed: while in impersonal market exchange situations people seemed to behave rationally in the constructivist sense, people were often found to deviate in situations of personal exchange, e. g. in two-person game situations in which people chose to cooperate where defection would have been the rational move but, nevertheless,

---

2 Evolutionary rationality is also called "ecological rationality" by some authors (cf. Smith 2003), however, the term "ecological rationality" often describes the rationality of an adaptive decision maker (cf. Todd and Gigerenzer 2003) whose behavior is the best response to the constraints of the decision environment in the real world and, thus, "ecologically" rational. This latter concept is already included in the concepts of institutional and evolutionary rationality, so that no further distinction shall be made here.

achieved cooperation by their counterpart, thus reaching a collectively superior outcome.

Such experimental and empirical findings which could not convincingly be explained by the constructivist view gave rise to perceiving the development of institutions "as an undesigned ecological system that emerges out of cultural and biological evolutionary processes" (cf. Smith 2003: 469). Thus, in sharp contrast to the concept of institutional rationality mentioned above, evolutionarily rational institutions need not be devised by conscious and cognitively effortful reasoning processes but have emerged from social processes in which agents, based on their experiences try new patterns of behavior that are subsequently selected or rejected on the basis of the desirability of the achieved outcome. In this evolutionary process the agents who introduce new patterns need not be rational in the instrumental or constructivist sense, they need not be able to apply conscious and consequent reasoning for determining their courses of action, they can be "naïve" and experience-based in their reasoning and still give rise to a new trial-and-error process that results in superior outcomes that subsequently get selected as institutions to persist. In an evolutionary process it is possible that institutions emerge that prove to be superior to institutions that would have been devised by constructivist rationality alone.[3]

**Figure 3-1:** Classification of rationality concepts in economics (own graph)

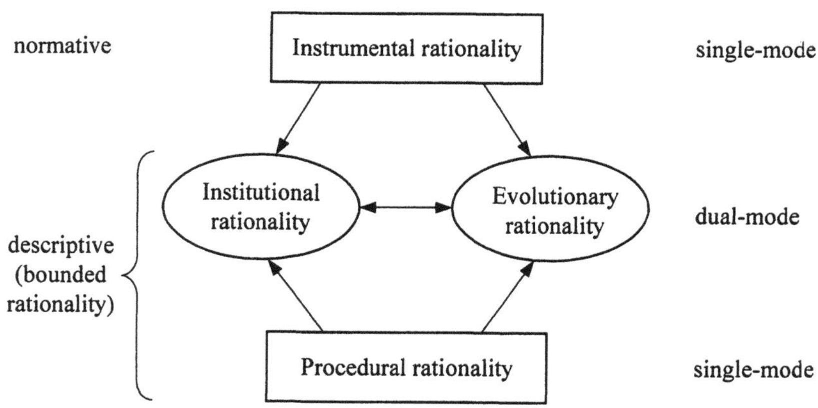


Figure 3-1 visualizes the connection of the rationality concepts described above. While instrumental rationality and procedural rationality represent antipodes in the sense of being mainly normative versus descriptive, respectively, both are

[3] See also Vanberg (2004) and Holland (1996) on evolutionary rationality where the evolutionary processes of rule creation and selection are made more explicit.

generally conceived as operating in one single mode. Since the hybrid concepts of institutional and evolutionary rationality draw on both single-mode concepts they can be classified as dual-mode concepts of rationality.

The field of descriptive rationality concepts derived from a more procedural perception of rationality shall be subsumed here under the term "bounded rationality". In the literature, no clear cut definition of what bounded rationality comprises and what it does not, has emerged. In any case, the central characteristic of bounded rationality is its requirement to be in line with the central findings of cognitive psychology regarding information processing in human brains, problem solving and decision making. As already mentioned in the section on procedural rationality as conceptualized by Herbert Simon, the use of decision heuristics in order to find a way out of the notorious infinite regress problem of rational choice is the main feature of the descriptive rationality concepts. Evolutionary rationality explains the emergence of such decision rules while institutional rationality provides an intuition as to when it is rational to employ conscious, cognitively effortful reasoning and when procedural, rule-following behavior seems to be more appropriate. Due to the importance of the overarching concept of bounded rationality for this study, the following section shall briefly review its development and evidence in the literature before addressing more specifically the kinds of decision heuristics employed by boundedly rational decision makers.

## 3.3 Bounded rationality

### 3.3.1 The emergence of bounded rationality in the literature

Even before the term "bounded rationality" appeared for the first time in the social science literature with Herbert Simon's book "Models of Man" (cf. Simon 1957), the concept developed in social science works under different terms. In a recent historiographic survey Klaes and Sent (2005) analyze the occurrence of related terms over the course of time. They identify a base field of expressions and technical terms setting the stage and preceding the occurrence of bounded rationality. The term *limited intelligence* appeared for the first time in the literature in 1840 in a Report to the Council of the Statistical Society and can be considered the starting point of the conceptual development of bounded rationality. *Limited intelligence* is later joined by a number of terms within the base field of bounded rationality, namely *finite intelligence*, *incomplete rationality*, *limited rationality* and *approximate rationality*. The numbers of occurrences of these terms of the base field in the literature up to now, along with those of subsequent concepts, are illustrated in table 3-1.

While limited intelligence was at that time far from being used as a technical term and rather carried along prejudicial and offending connotations with respect to other peoples or social classes, the term finite intelligence became a technical term largely confined to the philosophical literature as of the year 1880. It was mainly used to distinguish man's intelligence, thoughts and ideas from divine, perfect intelligence, thus closely associated with religious ideas. In the 1920s this term becomes mainly used to describe the limitations of human cognition with respect to the perception of the natural world.

**Table 3-1:** The development of the Bounded Rationality field from 1840 – 1995, from Klaes and Sent (2005: 30)

| | first occurrence | Total |
|---|---|---|
| Base field | | |
| Limited intelligence | 1840 | 73 |
| Finite intelligence | 1880 | 40 |
| Incomplete rationality | 1922 | 7 |
| Limited rationality | 1945 | 105 |
| Approximate rationality | 1948 | 9 |
| Bounded rationality | 1957 | 626 |
| Procedural rationality | 1963 | 124 |
| Finite rationality | 1972 | 17 |
| Constrained rationality | 1978 | 7 |

In 1922 the word "rationality" starts to be associated with discussions of *finite intelligence* in Oakeley's article "On the Meaning of Value" (cf. Oakley 1922, cited in Klaes and Sent 2005: 34) which is contrary to its title not an economic work but a philosophical treatise of how humans with their finite intelligence and limited knowledge of the world could possibly "comprehend ideals of value". In this sense, *incomplete rationality* is seen as a central property of, in this respect, limitedly endowed human beings. Whereas *incomplete rationality* was just very shortly and rarely used in the literature (see table 3-1), the expression *limited rationality* first used by Almond (1945, cited in Klaes and Sent 2005: 36) turned out to be a much more potent technical term for a further diffusion of the controversies on rationality. When Herbert Simon entered the discussion of rationality concepts in economics, he picked up *limited rationality* as the common term in the social science literature at that time in his groundbreaking article "A Behavioral Model of Rational Choice" in 1955 (cf. Simon 1955).

According to Klaes and Sent (2005) Simon seemed to experiment for some time with variations of rationality terms, in the process coining the term *approximate rationality*, until he finally created the technical expression *bounded rationality* which came to dominate the entire conceptual field in the subsequent decades. Simon intended "to use this expression as a label for the things that economists needed to pay attention to – and were not" (Simon 1999: 23, cited in Klaes and Sent 2005: 37). From hindsight, bounded rationality emerged as the dominating technical term for mainly two reasons: first, Simon elevated it to the rank of a principle, the "principle of bounded rationality" which seemed to motivate discussions and further research as to a deeper understanding of such a principle, and, second, the term "bounded" seemed to appeal to mathematically oriented economists who were used to thinking of optimization problems in terms of boundary conditions to some objective function. Thus, the limitations of the human mind were coined as a mere extension to the already existing boundary conditions of a mathematical optimization problem which made this concept easier to assimilate in economics. In the introduction to part IV of "Models of Man" (cf. Simon 1957: 196ff), where the term bounded rationality was supposedly used for the first time in the literature, Simon sets out the principle as follows: "The alternative approach employed in these papers is based on what I shall call the principle of bounded rationality: The capacity of the human mind for formulating and solving complex problems is very small compared with the size of the problems whose solution is required for objectively rational behavior in the real world – or even for a reasonable approximation to such objective rationality". Later, Simon (1987: 266) states that the concept is used to "designate rational choice that takes into account the cognitive limitations of the decision maker – limitations of both knowledge and computational capacity." Thus, the concept was intended as a criticism of neoclassical economics which used to model decision making generally in an environment of either perfect information or optimal risk taking under the assumption of unlimited computational abilities.

With his models based on the "principle of bounded rationality" Simon starts to provide a formal framework for modeling decision making under circumstances that are seen to be more appropriate in real-world situations and thus challenges the standard neoclassical models. He explicitly takes into account and includes into his models those conditions of the human mind and of his social, external environment that prevent human actors from making decisions in such a way that would even approximate the predictions of neoclassical economics. Instead of aiming only on the outcome of a decision problem, as this would be the focus under the concept of substantive or global rationality, bounded rationality stresses the importance of the process of decision making, of how people actually arrive at their decisions given their knowledge, computational capabilities and external constraints. In order to be able to arrive at suitable decisions at all, human actors seem to have developed simplifying strategies, based on tradition and experience, that have proved to be successful in the past. These rules of thumb, or heuristics, enable a decision maker to arrive at least at a satisfactory decision within the given constraints. For this search for merely satisfactory outcomes for which, after attained in the decision making process, any search for better outcomes is terminated, Simon has coined the term "satisficing". Under the satisficing heuristic a decision maker defines an aspiration level, i. e. a minimal level of well-being to be attained by some decision, and searches and evaluates the available alternatives, the budget set, until an alternative satisfying that minimal aspiration level is found. At that point, the search and evaluation of further alternatives is terminated and the decision maker settles with the (first) satisfactory outcome found along the search. In this simple procedure, the main concern of the principle of bounded rationality and its main point of criticism of neoclassical economics becomes apparent: the necessity to define at which point a search or a decision making process is finally terminated. The satisficing heuristic, therefore, represents a real-world operationalization of the common condition for search-stopping that the marginal benefit of further search should equal its marginal cost.

### 3.3.2 Evidence of bounded rationality in economics and the social sciences

Accepting the existence of bounded rationality in real-world decision making does not mean to assume that all decisions exhibit strong distorting effects that would entirely reject the results predicted by the standard theory of instrumental or substantive rationality. There are many situations in which the outcomes of economic decision problems are in conformity with the standard theory, i. e. where economic agents achieve optimal or nearly optimal outcomes. However, the literature provides a wide variety of examples in which the assumptions of the standard theory seem to fail systematically and where alternative approaches for explaining the observed behavior, like for example bounded rationality, need to be taken into consideration. This section will review some of the evidence of boundedly rational behavior found in the literature and will try to uncover some unifying pattern from these examples.

One line of evidence of boundedly rational behavior is based on direct experiments with single individuals in order to test whether they adhere to the assumption of substantive rationality in that experimental setting. The basic idea in many of such experiments is to confront individuals with a specific decision problem to which an objectively correct solution exists, such as dealing with probabilities and statistical evidence. These experiments demonstrate that individuals are susceptible to a number of systematic biases: e. g. they often seem to misunderstand statistical independence of given data, they mistake random data for patterned data and vice versa, they make errors in updating probabilities on the basis of new information (a violation of Bayes' rule), make false inferences about causalities and exaggerate the ex ante probability of a random event which has already occurred, just to name a few (see Conlisk 1996 for a detailed review of these effects). Other experiments do not make use of such a reference point of objectively correct answers but they test whether the observed behavior exhibited by test individuals in an experimental setting conforms to the expectation predicted by the standard rationality assumption. In these experiments it is often found, for example, that people place higher values on "status quo" options than would be expected, that they fail to discount the future consistently and that they fail to adjust repeated choices in the light of changing constraints (cf. Conlisk 1996). It is, thus, hypothesized that people systematically commit cognitive errors and use simplifying rules, or heuristics, when solving a given task.

The above mentioned results emerged from a body of literature mainly initiated by decision theory psychologists around Daniel Kahneman, Amos Tversky and Paul Slovic who started an extensive research program known as "Heuristics and Biases" (cf. Kahneman et al. 1982, Gilovich et al. 2002). Under the overarching theme of simplifying mechanisms of information processing leading to systematic biases of judgment and decision behavior, three basic heuristics were identified to be accountable for these effects: (1) availability, (2) representativeness, and (3) anchoring and adjustment. The *availability heuristic* refers to judgment errors caused by the ease of memory retrieval, e. g. the estimation of how frequently a specific event occurs would be biased by how recently such an event has occurred because recent events are more easily available in the mind than less recent ones.

The *representativeness heuristic* refers to judgment which is influenced by what one considers typical. A rather famous and widely controversially discussed example is the "Linda problem" which shall be cited here because of its prominence in the literature. In this example, test persons are given a brief description of a 31 year-old woman who is single, outspoken and very bright. As a student she majored in philosophy and was deeply concerned with issues of discrimination and social justice. Also, she participated in anti-nuclear demonstrations. After this description the test persons are asked to rank a number of statements about her according to their probability to be true. Surprisingly, a majority of test persons rank the statement "Linda is a bank teller and is active in the feminist movement" (T&F) more likely than the more general statement "Linda is a bank teller" (T). This judgment is a clear violation of the conjunction rule according to which the more specific category T&F cannot be more likely than the more general category T since the former is just a subset of the latter. Therefore, such biased judgment was termed "conjunction fallacy". It is argued that this behavior is brought about by the higher representativeness of the specific statement T&F in terms of the description of the personality, i. e. the description resembles that of a typical feminist (without even mentioning this trait explicitly) so that the more specific statement of Linda being a feminist bank teller is invoked more strongly than the one of being "just" a bank teller, for which the personality description is not at all typical. The conjunction fallacy could be replicated in a wide variety of experiments under different environments.

An often cited consequence of the representative heuristic is the phenomenon of preference reversals which have already been discussed in relation to reasoning errors in the CVM under risk and uncertainty in section 2.2.1. Preference reversals represent a violation of the fundamental principle of procedure invariance and are, thus, of great concern for any empirical application of economic decision making. For illustration, a simple example of preference reversals shall be given here using the following two gambles A and B:

Gamble A: 90% probability to win $8
Gamble B: 20% probability to win $30

In preference reversal experiments test persons are asked to state a minimum price at which they would sell each of these gambles (assuming they had acquired the right to play the gambles themselves) and to subsequently choose which gamble they would like to play. In this experiment, most people choose to play gamble A over gamble B, but at the same time a high proportion of people (40% - 50%) states a higher selling price for gamble B. This result is a clear violation of procedural invariance according to which it should not matter which method, pricing versus choice, is used for eliciting the preferences over these gambles. Preference reversals are usually explained by the compatibility effect and the prominence effect which can both be interpreted as being based on representativeness. The compatibility effect states that when monetary values are an available attribute of a gamble they have more influence on an evaluative response which is also in monetary units like a price. Thus, since $30 is much higher than $8 gamble B receives a higher price. On the other hand, when asked to choose a gamble to play a probability of winning of 90% features much more prominent than one of 20% so that people tend to make their choice, in this case correctly, based on the higher probability. The literature dealing with preference reversals is much too extensive to be reviewed here (cf. Irwin et al. 1993, List 2002, Safra et al. 1990, Seidl 2001).

The *anchoring and adjustment heuristic* refers to judgment which is influenced by what comes first, i. e. where "people make estimates by starting from an initial value that is adjusted to yield the final answer [and where] adjustments are typically insufficient" (cf. Tversky and Kahneman 1974: 1128). Such anchors, although randomly chosen and presented to test persons, were shown to influence judgments consistently in a wide variety of task environments. Thus, whenever anchors are chosen or provided in a biased way the outcome of a judgment based on anchoring and adjustment will be biased as well. The starting point bias in the dichotomous choice elicitation format is a good example for the use of the anchoring and adjustment heuristic in the context of the CVM. A number of results inconsistent with the traditional rationality assumptions, especially in judgments based on the correct application of the expected utility criterion, could be explained by these three underlying heuristics and as such form the conceptual basis for frequently observed judgment errors in CVM surveys.

It was found that certain cognitive errors could be avoided with increasing experience on the side of the individual decision maker and by making certain changes in the experimental design. From these findings, it was investigated under which circumstances the found systematic biases could be made to disappear (debiasing). It turned out that while setting clear economic incentives and punishing cognitive errors successfully eliminated some of the biases, others consistently kept occurring so that the possibilities for debiasing remained limited (cf. Grether 1992, Slonim 1994).

A second line of evidence of boundedly rational behavior is rooted in testing rationality assumptions using real economic data, either from actual transactions or from economic surveys. Thaler (1992) provides a comprehensive overview of anomalies in everyday economic life collected from a series of articles in The Journal of Economic Perspectives. In the field of consumer behavior it commonly occurs that households deviate substantially from the assumptions of standard life cycle theory of intertemporal choice. Smoothing of consumption on the basis of perceived life-time income is usually far from efficient in this sense so "that the young and the old consume too little, that consumption is unduly sensitive to short run income fluctuations, that consumption is not sensitive enough to expected future changes in income, and that consumption is improperly sensitive to the composition of wealth and income" (cf. Conlisk 1996: 672). A rich source of anomalies are the financial markets, e. g. the stock market and foreign exchange markets where investors exhibit anomalous behavior with respect to asset pricing. The development of asset prices generally deviates from the predictions of the efficient markets hypothesis according to which arbitrage should make price predictability impossible. However, a number of studies demonstrate anomalies like end-of-week, end-of-year, seasonal and holiday effects (cf. Thaler 1992: 139ff), excess fluctuation in prices relative to fluctuation in fundamental data and dramatic bubbles that cannot be explained by changes in fundamentals, just to name a few. Cutler et al. (1991) provide an extensive overview of such anomalies.

An anomaly already discussed in the context of environmental valuation (see chapter 2) seems to be present in other economic situations as well: that people attribute a higher value to a good if they are asked to sell it than if they were to acquire it, i. e. the disparity between willingness-to-pay and willingness-to-accept. This anomaly is at odds with standard utility theory and implies that an individual's indifference curve exhibits a kink at the status quo location. Such indifference curves whose location changes every time a different status quo is observed cannot conform to the basic assumptions of utility theory like e. g. transitivity. In their prospect theory Kahneman and Tversky (1979) have termed this kind of behavior "loss aversion" and "endowment effect". Since the development of the theory, prospect theory has been extended in a number of ways, e. g. allowing for uncertainty of status quo and reference points (see Schmidt et al. forthcoming for a discussion of refinements of prospect theory). A further example of frequently occurring anomalies is the phenomenon of overbidding, termed "winner's curse" by Thaler (1992). During auctions, experimental or real, it is a common phenomenon that the winning bid either exceeds the value of the offered stake or turns out to generate a disappointingly low surplus falling short of the opportunity costs of the investment. Numerous studies (e. g. Capen et al. 1971, Hendricks et al. 1987, cited in Thaler 1992) have been conducted on returns of oil drilling lease auctions documenting the losses and low returns for the winners. According to Thaler (1992: 62) "the key ingredient is the existence of a cognitive illusion, a mental task that induces a substantial majority of subjects to make a systematic error. [...] Whenever such an illusion can be demonstrated, the possibility that market outcomes will diverge from the predictions of economic theory is present."

In summary, the above mentioned behavioral anomalies demonstrate the fact that the standard assumption of substantive rationality is too idealistic to accommodate and explain many facets of behavior observed in the real world. As was shown in chapter 2 deviations from instrumentally rational behavior was also widely observed in the field of environmental valuation methods. This section demonstrated that the reasons for such anomalous behavior, whether in every day economic decisions, laboratory experiments or CVM surveys, are based largely on the same behavioral principles. Thus far, however, bounded rationality and its behavioral consequences were treated in a rather descriptive way. In order to understand and analyze boundedly rational behavior its underlying mechanisms need to be explored further. Since the main characteristics of bounded rationality as described above were found in people's limited cognitive and information processing capabilities explanations for boundedly rational reasoning should be found in the field of psychology, especially modern cognitive psychology. The following section of this chapter will, therefore, explore these foundations of boundedly rational information processing, specifically in relation to environmental valuation methods, by looking over the disciplinary fence into the neighboring field of psychology.

### 3.3.3 The psychological foundations of bounded rationality in environmental valuation

#### 3.3.3.1 Why deal with psychology?

Looking at human decision making behavior in general, evidence of decision not conforming to the assumption of full rationality is rather strong in real-world situations. As shown above, in many judgment and decision making environments people deviate systematically from the predictions made by standard theories based on the fully rational *homo oeconomicus*. One explanation for this behavior is certainly that deliberation comes at a cost to the economic agent so that these costs need to be included into models of optimal decision making. This approach, however, is limited by the infinite regress problem of optimal search mentioned in section 3.2.2 where Simon proposed the use of the satisficing heuristic to determine the point of equality of marginal benefits of further search and marginal cost in an intuitive way. Given these observations and given the fact that decisions are actually taken in the real world despite the impossibility of determining optimal stopping as defined above there must be other explanations of how people actually arrive at decisions, some even in very short time without possibly being able to check for the fulfillment of the mentioned marginal condition.

Relating the insights of the preceding sections of this chapter to the theme of this study, environmental valuation using direct valuation methods like the CVM, some important connections can be drawn between the rationality problems mentioned in chapter 2 and the concept of bounded rationality described above. It was revealed that CVM respondents are susceptible to produce systematically biased responses to the WTP elicitation question when particular characteristics of a questionnaire or an interview situation prevail. In case respondents were fully rational in the instrumental sense their responses to the WTP elicitation question would simply be guided by their evaluation of their preference ordering w. r. t. to market and environmental goods. Their response would, thus, be invariant to procedural characteristics of the survey as long as the environmental good to be valued remains the same. Obviously, this is not the case as demonstrated by a multitude of valuation studies systematically exploring biased response behavior.

Instead, respondents' WTP statements seem to be guided to some extent by characteristics of the survey that should have nothing to do with their "real" valuation of the environmental good. The initial bid in a dichotomous choice elicitation question or the presence of an interviewer during the interview appear to trigger certain behavioral programs within the respondent with which he reacts to these elements of the decision environment. It might be suspected that such behavior stems from certain rules the respondent has learned to apply in particular decision situations. For example, as is often suspected, an initial bid signals the respondent a reasonable amount that everyone would have to pay for the provision of an environmental good, like e. g. a fair share of the cost of provision. The behavioral rule activated in this situation might be to accept such a fair share although the respondent is not entirely certain of the actual benefits accruing to him in case the environmental good is provided.

For the respondent such a behavior must not be considered irrational, although it might be from a strictly instrumental point of view. Employing such a behavioral rule functions as a simplifying heuristic that allows him to evaluate an unknown situation that would otherwise require much cognitive effort with much less time and effort, instead. The respondent considers the use of such a heuristic as rational since it might have helped him in previous situations to make adequate decisions. Therefore, such observed behavior must be evaluated in the light of bounded rationality as discussed above.

In order to search for the underlying reasons for boundedly rational reasoning and human decision making behavior it seems promising to look into the neighboring field of psychology as a discipline that lies at the core of mental processes in human brains, the foundations of all behavior. The necessity to transgress the disciplinary boundaries of economics and search for explanations of boundedly rational behavior in psychology was prominently stated by Simon in two citations: "If the principle [of bounded rationality] is correct, then the goal of classical economic theory – to predict the behavior of rational man without making an empirical investigation of his psychological properties – is unattainable" (cf. Simon 1957: 199) and: "Theories of bounded rationality are more ambitious [than simply expected utility], in trying to capture the actual process of decision as well as the substance of the final decision itself. A veridical theory of this kind can only be erected on the basis of empirical knowledge of the capabilities and limitations of the human mind; that is to say, on the basis of psychological research" (cf. Simon 1987: 267). In the light of this necessity, after a long period of seemingly insurmountable gaps in their respective world views the scientific fields of economics and psychology have in recent times come increasingly closer in the way they perceive human decision making (cf. Handgraaf and van Raaij 2005). Behavioral economics (from the side of economists) and economic psychology (from the side of psychologists) are now well-established fields of interdisciplinary cooperation.

Broadly speaking, psychology aims at understanding mental processes of human beings and at explaining human behavior using this understanding. Exploring the link between the outside world with its many stimuli and the inner perception, experiencing and feeling of an organism with its subsequent consequences on that organism's behavior observable from the outside world constitutes the general interest of the discipline (cf. Ulich and Bösel 2005: 11ff). More particularly, psychology distinguishes "forces" like emotions and motives on the one hand from "functions" like cognition and action on the other (cf. Rohracher 1984). Forces are considered the more fundamental psychic phenomena, they form the basis of experiencing and give rise and reason to psychic functions. At the same time these psychic forces are difficult to observe and, therefore, remain largely inaccessible. Cognition is an expression for all processes of acquiring, organizing, storing, retrieving and utilizing knowledge (cf. Medin et al. 2005: 4), whereas action comprises purposeful, subjectively meaningful and conscious forms of behavior (cf. Ulich and Bösel 2005: 15). Thus, psychology analyzes the link between states of mind (motives), perception and processing of information and observable behavior, all of which also form the basis of economic action and decision making.

With respect to the objective of understanding the role of information search and deliberation as being the main feature of boundedly rational behavior in economics in general and of response behavior in environmental valuation surveys in particular, the field of cognition within the discipline of psychology seems most promising for discovering suitable concepts relating to decision making. Using economic terminology, the above mentioned forces "emotions" and "motives" can be interpreted as being part of or forming the preference ordering, e. g. between market commodities and environmental goods, of an economic agent. The function "action" or behavior, on the other hand, can be interpreted as an economic agent's expression of this preference, i. e. the result of an economic decision making process, for example a WTP statement in CVM. The function "cognition", then, serves as a link between an individual's preferences and his economic behavior since perception and information processing of outside stimuli influence an agent's emotions and motives for action. At the same time the cognitive system is responsible for finding those actions that are suitable to be in line with these motives, i. e. that best conform to the agent's preferences. Thus, cognitive aspects of psychology really lie at the heart of economic decision making in general and, consequently, need to be considered thoroughly in any kind of survey like the CVM.

It goes without saying that the discipline of psychology has seen over time a variety of different schools of thought that represented the most influential scientific paradigms within psychology at that time. Two of these schools, behaviorism and cognitivism, are of particular interest for research of environmental valuation survey methods like the CVM because their main paradigms are reflected in the approaches of dealing with rationality problems encountered in CVM surveys. In order to make this link between psychological schools of thought and survey research more explicit, the following section will give a brief overview of their main paradigms and illustrate their influence on the perception of rationality in CVM surveys.

### 3.3.3.2 Cognitive psychology and its relation to the discipline of psychology

Behaviorism has dominated psychology for at least fifty years in the first half of the twentieth century. The behaviorist school has developed in the United States as sharp contrast both to the psychoanalysis of Sigmund Freud which focused on unconscious conflicts within the life-history of individuals and to the method of introspection as practiced by the pioneer of psychology, Wilhelm Wundt, who established the first psychological laboratory in Leipzig, Germany in 1879. Wundt's "psychology of consciousness" was already mainly concerned with cognitive processes, however, his method of introspection which is based on detailed subjective reports of test individuals performing some predefined cognitive task led to increasingly contradictory and even irrelevant results. In contrast, the guiding principle of behaviorism had its focus on observed behavior. Any unobservable mental processes, especially aspects of cognition, were thought inappropriate in principle for scientific analysis. One of the founders and protagonists of behaviorism, John B. Watson (1878 – 1958), aimed at transforming psychology into a discipline of natural sciences. To this end he established an exact method of experimental psychological research which would generate quantitative data in accordance with the standards of those obtained in other fields of natural science, taking physics as an example. Behaviorists aimed at discovering the underlying principles of human behavior, the natural laws of the mind (cf. Watson 1968). The combination of stimulus and reaction, i. e. the relationships between observable behavior and the underlying conditions producing this particular behavior, was the main paradigm of behaviorist research. As such, behavior was regarded as an organism's adaptation to the various stimuli of the surrounding environment and all observed behavior was scrutinized as to its relationship to such adaptation. The mind was given the role to produce such adaptive behavior in reaction to the external stimuli (cf. Wertheimer 1971). In the course of behaviorist research, the human being as a subject was substituted by the rat as a suitable object of study.

From hindsight, however, it is astonishing that this strict behaviorism as described above has remained a closed field of psychology, especially in the United States of America, for such a long time. Even exact natural sciences like physics, the leading example for behavioral psychologists, were open enough to develop theoretical models of quantum mechanics without being able to access the realm of atoms with accurate measurements. However, the paradigm shift towards cognitive psychology and its focus on information processing did not occur before the beginning 1960s.

Cognitivism's view of human beings as active regulators of their behaviors is not self-evident and just a relatively recent change of paradigm in psychology. The motivation to perform some action is now perceived as a mostly active decision making process, in which acquisition and evaluation of information, formation of expectations and considering alternative consequences play the crucial roles. The main cognitive tasks that illustrate the paradigm shift from behavioral psychology to cognitive psychology can be seen as (1) anticipation of consequences, (2) estimation of prospects for success, (3) evaluation of own capabilities, (4) comparison of expected outcomes with prior objectives and (5) estimation of probabilities (cf. Ulich and Bösel 2005: 129). Thus, in contrast to behaviorism individuals are seen as largely independent from external stimuli and as being able to regulate their behaviors mainly by themselves.

In the 1970s cognitive psychology started to increasingly draw analogies to the fields of information theory and computer science, a considerable number of technical terms and concepts were derived from these fields and appropriated within cognitive psychology. An early but highly influential model of information processing was the so-called Sternberg paradigm by Sternberg (1966). He characterized an overall cognitive task as a sequence of abstract units of information processing with each unit of processing requiring a certain time so that the complexity of some task with an observable outcome could be represented by the overall time needed for this task. Subsequently, research of such processes of information processing became broader and increasingly complex. Anderson and Lebiere (1998) developed a framework of cognitive architecture with which entire cognitive systems can be represented by units of information processing.

In recent times one part of cognitive psychology has developed towards understanding the fundamental neurological processes of cognition and other psychological phenomena. This field of neuropsychology has emerged in parallel to the understanding of physiological processes in the human brain (cognitive neurosciences) and to technical improvements necessary for the measurement of brain processes starting with the electro encephalography (EEG) as soon as 1924 until the use of modern visualization technologies like positron emission tomography (PET) and functional magnet resonance imaging (fMRI) (see Medin et al. 2005: 24ff for details of these methods). These new fields of cognitive psychological research, however, shall not be pursued here any further.

This brief description of the main aspects of behaviorism versus cognitivism already sheds light on the fundamentally different perceptions of rational response behavior in CVM and the recommendations for improving the method of valuation. As described above, behaviorism is dominated by the stimulus – response framework. In the context of the CVM a particular scenario including the payment scheme would represent the stimulus given to the respondent in the course of the interview to which the interviewee should react with an appropriate response, i. e. the WTP statement that is in congruence with his expected utility change. This relationship between stimulus and response is simple, however, in practice it is often unduly disturbed by external influences, other stimuli, like the framing of the scenario, the presence of interviewers or payment vehicles, i. e. necessary elements of a CVM survey that should have no influence on the utility change accruing from the proposed project. In CVM research, the view that such disturbing external influences simply need to be investigated and eliminated in the survey design in order to obtain valid, i. e. rational, WTP responses reflects that behaviorist paradigm. However, this approach neglects crucial aspects of human information processing and reasoning inherent in the cognitivist paradigm so that its success for improving CVM surveys is only limited.

From the cognitivist perspective the mental processes during a CVM interview are more complex and cannot be reduced to a simple stimulus – response pattern as desired from the behaviorist perspective. The external stimuli mentioned in the preceding paragraph must be seen as integral parts of the decision environment unless they cannot be entirely omitted from the interview. CVM respondents process all the available information, maybe to different degrees depending on their motives and their computational capacities. Some information that the CVM researcher considers highly relevant for the evaluation of the scenario might be only of minor importance for the respondent due to the prominence of some other aspect, like the fairness of the payment vehicle employed. Consequently, the respondent might choose to employ simplifying decision heuristics and disregard essential scenario information. Respondents' attention may be limited, e. g. due to an inappropriate presentation of information concerning the CVM scenario. Further, the motivation of the respondent to consider the trade-off situation thoroughly might be rather low leading him to process the given information only superficially. Under the cognitivist perspective, all these aspects cannot simply be eliminated in the survey design but must be treated as being part of the respondent's particular decision environment, including his information processing capabilities and constraints. Therefore, the perception of rationality under the cognitivist view is clearly a bounded one since the respondent is regarded in a way that takes his decision environment into account realistically.

In order to better understand the cognitive capabilities and restrictions that respondents generally face in environmental valuation interviews the next section will explore some fundamental principles of modern cognitive psychology as they are relevant for the conceptual and empirical research in this study.

### 3.3.3.3 Fundamentals of cognitive psychology

Due to the relatively short history of cognitive psychological research the insights gained for an understanding of the human mind are still relatively limited and thus many fundamental questions remain unexplained to some extent (cf. Anderson 2001). However, a number of important concepts of the working of the human mind are already quite well understood and insofar as those concepts contribute to an understanding of CVM response behavior as investigated in this study they will be briefly described and discussed in the following.

*Attention*

The first cognitive process of importance for the present study is *attention* since it can be perceived as the gatekeeper of stimuli like e. g. visual or audio information entering the cognitive system. In general, there exists a system of various processing units like the perceptive, the motor and the central cognitive units that work largely in parallel, i. e. independently from each other. Also, each of these units has some capacity for parallel processing as well, e. g. performing some task with the hands while walking, or listening to music and a conversation at the same time. However, in each of these units there seem to be bottlenecks that limit such parallel processing which appears to be associated with limited attention capacity (cf. Medin et al. 2005: 115f).

These limits are especially pronounced in the auditive system where attention needs to be focused on those auditive stimuli that are required for subsequent processing in the cognitive system, i. e. where unnecessary information is filtered out (cf. Broadbent 1958). Neisser (1967) demonstrated experimentally that auditive information which the test person should not be attentive to, i. e. that was meant to be filtered out, is available only up to 5 seconds in a sensory store called *echoic memory*, subsequently this information is lost. This feature called *selection*, i. e. filtering of information after entering some kind of sensory memory, ensures that attention can be switched to that information input in case it becomes important somehow, e. g. when a key word with a special importance like a name comes up in a conversation of a neighboring table in a restaurant etc. (cf. Medin et al. 2005: 110, 117). However, it is still controversial whether this selection occurs early, i. e. after only rudimentary processing, or late, i. e. after considerable processing including semantic recognition. A similar mechanism exists for visual inputs (*iconic memory*), however, the storage time of visual data in the sensory memory is very short, usually much shorter than one second.

Apart from the findings that *within* a mode of perception, i. e. audio and visual, attention is mainly directed to one particular information at a time and other information is largely filtered out or ignored, bottleneck effects appear also to be present *between* those modes of perception. Karlin and Kestenbaum (1968) demonstrated that the time needed to process an auditive stimulus almost doubled if test persons were to process visual stimuli slightly prior to the auditive stimulus. Thus, there seems to be a central bottleneck of attention which sets limits to the parallel processing capabilities of the cognitive system. Consequently, attention needs to be shifted between competing requirements of information processing. For selective information processing it is now considered that both bottleneck effects filtering out superfluous sensory information, either early or late, and capacity effects allowing only for a certain amount of incoming information to be processed play a role (cf. Pashler 1998).

The role of attention in CVM interviews is rather obvious since the level of attention a respondent attributes to information presented to him decides about the amount of such information available for further processing and evaluation in the light of his economic preferences. Due to the mentioned bottleneck and capacity effects scenario-relevant information needs to be presented in such a way that the interviewee's ideally uninterrupted attention to it is assured. Here, two aspects are of particular importance. First, the interviewee might be distracted by other stimuli like e. g. noise or television in the background, children etc. Second, he might still be processing recently provided information while the next aspects of the scenario etc. are already presented, thus preventing him to be attentive for new pieces of information. In the CVM literature the concern of preventing "information overload" and "tiring" has also often been voiced in this respect.

*Representation of information*

The next cognitive concept of importance is the fundamental process of *representation of information* that has entered the human cognitive system through the gatekeeper of attention. According to the *theory of dual coding* (cf. Paivio 1986) visuospatial and verbal information are coded in fundamentally different ways. Visuospatial information of referents in the real world, like e. g. images, is generally represented in an *analog* way, i. e. the representation mimics the (spatial) structure of the referent. The spatial arrangement of the single elements of a visual input in relation to each other is retained in the memory. In contrast, verbal information is represented by *propositions*, i. e. "abstract assertions that are not tied to any particular sensory modality" (cf. Medin et al. 2005: 255). In these propositions only the relevant meanings are retained, superfluous information like details of a particular sequence of words is discarded (unless it carries a special meaning). Propositional structures, finally, can be seen as a logical network of such relevant meaning that are connected to each other. Altogether, such a network of propositions that carry the meaning of input information can be seen as the representation of the content of that verbal input within the cognitive system, i. e. in the memory.

The fact that verbal information is represented as abstract propositions highlights the importance of the translation process of the verbal description of a CVM scenario into the propositions stored for further processing. The recipient of verbal information, either text to be read by the interviewee himself or being read out loudly by the interviewer, needs to be able to filter out the important parts of the information in order to establish a propositional network that carries the essential facts about the presented scenario and payment scheme. This emphasizes the well-known recommendation that CVM researchers devote much time and effort especially on the design of verbal scenario information.

Further, the fact that visuospatial and verbal information is represented in different ways is underscored by the finding that different regions of the brain have been shown to be active depending on the processing of visuospatial or verbal information. Furthermore, Shephard (1967) and Standing (1973) have both shown that visual memory is superior to the memory of verbal information stemming from the assumption that analog representations are more easily retrievable than abstract propositional representations. This explains the well-known fact that it is easier to memorize verbal information if it is associated with a visual imagination of that information. Quite naturally, the combination of verbal and visual information in the presentation of a CVM scenario helps the interviewee to absorb and memorizes higher amounts and more complex information.

*Theories of memory: the role of elaboration*

Due to its importance for the storage of scenario information for further processing in the course of evaluating such a CVM scenario some remarks about the human memory system should be dropped at this point. Formerly, the human memory system was perceived as a sequence of storage units, namely the sensory memory as mentioned above from which the relevant information is transferred to the short-term memory through the filter of attention. Subsequently, contents of the short-term memory could be transferred by the active process of memorization into the long-term or permanent memory (cf. Broadbent 1958, Waugh and Norman 1965). It was hypothesized that the short-term memory had a limited capacity of about 6 – 8 elements, the so-called memory span, which can easily be determined by the number of elements, e. g. numbers, letters, words etc., that one can reproduce immediately after being presented. If one does not achieve the transfer of an element of the short-term memory into long-term memory by active memorization (e. g. constant repetition or rehearsal) that element would be overwritten by new, i. e. more recent information entering the short-term memory via attention. This theory which was in line with a lot of experimental data at the time was challenged by Craik and Lockhart (1972) who argued that the amount of information stored in long-term memory did not as much depend on the time spent on (mechanical) memorization, e. g. the number of repetitions, but on the depth with which this particular information is processed in the cognitive system. Their *theory of processing levels* states that memorization only increases the likelihood of storage in the memory if that information is memorized in a deep and meaningful way, i. e. passive memorization like pure repetitions will not lead to permanent storage.

Craik and Lockhart's theory and a number of experiments verifying this distinction (cf. Glenberg et al. 1977) led to the abandonment of the assumption of a separate short-term memory, it simply turned out to be superfluous for the explanation of memory processes. In place of short-term memory Baddeley (1986) proposed the concept of a *phonological and articulatory loop* for verbal stimuli in order to account for the existence of the memory span of 6 to 8 elements mentioned above. The articulatory loop represents the so-called working memory as the amount of information that can be kept in memory by constant repetition (loop) and it corresponds roughly to the amount of syllables that can be read (and repeated) within 1.5 to 2 seconds (cf. Baddeley et al. 1975). Whereas the articulatory loop represents the working memory for verbal stimuli, visual stimuli are kept available in the so-called *visuospatial sketchpad.* The task of the sketchpad is to keep constant track of changes of the spatial arrangements of objects surrounding us, i. e. determining one's own location in relation to the outside world. These two systems of working memory represent support systems for the central executive which coordinates attention and the systems of working memory and which utilizes their information for higher cognitive processes, for example the evaluation of a CVM scenario in the light of one's preferences. The distinction of these support systems to the concept of a short-term memory is that they work independently from each other and exhibit no interference. Thus, the phonological and articulatory loops and the visuospatial sketchpad are simply support systems to keep information available and accessible for further processing by the central executive.

As mentioned above primary sensory information is quickly translated into semantic information where especially the meaning of verbal information is represented in some kind of propositional structure while the superfluous details, like the exact wording in sentences, are erased, i. e. lost. It appears that this translation is crucial for a transfer of information to the long-term memory. Such translations occur the better the more meaning is given to the primary information, i. e. the more a person *elaborates* on it (cf. Medin et al. 2005: 155). *Elaborative processing* consists of an enrichment of the content to be stored by additional information that creates associations and thus embeds this content into a broader context. In line with the *theory of processing level* a higher degree of elaboration on sensory information increases the likelihood that this information is translated into meaningful propositional structures that are then more easily transferred to the long-term memory. The fact that information can usually be remembered better if it is considered to be personally of importance can also be explained by a higher degree of processing, by higher elaboration that creates a meaningful propositional structure and forms associations with other aspects of personal importance. In section 3.3.4 theories of information processing, especially the theories of dual-processes will be described in more detail since they form the underlying psychological theory of the research approach pursued in this study.

While the long term memory does not play an important role in the context of environmental valuation due to the short duration of CVM interviews storage of scenario information in the working memory is certainly a crucial aspect. In this respect the distinction between short term memory and working memory is mostly academic, however, the importance of elaboration is highlighted by the theory of processing levels. The more an interviewee elaborates on the provided scenario information and gives a personal meaning to it the better this information will be available in the working memory for further evaluation. An interviewee will elaborate more on the given information if it relates to his personal context so that the information carries meaning for his personal circumstances. In order to help interviewees to elaborate it is common practice in CVM interviews that the essential aspects of the scenario information are repeated before proceeding to the WTP question. For example, the respondent is asked to what extent he considers certain aspects of the presented scenario as important. Such an intermezzo forces the interviewee to reconsider the presented information and put it into a personal context, thus increasing its availability for further information processing, for example a monetary evaluation of the benefits generated by the CVM scenario.

This short introduction should serve to highlight some basic and relevant aspects of current knowledge of cognitive psychological processes of human beings in order to provide some necessary background for the more specific models of information processing and reasoning. It was shown how central aspects of cognitive psychology relate to crucial issues of the design of environmental valuation surveys. The field of cognitive psychology is developing rapidly and important and stunning insights into the functioning of the human mind are published at a high rate. These new insights are mainly due to the modern technologies of fMRI (see above) that allow almost a direct observation of the working of the brain. For a most recent textbook covering the entire state-of-the-art in cognitive psychology consult Medin et al. (2005). In the following section the basic concepts of cognitive psychology just presented will be employed in a set of theories and models of human information processing and reasoning forming the basis of the empirical research approach of this study.

### 3.3.4 Psychological models of reasoning: dual-process approaches

#### 3.3.4.1 The concept of dual-process approaches

After this discussion regarding the important connections between cognitive psychological aspects and response behavior in CVM surveys a specific class of theories concerning the process of reasoning and problem solving need to be addressed in detail. These theories form the conceptual basis of the empirical research of this study since they allow the formulation of survey instruments for an analysis of CVM response behavior in the light of bounded rationality of respondents. However, unlike the fundamentals of cognitive psychology described above the question of which basic processes actually guide our thinking, reasoning, inferring and problem solving is far from being settled. Experimental findings of reasoning have produced a number of theories each of which can claim some plausibility for explaining the observed data. Traditionally, the competition stretches from "models of mental phenomena to be built out of networks of associative devices that pass activation around in parallel and distributed form" (see e. g. McClelland et al. 1986 for models of parallel distributed processing) to the other extreme of "models built out of formal languages in which symbols are composed into sentences that are processed sequentially", in close analogy to the functioning of computers (cf. Sloman 2002: 379). However, there is a vast amount of evidence to strongly suggest that neither of these two extreme views holds the sole truth. Human thinking rather seems to be composed of building blocks from both of the above mentioned extremes each of which is sometimes more and sometimes less involved in a specific reasoning task.

This perspective is summarized in the field of cognitive research on the two systems of reasoning, i. e. on the so-called "dual-process" approaches. Until now, dual-process theories of reasoning do not form a coherent view w. r. t. the exact nature of reasoning, rather a multitude of specific approaches and conceptual models has arisen since the beginning of the 1980s each focusing on a more or less specific problem constellation. However, these models all have in common that they aim at explaining the puzzling facts, i. e. that people are "capable of being foolish one moment and wise the next, capable of behaving intransigently and then credulously in turn, capable of believing the right thing with their whole hearts while saying precisely the wrong thing with their whole mouths" (cf. Gilbert 1999: 4). The common perception of these models is the view that "two qualitatively different modes of information processing operate in making judgments and decisions in solving problems. In essence, the common distinction in dual-process models is between a fast, associative information-processing mode based on low-effort heuristics, and a slow, rule-based information-processing mode based on high-effort systematic reasoning" (cf. Chaiken and Trope 1999: ix). Not surprisingly, this distinction mirrors the dual-mode rationality concepts of institutional and evolutionary rationality mentioned in section 3.2.2 The multitude of models for these two different modes of information processing has also generated a multitude of names. Overall, one of these processes has been referred to as *intuitive, natural, automatic, heuristic, preconscious, schematic, prototypical, narrative, implicit, imagistic-nonverbal* or *experiential* while the other fundamental process is often termed *rational, thinking-conceptual-logical, extensional, conscious, deliberative-effortful-intentional, systematic, explicit* or *verbal* (cf. Epstein et al. 1996 and citations there).

In general, the dual-process models of reasoning are motivated by the *principle of least effort* (cf. Allport 1954) which describes people's tendency to achieve desirable outcomes by employing as little cognitive effort as possible due to their feelings that their own cognitive resources like e. g. attention, memory or logical thinking are naturally constrained. In an environment where constant and complex stimuli need to be evaluated and to which an individual possibly needs to react it is necessary to economize on those scarce cognitive resources. It has been described above that such scarcity is implied by the bottlenecks and capacity constraints in information processing, i. e. the competition among simultaneous cognitive tasks for processing capacity. It is thus argued that the default mode of information processing relies on simplification and learned automatic processes like e. g. the use of heuristics that have been acquired over time by dealing successfully with similar situations in the past. These simplifications "avoid effortful expenditures of cognitive energy" (cf. Moskowitz et al. 1999: 28) whenever possible in order to achieve satisfactory outcomes.

But how is this satisfaction level determined, what happens if it cannot be attained in the default mode of information processing? The underlying view in all dual-process models is that people seek sufficient rather than accurate knowledge of states, acceptable rather than optimal outcomes. As long as available information is seen as sufficient for a specific situation, e. g. explaining the motives of behavior of someone or deciding whether to undertake an action or not, and as long as the expected outcome of such an action is perceived acceptable, the default mode of processing will do. However, such economizing information processors become motivated to process information more deeply and systematically whenever a feeling of insufficiency arises, i. e. if their feeling of confidence in the automated heuristics and low-effort reasoning processes gets too low. In such situations, people will be motivated to take "a closer look", they will shift to more effortful, more systematic processes in order to overcome and alleviate this feeling of insufficiency. It has been argued that on the one hand such a shift generally occurs when the information at hand is perceived as being so inconsistent with prior structures that an individual's confidence in his judgment is seriously shaken. On the other hand, people might willfully choose to look closer in situations where they desire accuracy of information and judgment (cf. Tetlock 1985). Thus, people are seen to be "flexible processors", i. e. they are capable of more elaborate processing when they desire greater certainty. Each of the specific dual-process models that will be described in the next section has developed their own criteria for the shift of use of information processes, or their mix, so this issue will be discussed in detail there.

Before presenting selected specific dual-process models, a classification of the nature of these models shall be attempted. The basic distinction between the dual-process approaches concerns the way and the degree to which these two fundamental systems (for simplicity they shall be called *intuitive* vs. *rational* in the following) interact. Under the first view, only one of these two processing modes is involved in a given task, the second view holds that every outcome is ultimately produced by both modes. Following Gilbert (1999), the first view comprises two possible designs of interaction: (1) the selective design where the specific task at hand or outside stimuli activate one of the two processing modes selectively while the other remains dormant and (2) the competitive design where both processing modes are initially activated but the one with the stronger activation outcompetes the other at a specific state of processing which has no further part in the fulfillment of the task. An example of the latter could be seen in analogy to the simultaneous activation of the two meanings of the word "bank" where the specific context quickly decides which of the meanings is more appropriate, the river-bank or the financial institution. Under the second view two alternative designs of processing mode interaction are conceivable: (3) the consolidative design where any outcome is always a mix of both processing modes to a varying degree and (4) the corrective design where one of the two processing modes, preferably the intuitive mode, gets activated first but its outcome is subsequently subjected to a possibly corrective intervention by the other, the rational mode. Table 3-2 illustrates the distinction of these four possible designs of dual-processing modes.

To date the second view seems to be more prominent, therefore the majority of dual-process models that will be presented and discussed subsequently follows this view. However, the borderline between consolidative and corrective designs is often blurred in these specific models, in fact, as will be illustrated below, the described classification applies best to specific judgmental situations and not to entire dual-process modeling approaches.

**Table 3-2:** Features of the four elementary dual-process designs (adapted from Gilbert 1999: 7)

| | Are both processes activated? | Do both processes control output? |
|---|---|---|
| Selective design | No | No |
| Competitive design | Yes | No |
| Consolidative design | Yes | Yes |
| Corrective design | Sometimes | Sometimes |

In conclusion, the dual-process models of reasoning allow to address the often voiced reservation to perceive CVM respondents as fully rational decision makers more specifically. According to these models reasoning and information processing in CVM interviews can now be perceived to follow two different branches: the first branch conforms more to the concept of instrumental rationality where conscious evaluation of the available information using effortful sequential cognitive processes takes place, the second branch conforms more to the concept of procedural rationality where the "economy of cognition" leads respondents to employ simplifying heuristics in order to arrive at satisfactory outcomes. In the dual-process models the two branches are presumed to interact or rather to work in parallel to an extent depending on the specific circumstances of the cognitive task to be fulfilled. The analysis of the extent to which these two fundamentally different reasoning processes are employed during the perception and evaluation of a CVM scenario by a respondent, i. e. the degree of boundedly rational information processing, requires to look more specifically at selected dual-process models found in the literature. From these models the empirical survey instrument for the analysis of boundedly rational behavior in CVM surveys will be developed in chapter 4.

#### 3.3.4.2 Specific model approaches of dual-processes in the context of environmental valuation

From the multitude of conceptual models of dual information processing found in the literature, three selected models shall be described here in more detail. In conjunction, these three models allow to address a great variety of aspects of response behavior in CVM interviews and thus form a suitable framework for the analysis of bounded rational information processing in environmental valuation. Specifically, two of the three models have developed well-tested psychometric instruments which allow to classify individuals regarding the rationality concepts described above. These instruments shall be taken as the basis for the development of an empirical instrument to describe and analyze boundedly rational information processing in CVM.

Both the elaboration likelihood model (ELM) developed by Petty (1977, cited in Petty and Wegener 1999) as well as the heuristic-systematic model (HSM) by Chaiken (1980) deal explicitly with the question what determines the degree to which individuals employ deliberative, rational reasoning versus more intuitive, heuristic information processing. Specifically, the ELM distinguishes two processes, the "routes" to persuasion referring to changes of attitudes based on the intensity of elaborative processing of information, i. e. the degree of elaboration (see above). On the one hand the "central-route" attitude changes are those that are brought about by "relatively extensive and effortful information-processing activity" (cf. Petty and Wegener 1999: 42). Such "central-route" processing is associated with a deep scrutiny and analysis of the issues and information presented in order to uncover their "central merits". The term "elaboration" is used to suggest that people add something of their own to the specific information provided. On the other hand, attitude changes brought about by the "peripheral-route" are based on processes requiring less cognitive effort, such as processes that differ from the "central-route" process quantitatively, i. e. for example examining the same available information less carefully, or even qualitatively by using mental short-cuts like heuristics or schemas etc.

Regarding the degree of employing the central versus peripheral routes the critical concept of the ELM is the so-called "elaboration continuum". It signifies the range of degrees of elaboration by an individual faced with a judgment task. The points along the elaboration continuum at which a given individual operates in a given judgment or problem are determined by the strength of motivation and cognitive capability to elaborate on that situation, i. e. to scrutinize and evaluate information, to put new information in the context of existing information and/or to assess the likely outcomes of decisions taken. The ELM supposes that the degree of elaboration is directly related to the cognitive effort expended in a given task. The notion of an "elaboration continuum" implies that people elaborate to varying degrees, i. e. although people want to hold correct attitudes and make correct judgments, the amount and nature of elaboration in which they are willing and able to engage vary both with individual and situational factors.

Thus, personal motivation and mental ability are assumed to be the main drivers of cognitive effort, the more motivated and able people are the more likely they are to effortfully scrutinize all information available and relevant for the task at hand. However, "economy of cognition" decides to what extent the individual follows the peripheral and central routes of reasoning. In some situations where it does not "pay" to exert considerable mental effort it is advisable to behave as a "cognitive miser" (cf. Taylor 1981), i. e. as someone who tries his best to avoid cognitive effort. At other times, however, it is more appropriate for them to expend their cognitive resources more generously.

Compared to the ELM, the heuristic-systematic model (HSM) operationalizes the least-effort principle more specifically by transforming it into a *sufficiency principle*. It is assumed that people "attempt to strike a balance between minimizing cognitive effort on the one hand and satisfying their current motivational concerns on the other" (cf. Chen and Chaiken 1999: 74). To this end, the authors distinguish between an individual's *actual* confidence that he has in relation to a judgmental task and the *desired* confidence, i. e. that level of confidence that the individual would personally like to have when performing some judgmental task. This desired level of confidence is called *sufficiency threshold*. The authors claim that individuals will exert cognitive effort up to the point where actual and desired confidence coincide at which point then a decision is taken or an attitude is formed or expressed etc. In case low-effort heuristic processing alone does not achieve the closure of this gap between actual and desired confidence or where such processing is not possible due to the absence of any information that might serve as a cue for the activation of a heuristic, people are likely to adopt systematic processing in order to close this gap.

Furthermore, the HSM claims that it is in principle possible to predict whether a person is likely to employ either heuristic or systematic processing alone or to what extent and in which way those modes co-occur and interact given different patterns of cognitive, situational and motivational factors. On the one hand heuristic and systematic processing may be used in an *additive* way whenever both heuristic-cue information as well as other judgment-relevant information, so-called individuating information that describes a certain context in a more detailed and specific way, point into the same direction, i. e. are not contradictory. Such additivity is likely to occur for example in situations where consumers are asked to evaluate some product and where its brand name serves as a positive heuristic cue which is also in accordance with other individuating information about that product. In such a situation the brand name as a heuristic cue establishes an already quite high level of actual confidence on top of which some further systematic processing based on the individuating information closes the gap to the desired confidence. In cases where the "brand name" heuristic is not applicable, e. g. when the brand name is not given or that particular brand is not known to the person (non-availability of the heuristic) the level of actual confidence is quite low at the beginning so that systematic processing on the basis of the individuating information has to occur to a higher degree in order to attain the sufficiency threshold.

On the other hand, heuristic cues like e. g. the brand name can also lead to a *biased* processing of individuating information. In this case, systematic processing does not only occur to a lower degree than in the example above but individuating information is even seen in a more favorable light. Thus, in those cases when individuating information is ambiguous to some extent or even contradictory and would, therefore, require more complex reasoning about the task at hand, the presence of heuristic cues, e. g. positive ones like the brand name or negative ones like the doubtful quality of the source of information, can lead to systematic processing of the individuating information either in a more favorable or in a more unfavorable light. In both cases the outcome of the evaluation will be biased. Such effects were indeed found in experimental studies (cf. Chaiken and Maheswaran 1994, Chen et al. 1996). Similar effects occur when people are given information on the opinions of others, e. g. of representatives of their own peer group, on certain task-relevant issues, so that the "consensus" heuristic was shown to have a large biasing effect on systematic processing of individuating information.

All aspects of the ELM and HSM mentioned above are relevant in the context of CVM surveys. The level of motivation of a respondent to evaluate an environmental change scenario may depend highly on the specific good to be valued. In case the environmental change has a high personal relevance for the respondent he may be more highly motivated to scrutinize the given information and, thus, engage in the central route of information processing. On the other hand, an environmental change scenario showing a low degree of personal relevance may, therefore, trigger the peripheral route and lead to superficial information processing with a higher susceptibility to heuristic cues present in the scenario or payment scheme. The HSM addresses even more specifically the role of such heuristic cues. It highlights the role a positive heuristic cue, e. g. the participation of a well-known and respected non-governmental organization in the implementation of the environmental project, may play in the way a respondent processes and evaluates further project relevant, i. e. individuating, information. The presence of that organization may create a notion of trust where the respondent evaluates the given information in a more favorable light than he would otherwise do if that organization were not mentioned. Moreover, Chen and Chaiken (1999)'s findings on the consensus heuristic highlight the danger of including information about what other people think of project related issues into the questionnaire since people tend to follow the consensus in case they consider themselves as part of that group.

Another important feature of the HSM in relation to CVM response behavior is the "multiple-motive framework" which serves as a classification for people's motivations to engage in heuristic or systematic processing. Three basic types of motivation are distinguished: (1) *accuracy motivation* which claims that people are motivated to hold accurate attitudes and beliefs, (2) *defense motivation* which "refers to the desire to hold attitudes and beliefs that are congruent with one's perceived material interests or existing self-definitional attitudes and beliefs" (cf. Chen and Chaiken 1999: 77), and (3) *impression motivation* referring to a social goal, the need to be perceived by others in a certain way. This latter type of motivation addresses the considerations of people w. r. t. the interpersonal consequences of expressing attitudes or making judgments. In order to satisfy certain impression objectives people process information selectively where, again, certain cues might activate heuristics like "Go along to get along" which suppress any more systematic processing. In a CVM context the presence of such a motivation type could lead to social desirability effects or the tendency of "yea"-saying as discussed above.

These three different motives may be active at the same time in a specific decision situation. For example, a respondent in a CVM interview might predominantly be motivated to determine his true willingness to pay for the provision of improvement of some public good (accuracy motivation). At the same time he would like his answer to reflect his view of himself as being a good citizen who cares for society (defense motivation) as well as he would like to make a good impression on the interviewer who he assumes to expect him to show his care for the environment (impression motivation). All these three motivations will then influence the way the respondent processes the information presented to him in the CVM scenario. For example, informational uncertainties might not be strongly taken into account in the evaluation of the scenario due to the desire to make a good impression on the interviewer, his view of himself as a good citizen obliges him to contribute to the project although he has doubts regarding its environmental efficacy etc. Thus, the multiple-motive framework of the HSM corresponds well with socially interactive situations like CVM interviews and might help to better understand respondent behavior in such conflicting situations.

Cacioppo and Petty (1982) and Cacioppo et al. (1996) argue that there are individual differences in the degree of elaboration people generally engage in. Some people intrinsically enjoy thinking and problem solving, some people draw pleasure from effortful thought regardless of its practical use while other people don't. In order to measure such individual differences that do not merely vary between situations but as general traits between people Cacioppo and Petty (1982) developed a scale which they called "Need for Cognition" (NFC), i. e. "the tendency for an individual to engage in and enjoy thinking". Selected elements of the NFC scale will later be utilized for the empirical research in this study. The NFC is a self-report scale where test persons are asked to rate to what extent given statements concerning cognitive behavior, e. g. "I really enjoy a task that involves coming up with new solutions to problems" apply to them. From a multitude of such questions, an overall score for their individual need for cognition is computed. As such the NFC scale represents a one-dimensional bipolar measure of general cognitive disposition, i. e. a high score on the scale implies a high tendency of the individual for central-route processing and at the same time a low affinity to peripheral-route processing and vice versa. It has been found in various studies that the NFC scale produces a reliable measure of an individual's general cognitive disposition as perceived by the ELM and that it corresponds well to a number of objective indicators like the type of profession.

While the ELM and the HSM already highlighted essential aspects of employing the two systems of reasoning in general and in the context of environmental valuation interviews, the integrative framework of cognitive-experiential self-theory (CEST) developed by Epstein (1985) shall be used in this study as the conceptual backbone of this study. CEST shares with the other models the distinction of the two basic and different systems of information processing or reasoning: a preconscious system termed "experiential" and a primarily conscious system termed "rational". In general, the experiential system as the more basic system operates largely without much effort, employs associations and heuristics for rapid but mostly efficient reasoning for everyday life, while the rational system requires considerable cognitive resources and relies on a person's understanding of logical rules of inference.

An important integrative feature of CEST is the concept of four basic needs which incorporates the multiple-motive framework of the HSM. According to Epstein and Pacini (1999) the basic needs of an individual are: (1) to maximize pleasure and minimize pain (in accordance with other psychological theories), (2) to maintain a stable, coherent conceptual system for organizing the data of experience, (3) to maintain relatedness to others and (4) to maintain a favorable level of self-esteem. The interaction of these four basic needs is assumed to determine the actual behavior where, in general, a compromise between these needs has to be found since it is often not possible to satisfy all of them at the same time. Thus, this psychological concept corresponds closely to economic principles where it is assumed that an individual strives to find an optimal balance in the consumption of a variety of goods that is limited by an available budget. Just as the level of consumption of one good is traded off against the level of consumption of another in order to maximize the individual's well-being, the fulfillment of the basic needs is traded off so that an optimal balance is found for the individual. However, unlike in economics no formal theory w. r. t. this optimal trade off among basic needs has been developed in psychology so far, but the proximity to economics is striking in this respect.

Regarding interpersonal differences in the way people process information, the framework of personal beliefs, i. e. theories that are established by an individual about himself, the world and their connections, is of particular importance. In the rational system these theories are explicit in the sense that an individual is able to consciously state and explain them (explicit beliefs), while those beliefs that refer to the experiential system are not directly expressible, i. e. they are held implicitly (implicit beliefs) and are, therefore, often termed "schemas". Schemas represent generalizations that are derived from emotionally significant experiences of an individual in the past, they represent the individual's implicit model of the world. In the context of environmental valuation a respondent in a CVM interview might hold the explicit belief that e. g. contamination of the drinking water source with bacteria will most likely result in many cases of diarrhea. A typical belief that is held only implicitly, for example, is that an interviewer engaged in a CVM survey regarding a proposed environmental project like the improvement of water quality in an area has a personal interest in that project and, in turn, expects the respondent to state a favorable answer. However, the respondent would most likely not be able to state this belief explicitly and, in fact, it would not even be correct in most cases. Nevertheless, it can influence his response behavior by triggering a higher WTP statement for the project than he actually has.

Furthermore, in analogy to the four basic needs CEST postulates four basic beliefs which are formed by an individual's "intuitive assessments of the degree to which (1) the world is benign versus malevolent; (2) the world is meaningful (including predictable, controllable, and just) versus chaotic (including unpredictable, uncontrollable, and unjust); (3) relationships with others are supportive versus threatening; and (4) the self is worthy (including competent, good, and lovable) versus unworthy (including incompetent, bad, and unlovable)" (cf. Epstein and Pacini 1999: 464).

This implicit model of the world as composed of an individual's basic beliefs influences an individual's behavior in the sense that it determines the available and applicable heuristics and rules of thumb in the experiential system and influences the degree to which an activation of the rational system occurs. For example, an individual holding the implicit belief that the world is largely chaotic will have little trust in his own possibilities to influence outcomes and thus little motivation to engage in effortful rational cognitive processes. Individual differences in these implicit beliefs form the foundations for individual differences w. r. t. people's employment of experiential versus rational information processing. Such individual differences can be captured in empirical instruments like the rational experiential inventory (REI) that will be introduced in detail in chapter 4 and from which the empirical survey instrument for the analysis of boundedly rational information processing in this study is derived.

In summary, this section has presented and discussed a selection of psychological dual-process models that directly relate to the context of reasoning and decision making in environmental valuation studies, specifically in the context of CVM interviews. The ELM distinguishes between a central and a peripheral route of information processing where the level of motivation of an individual determines the cognitive effort, i. e. the elaboration, that is expended on a task. The HSM becomes more explicit in the description of the various processes in the two modes where the use of heuristics, rules of thumb, schemas etc. are perceived as relatively effortless processes that are assisted by more systematic reasoning only to the extent that some desired level of confidence, the sufficiency threshold, can be attained. Finally, cognitive-experiential self-theory CEST can be seen as an integration of the variety of dual-process models into a broader coherent theory of behavior

All of these models share the principle of *economy of cognition* or the *least-effort principle* which states that an individual possesses limited cognitive resources that have to be allocated to the two information processing systems in such a way that a judgment of satisfactory or sufficient quality is achieved, where the level of satisfaction or sufficiency is determined by personal and individual factors. It was shown that cognitive resources may be limited in two ways: on the one hand the capability of an individual w. r. t. systematic processing in principle may be limited; on the other the short time intervals between judgments and decisions to be taken usually limit the possibility for fully systematic processing which occurs serially and is thus subject to bottleneck effects. Therefore, a division of cognitive load occurs between those tasks that can be accomplished by a mostly parallely-operating low-effort system using heuristics, schemas and prototypes etc. that have been learned by past experiences and those tasks that require effortful serial and systematic processing due to their novelty (lack of sufficient previous experience) or complexity. All models argue that such a division of labor is highly adaptive to real-world decision environments while nevertheless in a number of situations systematic judgment and decision errors occur that leave an individual short of optimality.

Therefore, the dual-process models of reasoning fit the framework of bounded rationality as laid out in section 3.3 very well and provide a detailed cognitive psychological foundation for the observed limitations and non-optimal outcomes in real-world situations. These models also demonstrate that such behavior, even the obvious judgmental errors, should not be regarded as irrational behavior and, thus, as behavior outside the realm of economics, but that such a dual-process reasoning system must be regarded as an optimal adaptation to the limitations, both personal and situational, of the real world. As a result the insights gained from cognitive psychology and especially from the dual-process models of reasoning will be used in the research approach of this study in order to analyze decision making in environmental valuation under the perspective of bounded rationality.

## 3.4 Summary

This chapter presented and explored the rationality concept in economics and the development of the conceptual framework of bounded rationality in a broad perspective where a special focus was laid on its links to psychology. It was shown how the concept of instrumental rationality forming the main paradigm of neoclassical economics today has evolved from the rationality postulate by Adam Smith explaining economic agents' actions with the pursuit of their self-interests. The common set of rationality axioms of an agent's preference ordering form the foundations for analyzing economic actions in formal models. The main rationality principle of such preference orderings, consistency, as postulated by the transitivity axiom, however, has often been criticized since many instances of systematic violations of this principle were observed in economic choices in the real world. Instrumental rationality can thus be perceived as a normative, i. e. idealized, rationality concept.

Observations of violations of transitivity, especially in cases of decision under risk and uncertainty, gave rise to efforts to extend the neoclassical rationality concept where special focus was laid on a more realistic perception of economic agents. Herbert Simon was the first to systematically include economic agents' limited cognitive capacities into models of rationality where he emphasized the role of the procedures as opposed to the outcome of decision making resulting in the concept of procedural rationality. Instead of cognitively effortful analytical reasoning the use of simplifying heuristics or shortcuts leading to satisfactory as opposed to optimal outcomes is highlighted in this concept. The hybrid rationality concepts of institutional and evolutionary rationality incorporate both instrumental and procedural rationality while focusing more specifically on the development of such heuristic decision rules. These extended rationality concepts are often termed "descriptive" and, in conjunction, form the overarching concept of bounded rationality.

The main characteristic of bounded rationality is the co-occurrence of analytical and heuristic reasoning in real-world information processing and decision making. This puts the respective use of either reasoning processes in the center of research on boundedly rational decision making. Psychological models of reasoning, most notably from the field of modern cognitive psychology, provide a suitable framework for an analysis of this trade-off and the mental mechanisms at work. They show that the human mind performs an "economy of cognition" in that cognitive resources are allocated selectively to tasks according to whether they can be performed in a rather effortless way by making use of past experience and fast associations or whether they require a more effortful systematic processing due to their complexity, importance or novelty. This type of reasoning using two fundamentally different systems of information processing is captured in dual-process models like the elaboration likelihood model, the heuristic-systematic model and cognitive-experiential self-theory

The psychological models highlight the importance of information processing in CVM interviews. Cognitive psychology shows under which circumstances respondents may exhibit limited attention capacities due to bottleneck effects and may have problems in absorbing, representing and storing scenario information necessary for subsequent evaluation. Heuristic cues functioning as signals that it may be possible for the respondent to deviate from effortful information processing and make use of simplifying decision rules, instead, were identified as the main reasons why respondents may exhibit boundedly rational behavior and be susceptible to the procedural biases of the CVM presented in chapter 2.

The framework of bounded rationality with its connection to the psychological dual-process approaches to reasoning is, therefore, closely linked to the observed rationality problems of respondents in environmental valuation surveys. It provides a suitable basis for the analysis of information processing in CVM interviews. This task shall be approached in the following chapter.

# 4 Bounded rationality in environmental valuation

## 4.1 Review and outline of the chapter

The preceding chapters dealt with rationality as one of the central topics in economic decision making and put special emphasis on the role of rationality in environmental valuation. As was laid out in detail in chapter 2 a rational decision in the context of an environmental valuation interview using the Contingent Valuation Method requires that a respondent be able to evaluate whether he or she is better off after some proposed project with environmental consequences has been carried out than before. In addition, the response, i. e. the stated WTP or WTA, must be consistent with this personal evaluation of expected change in well-being resulting from the proposed project. It was shown, however, that in the practice of environmental valuation respondents seem to have difficulties conforming to these requirements of rational decision making. Often, the available time during such an interview is rather short so that the respondent may have trouble evaluating a complex environmental change scenario thoroughly enough to take all the personal consequences resulting from the project into account. Due to the novelty of the situation for a respondent in an environmental valuation interview the respondent may not even be certain what his preferences relating to the proposed environmental change are. Moreover, the design of the questionnaire, like e. g. the WTP elicitation question or the specific payment vehicle used, exerts a significant influence on the respondent's reasoning and decision making which results in numerous procedural biases well documented by an abundant literature.

In order to put these findings into the general context of decision making in economics chapter 3 explored violations of rationality in a broader perspective. The biases detected in environmental valuation interviews are largely consistent with findings from the field of behavioral economics where the concept of bounded rationality is used as a more realistic perspective on human reasoning. Psychological decision mechanisms like the *availability*, *representativeness* and *anchoring and adjustment* heuristics made famous by Daniel Kahneman and Amos Tversky were shown to be responsible for a wide variety of common reasoning failures. A closer look at central findings of cognitive psychology then revealed that human beings have developed and learned mental strategies to cope with the complexity of reasoning and decision making situations in the real world enabling them to make "reasonable" decisions, however often not based on exact judgment, with their limited cognitive capabilities. Such decisions seem to make use of a two-tiered mechanism of information processing where an analytical system requiring rather large amounts of cognitive resources and a more effortless intuitive system based on experience and learned decision rules,

i. e. heuristics, interact in a kind of "economy of cognition". It was also shown in chapter 3 that such psychological models of reasoning, the so-called dual-process models, may well be related to information processing and decision making in the context of environmental valuation interviews and, thus, have the potential to better explain and analyze procedural biases in CVM response behavior.

This chapter will now build on this literature review and the connection that has been established between psychological models of reasoning and response behavior in CVM surveys in order to gain a more realistic perspective of the way respondents process complex information in CVM interviews where both time and the available information are limited in principle. As described above, two aspects are of particular importance in this respect: (1) how respondents deal with preference uncertainty, and (2) whether and to what extent respondents make use of an "economy of cognition" and, consequently, base their decisions in CVM interviews on simplifying heuristics instead of thorough analytical reasoning.

In section 4.2 these two aspects will first be considered from a theoretical point of view. Regarding preference uncertainty, section 4.2.1 will present and discuss a modification of the traditional neoclassical model of preference orderings. The concept of fuzzy preferences will be used to describe the uncertainty over preferences with respect to environmental goods. It will be shown, however, that the practicability of this approach is rather limited since it is technically not possible to derive proper value functions for environmental goods like e. g. the Hicksian Compensating Variation which would be necessary for a quantitative representation of environmental values. Section 4.2.2 will then address the issue of information processing in CVM interviews from the perspective of bounded rationality and the dual-process models of reasoning described in chapter 3. From those models a specific set of expectations concerning boundedly rational CVM response behavior will be formulated which serves as the basis for the development of empirical instruments for classifying and detecting such behavior.

In section 4.3 these instruments will then be used in an empirical CVM study regarding the social benefits of an improvement of tap water quality in northern Thailand. The purpose of this empirical application is to test the usefulness of the developed instruments for the analysis of boundedly rational information processing behavior and for the development of recommendations for an improvement of CVM survey designs. The empirical study underlying this test was conducted as part of a subproject within an international collaborative research project in northern Thailand. Thus, section 4.3.1 will first describe the background and the design of the empirical research project conducted and will present the details of the implementation of the scales of bounded rationality within this project. Section 4.3.2 will present and discuss the empirical results of the project in general and, in greater detail, of the bounded rationality scales employed. Subsequently, the implications of the empirical results of the chosen research approach for the design of contingent valuation studies will be discussed.

## 4.2 Theoretical considerations

### 4.2.1 Dealing with preference uncertainty: a fuzzy approach

In section 2.2.2 of chapter 2 it was argued that it is plausible to assume that some respondents in CVM surveys are uncertain about their preferences toward environmental goods when having to state their WTP. Due to unfamiliarity with the good and the task to express rather abstract values people commonly hold for the environment in monetary terms it appears more reasonable to consider the existence of an uncertainty range within which respondents are not entirely sure whether they are truly willing to pay a particular monetary amount or not. Below that range respondents are certain that they would pay the proposed amount, above that range they are certain that they would reject to pay it. As was shown in the preceding chapter the methodological approaches to account for such a situation of preference uncertainty are manifold and deal with this quite uncommon situation in ways that appear rather *ad hoc*, i. e. they are not founded on an underlying coherent theory of preference uncertainty.

The purpose of this section is to consider an existing theory of preference uncertainty more thoroughly and to apply it to the context of environmental valuation in order to (possibly) rationalize the approaches described in 2.2.2 on the basis of a theory of preference uncertainty. To this end, a theory of preferences based on fuzzy set theory shall be unearthed from the rather unnoticed and inaccessible niche it has been occupying in the literature, mostly in highly specialized journals, so far. The advantage of fuzzy set theory for a description of preference uncertainty is its inherent concept of vagueness or ambivalence. Unlike in the two-valued logic where a statement is either true or false fuzzy set theory, or fuzzy logic as it is often called, allows intermediate states where a statement is neither fully true nor entirely false, just as one would assume a respondent in CVM to be neither fully sure about whether he would actually pay a proposed amount nor entirely certain that he would definitely not pay it, at least for amounts falling into his range of uncertainty. Therefore, fuzzy set theory and the existing theory of fuzzy preferences provide a suitable starting point for considering preference uncertainty in the context of environmental valuation.

4.2.1.1 Fuzzy logic and fuzzy preferences

Fuzzy set theory dates back to Lofti Zadeh (1965) who developed the concept of fuzzy sets building on the concept of multi-valued logic introduced by the Polish mathematician Jan Lukasiewicz in the 1920s. Multi-valued logic was successful in solving problems in quantum physics that could not be adequately addressed by the commonly used crisp sets of standard two-valued Boolean logic. In a crisp set A some $x \in X$ either is an element of some set A or it is not an element of that set, i. e. there exists certainty as to whether x belongs to A or not. Crisp sets are common in the real world: e. g. from a number of objects, let's say cars, bicycles and boats, it can usually be determined without doubt which ones are classified as land transportation vehicles and which are water transportation vehicles.

In the case of a fuzzy set $\tilde{A}$, however, a given element $x \in X$ may not fully belong to the fuzzy set but only to some degree while it may belong to some degree to some other fuzzy set $\tilde{B}$, i. e. following Ott (2001: 14) a fuzzy set $\tilde{A}$ can be defined as

$$\tilde{A} = \{(x, \mu_A(x)) | \ x \in X\} \text{ where } \mu_A(x): x \longrightarrow [0,1]. \qquad (4\text{-}1)$$

The function $\mu_A(x)$ denotes the degree between 0 and 1 to which the element x belongs to the fuzzy set $\tilde{A}$. $\mu_A(x)$ is often called "characteristic function" or "membership function" of x to $\tilde{A}$ (cf. Zimmermann 1996) . Let's consider as an example the set "high income", a possible category in economics. When this set is to be crisp we need to define a lower threshold income above which income is classified as "high income". It is obvious that such a threshold is purely arbitrary since if the figure 100,000 Euros per year is defined as threshold for high incomes it would be hard to justify why an income of 99,000 Euros should not be classified as "high income", as well. Here, "high income" could instead be defined as a fuzzy set where all incomes at or above 100,000 Euros assume a value of the membership function of 1, i. e. $\mu_A(x \geq 100{,}000) = 1$, whereas values between, let's say, 50,000 and 99,999 Euros assume membership values to the fuzzy set $\tilde{A}$ between 0 and 1, i. e. $0 < \mu_A(50{,}000 \leq x \leq 99{,}999) < 1$ and incomes below 50,000 Euros assume a membership of 0, i. e. strictly do not belong to the category "high income". Figure 4-1 graphically illustrates such an exemplary fuzzy set "high income".

**Figure 4-1:** The fuzzy set "high income" (adapted from Ott 2001: 15)

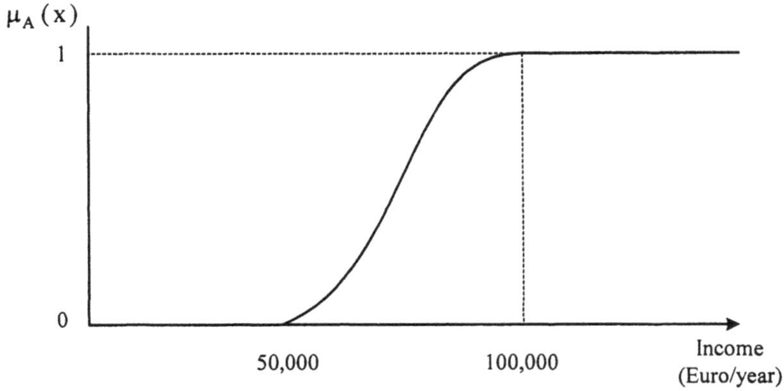


Obviously, fuzzy sets are often used for linguistic categories that are vague by definition, i. e. categories without a clear natural boundary of what belongs to them and what does not. Another example is the classification of thermal states like "cool", "warm" or "hot". There is no clear boundary between these states since they represent subjective feelings so that a specific temperature might still belong to a certain degree to the state "cool" and to some degree to "warm" already. In these cases it has proven very useful to be able to specify the degree to which some element is a member of that linguistic category. However, fuzzy sets and fuzzy logic have also become favorite concepts in the field of technology whenever complex technical processes are controlled by automated computer programs (cf. Klir and Yuan 1995 for examples). The mathematics of fuzzy sets, however, has become quite complicated and is a field of fast development where many fundamental theorems have not yet been proven. This section will, therefore, make use of only simple fuzzy mathematics in order to illustrate the basic features of fuzzy preferences.

An important concept of fuzzy logic necessary for a simple representation of fuzzy preferences are fuzzy relations (cf. Ovchinnikov 1981, Ovchinnikov and Roubens 1992). In the crisp, i. e. non-fuzzy case a relation between two elements $x, y \in X$ is clearly determined, i. e. either x is greater than y or it is not, there is no ambivalence. In the case of fuzzy relations this is different: here, x may be greater than y only to some degree, let's say a degree of certainty. To some degree of certainty it may also be that y is greater than x, it is thus ambivalent. Formally, this can be expressed by a fuzzy relation r which is a mapping from the two-dimensional space $X^2$ to the closed interval between 0 and 1, i. e. $r: X^2 \longrightarrow [0,1]$. In the case of fuzzy preferences, for example, such a vague comparison may occur in case the evaluation of goods is ambivalent, i. e. in case an individual is uncertain regarding his preference of x over y.

Fuzzy preferences can thus be defined as fuzzy preference relations (cf. Salles 1998: 322ff). Let $x, y \in X$ be two commodity bundles from the non-negative commodity space X, then $r(x, y) \in [0, 1]$ denotes the degree to which an individual considers x to be "at least as good" as y, i. e. $x \succsim y$, whereas $r(y, x) \in [0, 1]$ denotes the degree to which y is considered "at least as good" as x, i. e. $y \succsim x$. Obviously, the crisp preference relation $\succsim$ is the limit of the fuzzy preference relation r where the relation would only take values of 0 or 1 (cf. De Wilde 2003). While it appears odd at first sight to assume that the weak preference relation $\succsim$ between two commodity bundles can only be determined to a degree between 0 and 1, the common interpretation of such a degree is how certain an individual is that bundle x will generate at least as much utility as bundle y, thus the fuzzy preference relation $r(x, y) \in [0, 1]$ represents a measure of preference uncertainty of the bundles x and y. This uncertainty of assessing whether x is at least as good as y may stem from unfamiliarity with the commodity bundles, i. e. some commodities have not been consumed before and the individual is still uncertain about the utility they generate, or it may stem from difficulties in comparing the utilities some of the commodities in bundle x generate with the utility other commodities in bundle y generate, thus a difficulty with the trade-off of some commodities against others.

A fuzzy relation that satisfies the properties of reflexivity, strong completeness and transitivity as defined below can be considered a fuzzy binary preference relation (cf. Barret et al. 1990: 198, Ott 2001: 97):

Reflexivity: $$r(x, x) = 1 \quad \forall\ x \in X$$

Strong completeness: $$r(x, y) + r(y, x) \geq 1 \quad \forall\ x, y \in X$$

Transitivity: $$r(x, z) \geq \min\left[r(x, y), r(y, z)\right] \quad \forall\ x, y, z \in X$$

The definition of reflexivity is straightforward and implies that there is no uncertainty that the same bundles are actually the same bundles. The property of strong completeness is already a quite strong one. It can be interpreted as a plausibility assumption of the individual's reasoning about the relation between the two bundles: the degree of doubt that $x \succsim y$ must be explainable at least by the degree of confidence that, in turn, y could be at least as good as x (i. e. $y \succsim x$). The transitivity definition used here is the most commonly used definition of transitivity in the theory of fuzzy preferences and follows Barrett et al. (1990: 198). However, there are a number of alternative definitions that differ to some degree from the definition above (cf. Salles 1998, Dasgupta and Deb 1996). The meaning of transitivity is that the degree of preference of x over z cannot be smaller than the weakest degree of preference of x over y or of y over z. If this condition were violated the individual would be "too uncertain" regarding his preference of x over z, i. e. the preference uncertainty between x and z could not be explained by the uncertainty between x and y and y and z alone and would thus be "irrational".

#### 4.2.1.2 Is it possible to assess fuzzy preferences regarding the environment?

The theoretical concept to express uncertainty over preferences between commodity bundles in terms of fuzzy binary preference relations as defined above seems quite attractive at first sight. As opposed to other approaches of preference uncertainty (cf. Li and Mattsson 1995, Wang 1997) that define uncertainty in an *ad-hoc* fashion fuzzy relations allow to express uncertainty in a fuzzy preference ordering that fulfills the usual properties of (quasi-)orders reflexivity, completeness and transitivity in their fuzzy definitions. However, and this is bad news for environmental valuation, no suitable concept of fuzzy utility functions has been derived so far from fuzzy preference orderings as defined above.

The Hicksian welfare measures presented in chapter 2 forming the basis for expressing welfare changes resulting from changes in environmental quality are, however, not based on the (direct) utility function but on the expenditure function. But, again, it is also not possible to derive a fuzzy version of the expenditure function since this would require a suitable definition of a fuzzy utility level or an upper contour set for the expenditure minimization (cf. Ahlheim and Rose 1989: 264). For the expenditure minimization problem the restriction, i. e. the upper contour set, must be a convex set, a requirement which is as such not fulfilled in the fuzzy case due to the uncertainty over preferences. Thus, a derivation of welfare measures in analogy to those usually employed when preferences are crisp, i. e. certain, remains elusive.

It appears, therefore, that a formal treatment of preference uncertainty in the context of environmental valuation is not possible and that the various *ad-hoc* approaches described in chapter 2 to take such uncertainty of respondents into account remain the only practicable way. However, due to the lack of a clear reference point how such uncertainty should be treated none of the proposed approaches can be recommended as being a good representation of preference uncertainty. Moreover, the direct assessment of how certain respondents are that they would actually pay a proposed or stated amount of money must be seen very critical. It must be suspected that respondents do not want to reveal their uncertainty of whether to pay or not, especially not in the presence of an interviewer and when the good under consideration is a public good, i. e. a "good cause". In such a situation, respondents are likely to understate their uncertainty, especially when assessed after the WTP question.

An ideal way of assessing preference uncertainty, therefore, would be to avoid any personal statements regarding the level of uncertainty but, instead, to repeatedly assess the same respondent's WTP for the proposed project. In case the response varies over time one could use this information to compute a measure of uncertainty. However, such an approach is certainly not practicable since respondents would be annoyed if their WTP for the same project were assessed every few weeks or so. Instead, it appears more sensible to concentrate on indirect approaches for detecting uncertainty, i. e. some proxy variable that is strongly correlated with uncertainty but at the same time not as problematic to assess directly as the personal uncertainty statement used in many CVM surveys. As mentioned in section 2.2.2 the existence of preference uncertainty might be an important factor for explaining the occurrence of common procedural biases in CVM like the starting point bias, the social desirability effect and the embedding effect. Uncertain respondents being forced to give a precise WTP statement in the DC or the PC question format, for instance, are likely to make use of reference points, frames or circumstances of the interview in order to narrow down the sensible figures from their range of uncertainty. Therefore, the measurement of a respondent's uncertainty level might be useful in two ways: (1) to explain the occurrence of procedural biases, and (2) to serve as a test for the reliability of WTP statements in CVM surveys.

In the following section such a proxy variable for the assessment of respondents' levels of uncertainty will be developed and included into an integrated empirical instrument to detect and classify boundedly rational information processing and decision making in CVM.

### 4.2.2 Considering bounded rationality in environmental valuation

Building on the research on bounded rationality in the field of cognitive psychology the central objective of this study is to analyze the role different kinds of information processing play in environmental valuation surveys. In chapter 3 it was discussed that responses in a CVM interview could depend heavily on the way information is received, stored and processed in the human brain and that the specific situation of such interviews puts more or less serious pressure on respondents' limited cognitive capacities. It can be argued that these limitations play an important role for the occurrence of the procedural biases described in detail in chapter 2. The research approach taken here, therefore, aims at applying the theoretical framework of bounded rationality as described by cognitive psychological models of reasoning and information processing to the context of CVM surveys in order to scrutinize the rationality assumption of respondents in environmental valuation interviews. It is expected that the adoption of this perspective leads to new insights regarding so far unexplained non-rational response behavior, i. e. the observed procedural biases, in CVM surveys. Finally, these insights shall lead to recommendations for an improvement of the design of CVM surveys.

First, a normative view of how respondents should behave and perform in such interviews so that valid and reliable results are achieved will be laid out. This normative view will then serve as a reference for the assessment of the influence of boundedly rational behavior and of the impact on the validity and reliability of CVM results. Subsequently, the specific research questions following from the analysis of expected problems resulting from bounded rationality in CVM surveys will be developed. These research questions, then, will lead to the construction of an empirical survey instrument that is suited for detecting boundedly rational behavior and analyze specific kinds of information processing in empirical CVM studies. This survey instrument will be derived from the rational experiential inventory (REI) which is based on cognitive-experiential self theory (CEST) presented and discussed in detail in the preceding chapter. In order to fit the needs and specifics of contingent valuation studies, the existing REI will be adapted so that a new empirical tool for the assessment of the degree of individual differences in the type of information processing and decision making in environmental valuation studies based on CEST will be available.

#### 4.2.2.1 What constitutes rationality in environmental valuation? The normative view

Chapter 3 presented an ambivalent view of bounded rationality: on the one hand the cognitive limitations and the ensuing simplifying heuristics and mental short cuts were seen as sources of biases and systematic errors in human judgment and decision making. Many empirical experiments where people's behavior in decision tasks was tested against objective criteria of decision quality exhibited those effects consistently and a number of experimental setups that facilitate the occurrence of such biased behavior were identified. This is the main view of the heuristics and biases research program around Daniel Kahneman and Amos Tversky. On the other hand, as argued in line with the descriptive rationality concepts presented in section 3.2.2, the employment of simplified decision rules represents an evolutionary adaptation to the complexity of real-world decision environments. In order to be able to deal with the multitude of everyday decisions, individuals make use of mechanisms that have turned out to be successful in the past. As a result, it is sometimes argued that such simplifying heuristics are not a source of bias in comparison to normative decision strategies but instead necessary means to achieve, on average, the best outcomes possible in such real-world environments (cf. Payne et al. 1993, Todd and Gigerenzer 2003 for details regarding ecological rationality in the real world). Thus, "economy of cognition" is not necessarily a source of bias, as argued by Kahneman and Tversky, but an ecologically rational behavior adapted to the structure of decision environments outside of the laboratory. As a result, there are two conflicting views w. r. t. the role of bounded rationality in human judgment and decision making and both rest on a firm experimental basis.

The question that invariably arises is which of the perspectives on bounded rationality applies to the context of environmental valuation studies employing empirical assessment methods like for example the CVM. Under the first perspective any boundedly rational behavior would introduce systematic errors and biases into the empirical data which would result in invalid and unreliable benefit estimates. Under the second perspective, any use of boundedly rational decision making strategies would have to be considered as ecologically rational, i. e. the resulting estimates would have to be regarded as valid and reliable since they are a product of respondents' "economy of cognition" and, thus, well adapted to the constraints of the particular decision environment.

From a normative perspective, however, the concept of ecological rationality based on the "economy of cognition" should clearly be discarded as a reference for the rationality of decisions in environmental valuation interviews. Since the aim of environmental valuation is the elicitation of people's true preferences w. r. t. an environmental, i. e. a public, good any type of information processing circumventing thorough and differentiated reasoning about the elements of a CVM scenario cannot be considered to be an appropriate way for individuals to evaluate and express their preferences. Thus, it is clearly not in the interest of environmental valuation surveys to allow respondents to strategically employ mental shortcuts and heuristic reasoning in order to deal with the complexity of a CVM scenario since such behavior would prevent them from expressing their true preferences for the proposed environmental good. Instead, a CVM survey should be crafted in a way that respondents are able to fully reflect on the proposed scenario and express their preferences on the basis of thorough reasoning.

#### 4.2.2.2 Why is bounded rationality a problem in environmental valuation?

Having established the reference of fully rational reasoning as the rationality concept of choice in environmental valuation it must be discussed in what ways respondents in CVM surveys can be expected to deviate from such information processing. In chapter 2 it was shown that respondents in CVM interviews are susceptible to a number of procedural biases of which the most prominent are the embedding effect, the warm glow of giving, the hypothetical bias, framing effects and the starting point and range biases. The occurrence of these biases reflects the fact that respondents often do not behave fully rational and give rise to the suspicion that important scenario information is processed in some limited way. As mentioned in chapter 3 an explanation for such limited information processing is provided by the dual-process models of reasoning which state that human beings try to economize on the cognitive resources employed for solving a decision problem.

The heuristic-systematic model (HSM), for example, provides an explicit explanation for the mechanism of choosing the type and level of information processing based on the gap between the actual and the desired levels of confidence w. r. t. a decision. It is argued that actual confidence is determined by a quick assessment of the available information and the search for heuristic cues within this information that will give the decision maker a first orientation of how he should decide. Actual confidence will be high if one strong heuristic cue, i. e. a piece of information that is perceived by the decision maker to be a reliable indicator for his choice or a few cues pointing in the same direction can be found. If information is perceived to be contradictory or unreliable, or if no or few heuristic cues exist in a decision environment, the level of actual confidence will be low. The amount of systematic processing, i. e. of thorough assessment of the given decision situation in the light of the available information, is determined by the gap between this actual confidence after the assessment of heuristic cues and the level of confidence that this particular decision maker feels comfortable with in order to make a decision.

Given the findings of the dual-process models it must be assumed that a similar mechanism of "economy of cognition" determines information processing and decision making in the context of contingent valuation interviews, as well. Thus, decision makers automatically search for, or at least are attentive to, such heuristic cues present in the information on the given decision problem in order to keep the cognitive effort that needs to be employed for the decision task as low as possible while achieving a desired level of confidence concerning that decision. In this line of thought the above mentioned procedural biases of the CVM could be interpreted as instances of simplified, i. e. heuristic information processing and decision making, that was triggered by the presence of heuristic cues in the given information and decision context. Non-contradictory heuristic cues would lead to an already high level of actual confidence and the remaining confidence gap to the confidence level desired by the respondent would be filled by analytical processing. Instead, an absence of such heuristic cues would have led to a lower level of actual confidence so that more analytical information evaluation processes would have been necessary in order to achieve the desired level of confidence.

As has become obvious from this discussion about known procedural biases of the CVM a wide variety of pieces of information contained in the design and specification of a CVM scenario have the potential to serve as heuristic cues. These cues could subsequently lead to some form of limited information processing and decision making which is not based on the full set of the information provided in the contingent decision setting. As a result, it is of high importance to avoid heuristic cues in the specification of CVM scenarios. However, certain cues might not be avoidable, e. g. the context in which a scenario is framed. Another issue deserves attention, as well: CVM scenarios typically contain a considerable amount of information since in a first stage the reference situation has to be described with all its attributes so that subsequently in a second stage an alternative situation to be valued can be sensibly specified. In order to obtain responses in CVM interviews that are based on all these pieces of information it is necessary that this information be correctly perceived and transferred into the working memory of the respondent. As is known from cognitive psychology, the bottleneck effects might limit the uptake of information into the working memory. Further, the amount of information that can be stored in the working memory for further processing is limited as well (see 3.3.3.3 on the articulatory loop and the visuospatial sketchpad). From these limitations of attention and memory it follows that heuristic cues contained in the presented information gain importance the greater the load of information becomes.

Considering the type of boundedly rational information processing in CVM interviews described above, what are the specific heuristics that respondents in such interviews may be expected to utilize? On the one hand, heuristic information processing may be triggered by heuristic cues present in the survey design or the scenario information and, on the other hand, simplified reasoning may be used in case respondents are uncertain, e. g. due to the lack of experience or information of the environmental good or time limitations during the interview. As mentioned above, a fully rational respondent in a CVM interview would employ analytical and systematic reasoning, following the central route of information processing, as described in the dual-process models like the ELM or the HSM in section 3.3.4. Such a respondent would consider all aspects of the proposed scenario and evaluate the consequences resulting from this scenario for him personally where some aspects would be likely to be of greater importance to the respondent than others. Subsequently, the WTP statement would follow directly from such an evaluation where the format of the WTP elicitation question or the presence of an interviewer have no influence on the amount stated.

This fully rational response behavior of an ideal respondent can be contrasted to an information processing and evaluation making use of intuition and simplifying heuristics. First, a respondent may not engage in much consideration about the proposed scenario at all and state his WTP on the basis of the first impression he gets when the scenario is presented to him. Such a WTP statement would simply rest on the intuition of the respondent, his "gut feeling". Intuitive responses are characterized by a rather quick and effortless decision on how much the respondent would be willing to pay, i. e. whether to accept or reject a proposed bid in the dichotomous choice format or which payment interval to select from the list of intervals on a payment card. Intuition may either refer to the quick formation of the impression the respondent gets from the proposed project, i. e. whether he likes it or not, or it may refer to which answer to the WTP question is appropriate. In the dichotomous choice format intuition may, for example, tell the respondent not to accept to pay any amount if the improvement of environmental quality in return for this payment, although in the future, is not sufficiently guaranteed. That means, intuition may tell the respondent to be skeptical regarding the proposed project and, thus, reject a proposed bid that would still be below his personal valuation of the scenario. In the case of the payment card format, intuition may tell the respondent to select an interval from the full range of the payment card that corresponds to his "fair share" in relation to his own position in society, i. e. for example select an interval in the mid-range in case he considers himself to belong to the middle income group within society.

Second, a respondent may fail to balance the single aspects of the complex project scenario and consider all aspects of equal importance for his decision. Such behavior would reflect a lack of elaboration on the proposed scenario which could be a result of bottleneck effects in the acquisition of information so that the respondent does not even obtain a clear picture of the proposed scenario. Furthermore, due to the general impression the respondent gets from the scenario he considers it of low personal relevance so that the reasoning process when asked to give a monetary valuation follows the peripheral route of information processing. The behavior of giving equal importance to the scenario elements is related to the intuitive decision making mentioned above, however, it is characterized by a generally low personal interest in the proposed scenario. The reaction to the WTP elicitation question may be quite similar to the intuitive decision maker, though, and thus follow the route described in the preceding paragraph.

A third specific type of limited information processing is the respondent who bases his WTP statement only on a few aspects that appear relevant to him. While he attributes different importance to the aspects of the scenario, just like the fully rational respondent would most likely do, he fails to consider the full set of aspects and simply concentrates on the ones that feature most prominent in the complex scenario. His WTP statement would, therefore, not reflect those aspects of the scenario that were left unconsidered. It may be argued that it is normal that some aspects are considered important and others not. However, a valid CVM response requires that all aspects are actually considered and in the situation where an environmental change scenario is presented with which the respondent has little prior experience some aspects may require deeper consideration before it is discovered that they actually do have some personal relevance to the respondent. A WTP statement based on the consideration of only few aspects, therefore, reflects a tendency toward limited information processing and gives rise to the suspicion that not all aspects of the scenario were well-understood by the respondent so that the response cannot be based on a thorough evaluation of all aspects of the scenario.

As mentioned above the described three specific types of limited information processing may be facilitated by the lack of sufficient information about the valuation scenario so that the respondent cannot obtain a clear picture about what is to be valued and by time constraints in the interview situation, especially when asked to think about his WTP. Both of these aspects may add to the respondent's feeling of being uncertain about the relevance of the scenario and, thus, his personal WTP for the project. Any analysis aiming at detecting the influence of limited information processing must, therefore, take information and time limitations into account, as well.

The dual-process models of reasoning assume the existence of individual differences in the way cognitive resources are allocated to decision tasks. It has been shown that there exist individual differences in cognitive abilities (as measured e. g. by the intelligence quotient, cf. Anderson 2001, or the Cognitive Reflection Test, cf. Frederick 2005) as well as in the kind of experiences individuals have made in the course of their lives with the applicability of heuristic versus analytical information processing (cf. Epstein et al. 1996). Thus, it has been shown that different individuals have developed different strategies regarding the application of simplifying heuristics. In addition to these differences inherent in the particular person, situational factors of a decision environment, e. g. personal involvement with the issue at hand, will lead to individual differences in the activation of intuitive-heuristic versus systematic-analytical processing. As a result, it must be expected that different respondents will react to the same situational factors like e. g. heuristic cues contained in the design of a CVM study in individually different ways. Some respondents will process the given information mostly analytically while others make extensive use of the possibilities of limited information processing. The issue of individual differences in information processing in CVM interviews will form the core of the empirical research in this study.

#### 4.2.2.3 Research questions and hypotheses

The discussion on the importance to consider bounded rationality in environmental valuation gives rise to a number of specific research questions for investigating the type of information processing and decision making in CVM interviews in practice. From the cognitive psychology literature on dual-process models two aspects can be extracted that form a suitable starting point for the derivation of such research questions: (1) the existence of an "economy of cognition" in real-world decision situations where individuals economize on their limited cognitive capacities in any given task, and (2) the existence of individual differences in the way given information is processed. Concerning the latter, it was shown that individual differences exist both in the general cognitive disposition, i. e. whether individuals show the tendency for intuitive-heuristic processing in general or whether they have an affinity for systematic-analytical reasoning, on the one hand and differences in the way individuals deal with a specific decision task on the other, i. e. whether they base their decisions on the heuristic cues provided in that task or not. In general, one would expect that these two types of individual differences are systematically related, i. e. that those individuals having a general cognitive disposition for intuitive-heuristic processing will, on average, be also those who make use of heuristic cues more often in a specific decision task.

Taking these distinctions as a starting point for an investigation of the importance of boundedly rational behavior in environmental valuation surveys, the following four research questions can be derived:

(1) Do respondents in CVM interviews perform an "economy of cognition" and, as a result, exhibit boundedly rational information processing?

(2) If yes, how can such boundedly rational information processing be detected and measured, i. e. what are suitable instruments for identifying boundedly rational decision makers and the types of information processing they use?

(3) What are the relationships between those classifications of rationality and stated WTP on the one hand and the occurrence of procedural biases on the other?

(4) What can be learned from the investigation of the influence of boundedly rational information processing for the design of future CVM surveys?

The first research question addresses the suspicion that the inconsistencies in CVM response behavior found in many empirical studies may in principle result from cognitive processes that are rooted in the selective employment of analytical versus limited information processing depending on respondents' feelings of how to optimally allocate cognitive resources to a decision task. As such, this research question represents the overarching direction of the research approach taken here. If such an "economy of cognition" is not found, i. e. if respondents are shown not to employ, at least to some extent, strategies of limited information processing as laid out in the preceding section, this cognitive psychological concept of dual-processes of reasoning is not suited for explaining the still controversial issues in CVM research.

The second research question focuses on the issue of an empirical determination of boundedly rational behavior in CVM interviews. In order to detect such behavior it is necessary to develop empirical survey instruments to be employed within a CVM survey so that specific types of information processing can be made visible, can be classified into general categories and can finally be attributed to every single respondent of the survey. Following the discussion of individual differences in information processing it shall also be determined which is the best way to describe these individual differences in the context of CVM interviews: either by general cognitive dispositions or by the task-specific differences in the use of heuristic cues. Aiming at the explanation of CVM response behavior, it is not evident a priori whether it suffices to characterize individuals by their general cognitive dispositions to process information more analytically or more intuitively or whether it is more appropriate or even necessary to consider specific task-dependent strategies of limited information processing. In order to explore this issue, separate empirical instruments for the measurement of general cognitive dispositions and of task-dependent information processing shall be developed. As mentioned above, it may be expected that these two different approaches are related to each other.

The purpose of the third research question is to scrutinize the open and controversially discussed issues of CVM response behavior, i. e. mainly the procedural biases described in chapter 2, using the newly developed empirical instruments for the classification and measurement of types of information processing in CVM interviews. First, it shall be investigated whether the general cognitive dispositions or the task-dependent information processing strategies are systematically related to the WTP stated by respondents. Again, no clear a priori hypothesis exists as to whether respondents exhibiting higher degrees of boundedly rational information processing (see section 4.2.2.2) have a higher or a lower WTP for environmental projects than respondents taking all aspects of a scenario fully into account and employing differentiated analytical reasoning. However, one may expect a tendency that in well-crafted and credible CVM scenarios thorough analytical processing will lead to higher WTP as compared to the limited information processors. This expectation arises from the fact that many aspects of environmental scenarios involving non-use values were shown to be rather complex and often unfamiliar to the average respondent so that these aspects require deeper thought before they are perceived to be of substantial personal relevance. Limited information processors that are characterized by a superficial and selective evaluation of the given scenario information, therefore, can be expected to attribute less personal relevance to an environmental scenario as compared to more analytical respondents and might state a lower WTP as a consequence. This rather tentative hypothesis shall be tested in the empirical example of this study.

Clearer hypotheses, however, can be formulated regarding the relationships between the types of information processing and the occurrence of procedural biases in CVM. Expecting clear distinctions between analytical and intuitive respondents both regarding general cognitive dispositions and task-specific types of information processing intuitive respondents are expected to show a higher degree of susceptibility to biases. Regarding the starting point bias in the dichotomous choice question format analytical respondents should have developed a clearer picture about the valuation scenario and, thus, their response should not be influenced (as much) by the varying starting bids as the response of intuitive individuals (see also section 4.2.2.2). The same should hold for the range bias in the payment card format. As a general hypothesis, therefore, it shall be expected that analytical-rational respondents are less prone to procedural biases in CVM surveys than intuitive-heuristic respondents. This hypothesis will also be tested in the empirical study below.

The fourth research question addresses the consequences of the investigation of boundedly rational CVM response behavior for CVM surveys. From the results of the empirical study below some generalizations shall be deducted that may turn out to be useful as a guideline for the improvement of future CVM survey designs. It is not the aim of this research to develop a mechanism to correct "erroneous" WTP statements, such an approach would require to know either "how wrong" the WTP statements of limited information processors are or, alternatively, to clearly identify untrustworthy responses and exclude them from the sample. Both approaches appear neither realistic nor desirable. In contrast, it shall be tried to improve the design of CVM surveys so that respondents with a tendency to employ strategies of limited information processing increase their use of analytical reasoning in the context of environmental valuation surveys.

## 4.3 Development of empirical instruments for analyzing bounded rationality in CVM

On the basis of the above discussion an empirical instrument to be included as a standardized part of an empirical CVM survey shall be developed in this section in order to be able to investigate the research questions stated above. In a first step, these instruments shall be developed in a general form in order to be applicable and adaptable to any empirical environmental valuation study based on stated preferences. In a second step, the developed instruments will be applied in an empirical CVM study in section 4.4 and the research questions stated in 4.2.2.3 will be investigated. In the following section, a measure of individual differences in information processing and decision making which is derived from cognitive-experiential self-theory will be described. This measure will form the basis for the specific development of the empirical instruments.

### 4.3.1 A measure for individual differences in decision making: the rational experiential inventory (REI)

As the basis for the detection of individual differences in information processing and decision making a self-report measure developed by Epstein et al. (1996) derived from their cognitive-experiential self-theory (CEST, see 3.3.4.2) will be used. In general, CEST proposes the existence of two fundamental and independent modes of reasoning, one based on intuition and personal experience and the other based on systematic and analytical cognitive processes. The interaction of these thinking styles produces the observable behavior in specific decision tasks, where it is assumed that while both styles are active, one usually dominates over the other to varying degrees. In addition, individuals are expected to differ in the degree to which these thinking styles are in general being employed, i. e. in their personal cognitive disposition. The rational experiential inventory (REI) was developed as a self-report measure to assess the degree to which individuals are confident with employing either thinking style in general. Further, it was designed by the authors to provide evidence for the assumption that the two thinking styles or information processing modes are actually independent from each other and interactive as postulated in CEST instead of being simply inversely related (like the NFC).

In order to test the assumption of CEST that the two processing modes operate independently, the REI consists of two distinct sets of questions assumed to characterize either mode. The first set of questions refers to the degree to which an individual perceives to employ the analytic-rational thinking style. The elements of this set are taken from the Need-for-Cognition (NFC) scale developed by Cacioppo and Petty (1982) as a measure for the likelihood of elaboration in their ELM framework (see 3.3.4.2). The second set of questions is used for measuring respondents' tendency to employ the intuitive-heuristic thinking style. These questions were developed by Epstein et al. (1996) and termed Faith-in-Intuition (FI). In conjunction, the NFC and the FI question sets form the rational experiential inventory (REI) as a total of 31 questions (items) where 19 items are selected from the original NFC scale and 12 items make up the FI scale. These questions are presented to test persons in a self-report test who are asked to rate each given statement on a five-point Likert scale ranging from 1 = completely false to 5 = completely true. The items of the REI are listed in table 4-1 where (R) indicates that the particular item is formulated in reverse sense to the level of need for cognition, i. e. a high rating on that item would mean a low association with need for cognition.

**Table 4-1:** The Rational Experiential Inventory (adapted from Epstein et al. (1996: 394)

| Scale and item | 1 | 2 |
|---|---|---|
| **Need for Cognition (NFC) – analytical scale** | | |
| I would rather do something that requires little thought than something that is sure to challenge my thinking abilities. (R) | **.74** | -.08 |
| I don't like to have the responsibility of handling a situation that requires a lot of thinking. (R) | **.71** | -.05 |
| I would prefer complex to simple problems. | **-.66** | -.02 |
| I try to anticipate and avoid situations where there is a likely chance I will have to think in depth about something. (R) | **.65** | -.06 |
| I find little satisfaction in deliberating hard and for long hours. (R) | **.63** | -.04 |
| Thinking is not my idea of fun. (R) | **.59** | .11 |
| The notion of thinking abstractly is not appealing to me. (R) | **.58** | -.02 |
| I prefer my life to be filled with puzzles that I must solve. | **-.57** | .01 |
| Simply knowing the answer rather than understanding the reasons for the answer to a problem is fine with me. (R) | **.57** | .16 |
| I don't reason well under pressure. (R) | **.55** | -.10 |
| The idea of relying on thought to make my way to the top does not appeal to me. (R) | **.51** | .12 |
| I prefer to talk about international problems rather than to gossip or talk about celebrities. | **-.49** | -.13 |
| Learning new ways to think doesn't excite me very much. (R) | **.49** | -.18 |
| I would prefer a task that is intellectual, difficult, and important to one that is somewhat important but does not require much thought. | **-.49** | .04 |
| I generally prefer to accept things as they are rather than to question them. (R) | **.46** | .00 |
| It is enough for me that something gets the job done, I don't care how or why it works. (R) | **.44** | .20 |
| I tend to set goals that can be accomplished only by expending considerable mental effort. | **-.42** | -.18 |
| I have difficulty thinking in new and unfamiliar situations. (R) | **.36** | -.32 |
| I feel relief rather than satisfaction after completing a task that required a lot of mental effort. (R) | **.36** | .00 |

*Table 4-1 continued*

| Scale and item | 1 | 2 |
|---|---|---|
| **Faith in Intuition (FI) – intuitive scale** | | |
| My initial impressions of people are almost always right. | .02 | **.76** |
| I trust my initial feelings about people. | .21 | **.76** |
| When it comes to trusting people, I can usually rely on my gut feelings. | .18 | **.72** |
| I believe in trusting my hunches. | .18 | **.64** |
| I can usually feel when a person is right or wrong even if I can't explain how I know. | .10 | **.56** |
| I am a very intuitive person. | -.16 | **.53** |
| I can typically sense right away when a person is lying. | -.12 | **.46** |
| I am quick to form impressions about people. | .20 | **.42** |
| I believe I can judge character pretty well from a person's appearance. | .22 | **.40** |
| I often have clear visual images of things. | -.09 | **.35** |
| I have a very good sense of rhythm. | -.07 | **.34** |
| I am good at visualizing things. | -.19 | **.34** |

In empirical tests the reliabilities of the NFC and the FI scales as measured by Cronbach's alpha[4] (α) have been found to be very good (α = .87 for NFC and α = .77 for FI).Epstein et al. (1996) present an empirical study of the REI scale on a set of 184 test persons in order to test its validity. For a test of the independence of the two postulated thinking styles, the responses of this test sample are subjected to a factor analysis. This statistical method is widely used to detect systematic patterns in datasets with many variables by exploiting the correlation structure between those variables. It is often employed to reduce the dimension of a dataset, i. e. it determines so-called latent factors which represent underlying, but unobservable variables.

Factors are formed by a number of observed variables that are substantially correlated with each other so that it can be assumed that they in conjunction have a common meaning, the interpretation of the factor. Each variable is related to each factor to a certain degree, the "factor loading", which can be interpreted as how strongly the meaning of the particular variable coincides with the "real" meaning of the factor to be interpreted. The meaning of the factor can thus only be inferred to be the common denominator of meanings of all the variables, i. e.

4 Cronbach's alpha is a statistical measure of reliability of factor scales and is based on the correlations between the various items of the factor. Values of .70 and higher are generally considered as sufficiently reliable, however, no convention of a threshold value for reliability exists (Janssen and Laatz 2003: 525).

items, that make up the particular factor. Table 4-1 shows that two factors could be generated or extracted from the dataset of the test sample. The numbers represent the factor loadings of the respective item where the bold figures indicate to which factor the particular item belongs, the one on which it loads highest. The factor loadings can assume values between -1 and 1 which can be interpreted as correlation coefficients of the items with the respective factor. Thus, in table 4-1 the items are ordered according to their strength of relation with the respective factor and not according to their sequence in the self-report questionnaire. Finally, it is possible to compute individual factor scores, i. e. a measure to what extent each individual is characterized by each of the extracted factors.

As expected the factor analysis groups the question items according to the NFC set on the one hand and to the FI set on the other. Respondents with a high rating on one NFC item have shown, on average, a tendency to rate the other NFC items also high (or low in case the item is formulated in reverse as indicated by (R)). The same applies for the FI items so that the correlation structure of the responses yields a clear distinction into two separate factors representing NFC and FI, respectively. A useful property of factor analysis is that all factors that are extracted from the underlying dataset are statistically independent from each other. As a result, the score on the NFC factor is not systematically related to the score on the FI factor, i. e. a high NFC score does not imply a low FI score for any given individual.

Therefore, Epstein et al. (1996) conjecture that there exist indeed two fundamental reasoning processes that, in general, operate independently from each other. At least it can be said that NFC and FI measure two different and independent processing modes. The very low and insignificant correlation between the NFC and the FI of $r = -0.07$ underscores this independence. This implies that people should not be considered to be either intuitive-experiential or cognitive-rational thinkers as would have been the case if NFC and FI had been found to be inversely related. Rather, people must be conceived as exhibiting both a certain degree of need for cognition as measured by the NFC score and of faith in intuition as measured by the FI score. These scores can be both high, both low or any possible combination of the two scales (see figure 4-2).

However, what does this independence really mean, how can it be interpreted? Can people be both analytical-rational and intuitive-experiential at the same time or, on the other end, not at all? From the formulations of the questions of the NFC and the FI scale in table 4-1 it becomes obvious that the REI does not intend to measure the actual employment of either thinking style objectively, i. e. to what extent individuals actually employ analytical or heuristic information processing. The object of measurement, rather, is the perception and the attitudes of individuals w. r. t. their own ease and success of using either mode in real life. The scores on NFC and FI mirror the experiences that respondents have made in their lives with either mode. Thus, some people have made good experiences with analytical thinking, they enjoy problem solving and have, most probably, even solved problems successfully in this mode. At the same time, they have confidence in their intuitions and hunches when it comes to making judgments and taking decisions.

**Figure 4-2:** Possible combinations of NFC versus FI scores

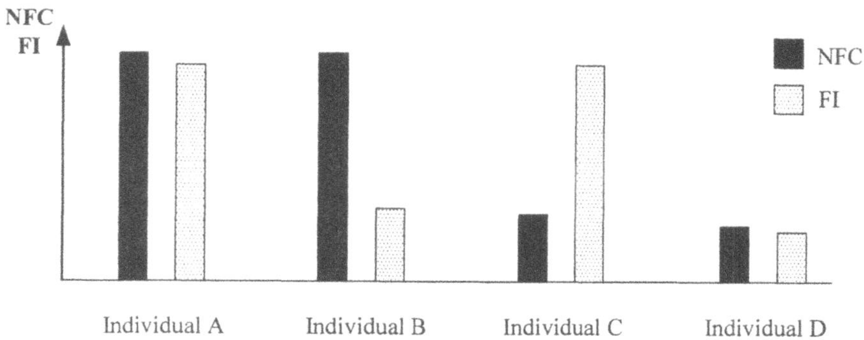


Such people like individual A in figure 4-2 would, thus, score high on both scales of general cognitive disposition. However, when actually taking decisions in a specific task context they would apply the tradeoff of information processing modes as indicated by the concept of economy of cognition laid out by the dual-process models in chapter 3. Here, the actual degree of employment of one mode versus the other depends critically on the structure of and the information provided in the specific task. The presence of heuristic cues would activate simplifying rules and analytical processing would be used to close the confidence gap (see chapter 3). However, the employment of cognitive resources would differ substantially from other kinds of people who score high on NFC and low on FI (individual B) or vice versa (individual C), or even score low on both scales (individual D). Those people have different levels of confidence in their information processing modes and perceive either one of the two modes as less reliable for decision making or they may even have little confidence in their cognitive abilities, analytical or intuitive, altogether due to continuous lack of success with their decisions.

A reasonable interpretation of the NFC and FI scores would be, therefore, that they measure the cost of information processing in terms of cognitive resources employed in either processing mode where the higher the score on the scale the lower the cost associated with the respective mode. For example, when an individual scores high on FI but low on NFC like individual C in figure 4-2 it indicates that the cost of analytical information processing is perceived as relatively high, i. e. relative to his own intuitive-experiential processing and relatively higher than someone else who scores higher on NFC and, therefore, has more ease with and confidence in such processing. In a specific task individual C would generally tend to rely to a higher extent on heuristic processing if made possible by the presence of heuristic cues where such heuristic processing would also generate a higher level of confidence than would be the case for other people scoring higher on NFC. High NFC indicates the ability to question the outcomes of heuristic processing and probably correct them in the light of other individuating information (see 3.3.4.2). The "relative cost" of such analytical processing as perceived by the individual would then determine the degree to which it is employed in specific tasks.

When comparing the cognitive dispositions of individuals A and D for which analytical processing has the same cost relative to heuristic processing the difference of processing in specific tasks would result in different levels of confidence in their decisions. Individual A must be expected to be quite confident of his decision, i. e. quite sure that his decision was correct, since he feels that he can rely on his intuitions and likes to employ more effortful cognition to scrutinize his hunches and to carefully consider the available information. Individual D, on the contrary, the classical cognitive miser, has little trust in either processing mode and would, therefore, be expected to have little confidence that his decision will actually be correct. Thus, staying within the terminology of the HSM it is expected that individuals A and D differ in their desired levels of confidence in decision making.

The REI is, therefore, considered to be a suitable starting point to develop measurement instruments for the assessment of individual differences in cognitive dispositions in CVM studies. In the following section, the REI as specified above will be adapted and extended in order to fit the research questions stated above.

### 4.3.2 Adaptation of the REI to the context of the CVM

The main objective of a measurement instrument of bounded rationality is the analysis of individual differences in heuristic information processing in CVM surveys. Considering this objective, it is necessary to analyze respondents' information processing on two levels: first, in analogy to the REI a method to measure respondents' general dispositions to engage in intuitive-experiential and analytical-rational information processing needs to be available. Such a task independent scale provides an indication of respondents' thinking styles regardless of the task at hand. Second, an instrument for the measurement of heuristic versus systematic information processing specific to the actual task that respondents have to perform is needed, in this case the particular environmental valuation study using the contingent valuation methodology. This task dependent scale of information processing creates the basis for an identification of the specific activation of heuristic responses due to the heuristic cue information provided in the specific CVM design as laid out in section 4.2.2.2. Thus, in conjunction the two individual scales of information processing generate a pattern of individual information processing and decision behavior that takes both the general dispositions to employ either thinking styles and the specific situation of a particular CVM task environment with its heuristic cues into account.

As laid out in section 4.2.2.3 it is not unreasonable to expect that the two individual scales of information processing are correlated to a certain extent due to the fact that respondents with a high propensity for intuitive-experiential processing are likely to employ such a thinking style in the specific CVM interview as well. Thus, it could be argued that one single scale on respondents' information processing types would suffice for detecting boundedly rational behavior in CVM studies. However, it was argued by all of the dual-process models of reasoning and the models of boundedly rational decision making described extensively in chapter 3 that "economy of cognition" implies that individuals adapt their information processing to the specific decision environment. In environments providing a high number of non-contradictory heuristic cues such intuitive-experiential processing would be facilitated so that people would be expected to exhibit a higher degree of employment of heuristics independently of their general types. On the contrary, if only few or contradictory heuristic cues are given, actual confidence will be low and decision makers will have to make up for this by employing more cognitive resources for systematic, analytical-rational information processing and decision making. Hence, although they may be correlated to some degree, the two separate indicators for individual thinking styles and information processing, one general and one specific to the task at hand, are necessary for the investigation of bounded rationality in CVM interviews. In an ideal CVM design where only a minimum number of heuristic cues is present so that procedural biases are avoided the task dependent scale is expected to indicate very low levels of heuristic processing while the task independent scale of general individual thinking styles still exhibits the usual distinction within the general population.

The task independent scale of information processing is adapted from the REI to fit the context of the interview situation of an environmental valuation study better than the original version. First of all, the original REI contains too many items, i. e. the application of the full REI scale would be unreasonable in a typical CVM interview since it would take too much time in relation to the remaining questions and respondents would be reluctant to answer due to the obvious lack of connection between the issue of environmental valuation and thinking styles. Therefore, the first task was to select from the REI a small number of representative items that could then be further adapted. Second, environmental valuation interviews are typically characterized by time pressure since such an interview almost always represents an unwanted interruption of other tasks the respondent is momentarily engaged in. Therefore, it is desirable to introduce the issue of information processing and decision making under time pressure into the task independent measure. This aspect is included in the original REI only to a limited extent.

Table 4-2 presents a suitable question for the elicitation of such a task independent scale. In this question, respondents are told in a short introductory passage that the researcher is interested in the individual decision making process. Subsequently, the respondent is asked to what extent some statements regarding his personal attitude are true, i. e. the respondent is expected to give an individual rating of how much these statements apply to him. Here, a five-point Likert scale where e. g. "1" means "not true at all" and "5" means "fully true". Depending on the general intellectual background of the sample population it is also conceivable to use smaller or larger scales. In question 1, items A, B, D and E represent reformulations and summaries of question items from the NFC scale of the original REI (see above) where it was focused on those question items that had shown a high factor loading in table 4-1. It is expected that four items eliciting the same underlying thinking style in different alternative formulations should be sufficient for the purpose of this concise instrument. Items were reformulated for better understandability in many socio-economic and educational contexts. However, it must be expected that E might not be applicable in all societies, as will be seen later in the empirical study performed in Thailand.

Item C refers to an individual's role and behavior in a social context with the intention to elicit a respondent's tendency to be a leader or a follower and, connected to this, the ease of being persuaded in a social context. It is closely related to the original REI item "I generally prefer to accept things as they are rather than to question them" but it was intended to focus on the aspect of behavior in a group. Items F and I refer to the issue of information processing and decision making under time pressure and are related to the original REI item "I don't reason well under pressure". Items G and H are directly taken from the FI scale of the original REI since they were considered to be suitable and concise formulations. Also here, the items with the highest factor loadings were concentrated on. Item J is based on the FI-item "I can usually feel when a person is right or wrong even if I can't explain how I know" used in an interpersonal context. However, for the purpose of this study it was reformulated to fit intuition in a more general context, i. e. independent of judgments w. r. t. people. Altogether, this compilation of 10 items is expected to be a suitable basis for computing a measurement scale of general task independent information processing types to be included in any CVM survey questionnaire.

**Table 4-2:** Task independent scale – the question items

| | |
|---|---|
| | Question 1:<br>I would like to know how you reached your decision. How true are the following statements regarding your personal attitude? |
| A | Thinking hard and for a long time about something bores me. |
| B | I enjoy doing something that challenges my thinking abilities like for example playing chess (*or some other typical game that requires hard thinking*). |
| C | In a group of friends I generally trust the arguments of others without always questioning where they come from. |
| D | A complex problem is a challenge to me rather than a nuisance. |
| E | Doing quizzes and cross-word puzzles are a pleasant form of entertainment for me. |
| F | Time is money, so I take decisions quickly. |
| G | I believe in trusting my hunches. |
| H | My initial impressions of people are almost always right. |
| I | I hate to make important decisions under time pressure. |
| J | Often, when I take decisions, I don't know why but I feel that I'm right. |

The second, i. e. task dependent measurement scale of information processing and decision making, is not based on any pre-existing scale. It was specifically developed for the task of measuring the level of response behavior based on heuristic cues contained in a CVM design and is oriented at the expected limited information processing strategies described in section 4.2.2.2. In an introductory sentence people are told to reconsider the way they had taken their decision whether or not (or alternatively *how much*) to contribute to the proposed environmental project. They are then asked to state whether the items given are true or false. The question items developed for the task dependent scale are listed in table 4-3.

**Table 4-3:** Task dependent scale – the question items

| | |
|---|---|
| | Question 2: When you think about your decision whether and how much to contribute to the proposed project, are the following statements true? |
| A | I made my decision based on my first feeling about this program right after it was presented to me. |
| B | I really thought very hard about every single aspect of the program before making a decision of how much to pay. |
| C | The first impression that I had about this program changed on a second thought. |
| D | I would have liked to have more time for making a decision about my contribution to this program. |
| E | All aspects were equally important for my decision. |
| F | With the given information about the project I found it very hard to make a good decision. |
| G | There are so many aspects in this project but only a few of them were really relevant for my decision. |
| H | Even if I had had more time available for thinking about this program I don't think that my decision of how much to contribute to it would have been different. |

Items A, B, E and G refer to the amount of information that was considered in the decision making process where item A stresses particularly the role of intuition, i. e. the immediate associations with the presented project. In general, it is expected that respondents who state to have used little information processing reveal a high degree of response to heuristic cues. Item C addresses the process of a correction of the first impression, i. e. the immediate associations of the experiential system, by the analytical-rational system. This refers to the possible corrective design of dual-process models (see 3.3.4.1). A "yes"-answer would thus indicate a high degree of analytical-rational processing. Items D and H refer to the available time in this specific task, i. e. whether the respondent felt to be under time pressure. Time pressure would indicate a high degree of heuristic information processing. Analogously, item F addresses the respondent's perception of whether sufficient information was provided. It is expected that respondents who say "yes" to this question were not seduced to short cut decision making by the presence of heuristic cues. Altogether, the items compiled in question 2 (table 4-3) are considered to represent a number of important aspects of possible heuristic decision making specifically in CVM studies. With slight adaptations of the formulations of these items, this question could be incorporated as a heuristic cue test in any CVM survey questionnaire.

Summarizing the main topics of discussion and developments of this chapter up to now, sections 4.2.2 and 4.2.3 have applied the insights gained from the cognitive psychological models of reasoning to the context of environmental valuation studies employing the contingent valuation method. It has been discussed that due to the purpose of environmental valuation studies to assess the social value of a public good that will be of benefit for the considered society as a whole it is of great importance for the validity and reliability of CVM results that responses be based on a consideration of all the presented information and as little economizing behavior resulting from heuristic cues present in the CVM design as possible. It is thus the general objective of the research approach followed in this study to develop an instrument that is suited to analyze the influence of the different forms of information processing on responses in CVM studies. Ideally, the developed instrument should serve to provide guidelines as to how future CVM design can be improved so that the use of strategies of limited information processing is minimized.

To this end two separate measurement scales based on individual differences in information processing and decision making were developed, where the task independent scale elicits the general disposition to employ the intuitive-experiential and the analytical-rational thinking styles and the task dependent scale elicits the degree to which simplified and limited information processing was actually applied in the specific CVM study. Factor analytic evaluations of the two separate sets of questions are expected to reveal patterns of information processing and decision making types both on the general, task independent and on the specific, task dependent level.

In the remainder of the chapter, these newly developed scales of bounded rationality will be applied in an empirical CVM study of a household tap water improvement program in northern Thailand. This study will demonstrate in detail how these measurement scales are to be used and whether the theoretical expectations associated with the particular response behavior to the items contained in the scales will be confirmed.

## 4.4 An empirical example

### 4.4.1 Background of the empirical research project: The Uplands Program

The empirical CVM survey for applying and testing the scales of bounded rationality developed in the preceding sections was conducted as a part of a research project which formed a subproject within the Collaborative Research Center (Sonderforschungsbereich, SFB) 564 funded by the German Science Foundation (Deutsche Forschungsgemeinschaft, DFG) from July 2003 to June 2006. This SFB represents an international and interdisciplinary conjunction of research projects with the aim to advance scientific knowledge for sustainable land use and rural development in the regional context of mountainous Southeast Asia (Uplands Program). The research areas of this SFB are located in northern Thailand around the provincial capital of Chiang Mai and in northern Vietnam mainly in the province of Son La. Since the part of subproject F1.2 on which the present empirical application of the scales of bounded rationality is based is exclusively located in Thailand, only the general research aspects of the Thailand part of the SFB 564 will be presented here subsequently.

In Thailand, research on the sustainability of fruit tree production systems in the uplands with a focus on lychee, longan and mango as the dominating fruits represents the thematic core of the SFB. In particular, possibilities for an increase in farmers' incomes from these production systems under the condition of preventing adverse effects to the fragile mountainous ecosystems and downstream lowland communities are investigated. Apart from issues of off-season fruit production, improved fertilization and pest management, erosion control measures and post-harvesting technologies one focus of the research collaboration is on social science and economic aspects in order to obtain a comprehensive understanding of the institutional circumstances under which such farming activities in the uplands occur. In this respect land use activities that are performed in the uplands and have shown to be associated with adverse environmental consequences for lowland communities in the valley bottoms or at the outlets of the respective water catchments are of particular concern since they give rise to ample discussions within the Thai society about such negative externalities. Subproject F1.2 deals with these upstream-downstream externalities in particular by analyzing the social benefits arising from an improvement of this situation in a specific water catchment. This approach and its specific empirical research will be described in the following.

## 4.4.2 General research ideas and hypotheses of the subproject in northern Thailand

### 4.4.2.1 Problem definition

Farming activities in the uplands of northern Thailand are associated with a number of adverse effects on the local environment. These include (1) the application of pesticides that are harmful to organisms in the surrounding ecosystems and to human health, (2) the occurrence of soil erosion due to a lack of vegetation covering the steep fields and plantations on the mountain slopes and (3) large amounts of water used for irrigation. These effects have consequences for communities that are located in lowland areas downstream due to their connection to the upstream farming areas by the rivers of the water catchments carrying the load of pesticides and sediments. Under these circumstances, lowland communities are usually affected by the upstream farming activities in a variety of ways: pesticide contamination of the water bodies from which the water for household use is taken, red color of the household water especially during the rainy season, contamination of fruits and vegetables consumed by the households, the accumulation of pesticides in the surrounding ecosystem harming animals and plants living there and periodical water shortages toward the end of the dry season.

Subproject F1.2 on which the empirical application of the scales of bounded rationality is based considers the situation of a particular water catchment that is characterized by the typical situation described in the preceding paragraph. The water catchment under consideration, the Mae Sa valley, is located about 20 to 45 kilometers north-west of the provincial capital of Chiang Mai in northern Thailand. Its total area comprises 147 $km^2$. The main river flowing through this valley is called Mae Sa river. In the town of Mae Rim, a suburban area of about 26,237 households (official 2003 data) located 10 – 15 kilometers north of Chiang Mai, the Mae Sa river flows into the Ping river, one of the main streams of northern Thailand passing the city of Chiang Mai on its way to the South. A three-dimensional scheme of this water catchment based on GIS-data is provided in figure 4-3.

The empirical objective of this subproject is to assess the social value accruing to a specified part of the population of Mae Rim from a project to improve the quality of the household tap water supply so that it would be safe at all times to drink tap water without further treatment. Furthermore, no water shortages or low water pressure should occur at any time. Before specifying the details of such a project the situation of household water supply in Mae Rim needs to be described more closely. In Mae Rim water use is complicated by the existence of parallel systems of water supply. As a most important source for the provision of household tap water there is the publicly owned municipal water provider, the Mae Rim Water Works (MRWW). For a number of approximately 4500 households in Mae Rim that are located within the area marked "study area" in figure 4-3 MRWW uses surface water of the Mae Sa river as their exclusive water source. Thus, these households are most directly affected by the farming activities in the upland areas. The households in other areas of Mae Rim receive their water from the Ping river. The water taken from the Mae Sa river is treated to drinking water quality, without, however, taking into account the pesticide concentration which cannot easily be reduced by common water treatment processes. The water reaching the households, however, has already deteriorated in quality due to the existence of holes and leaks in the water distribution system which is a patchwork of pipes of different materials and different age. Through these leakages biological contaminants can enter the distribution system and pollute the tap water leading to episodic outbreaks of diarrhea and other diseases in certain areas. Due to this unreliable water quality of the MRWW tap water most households refrain from using it for drinking or even cooking and buy bottled water instead. Either they buy it in the stores themselves or they have it conveniently delivered to their homes.

**Figure 4-3:** Three-dimensional view of the study area in Chiang Mai province, northern Thailand, schematic delineations of the Mae Sa water catchment and the survey area

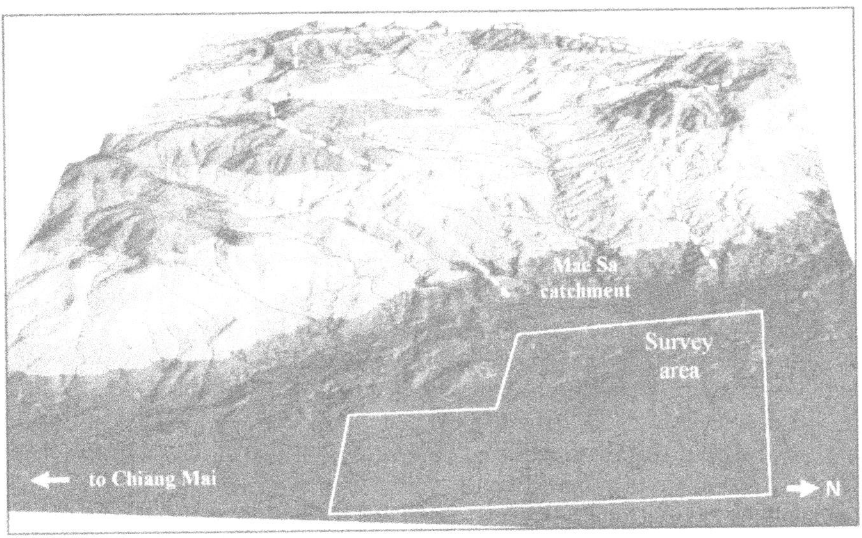


(Source: The Uplands Program, map composed by Peter Elstner)

Apart from the MRWW tap water system there exist two further systems or possibilities of household water supply in certain areas. Some villages within the municipality of Mae Rim have established their own village water systems, usually simple systems where water is pumped from the ground water body, stored and treated by simple means and subsequently distributed to the households. This water, however, cannot be used for drinking. Some households, moreover, have established their own systems of water supply by drilling a well or installing a ground water pump. Some households are connected to the MRWW system as well as to their village water system, others use MRWW water and water from their own sources. Only those 4500 households connected to the MRWW distribution system receiving their water from the Mae Sa valley are taken as the relevant population for this empirical study.

Given this complex situation of household tap water supply an improvement of water quality to the level where it can be directly consumed for drinking and cooking in the households at all times requires two sets of measures: first, the distribution system of MRWW needs to be repaired, modernized and continuously maintained in order to avoid biological contamination during distribution, second, upland farming activities have to be changed and improved to an extent where they do not adversely influence the quality of the Mae Sa river from which the water is taken, i. e. techniques have to be applied that reduce pesticide and sediment loads substantially. A program that ensures the complete implementation of these two kinds of measures would finally lead to the desired quality of household tap water. Additionally to these direct benefits to the MRWW customer households indirect benefits would accrue to those households as well as to the entire population of Mae Rim and to the people living in the upland farming areas: (1) less pesticides would accumulate in the ecosystems creating a benefit to future generations, (2) less pesticide residues would be contained in fruits and vegetables from the upland farming areas, and (3) soils in the uplands would be conserved due to reduced soil erosion. Whereas the direct benefits of drinkable water quality in the households constitute solely use values, the benefits described in (1) to (3) constitute mainly non-use values to the MRWW customers since those benefits are to the largest part experienced by other households including those that are not connected to the MRWW system or even by future generations. In this respect, the measures proposed here would lead to the improvement of both a private good and a public good.

The described problem state of municipal household tap water quality where part of the problem arises from a negative external effect created by upland farming and the other part from a partly rotten distribution system in the lowlands forms the basis for an empirical valuation study employing the contingent valuation method. The empirical aim of this study consists in the assessment of the direct and indirect benefits accruing to those households connected to the MRWW system using the Mae Sa river as a water source. Apart from the empirical aim, this study pursued a number of methodological aims in relation to the applicability of the CVM in the socio-economic and cultural context of Thailand and in relation to the possibility to develop a methodology to conduct valid and reliable CVM mail surveys. These methodological issues are treated in detail in Ahlheim et al. (2007); most of them shall not be presented and discussed here since they are not directly related to the specific topic of this study. Nevertheless, two of these methodological issues are of importance for this research. They shall be briefly touched on here since they form part of the empirical design of the CVM study described in detail below.

The first of these methodological issues is the testing of the performance of two alternative WTP elicitation question formats in the Thai context, i. e. the dichotomous choice (DC) question format and the payment card (PC) format (for a detailed discussion of such question formats see chapter 2). The second methodological issue arises from the well-known social desirability effect and the results of a previous comparison between a CVM study conducted with personal interviews and as a mail survey where the mail survey yielded much lower WTP results (detailed results will be shown below). In search for an explanation for this result it was hypothesized that the observed difference is due to the social desirability effect in that respondents give an answer that they consider socially desirable, i. e. that the interviewer wants to hear. This phenomenon should disappear if respondents are given the opportunity to state their WTP secretly on a separate sheet of paper so that their response would not be known to the interviewer. This latter assumption will also be tested in the empirical study conducted here. In the following the empirical design of the CVM study will be specified in detail.

#### 4.4.2.2 The empirical design

The questionnaires employed in this CVM study consist of five parts (the complete questionnaire is provided in the appendix). The first part contains warming-up questions in order to reduce tensions that the respondent might feel due to the sudden interview situation and in order to obtain specific information on household water use. A number of questions are asked w. r. t. the purposes the MRWW water is used (washing, bathing, gardening, cooking, drinking etc.), how long the household has been connected to the MRWW system, whether particular problems like low pressure and interruptions of water service occur and how frequently they are experienced. Moreover, information is obtained on the household's primary source of drinking water and why that specific source was chosen. Subsequently respondents are questioned on their opinions concerning the water quality and the service of MRWW and whether they worry about catching specific water-borne diseases if they were to drink the MRWW water.

Box 4-1: Scenario description of the tap water improvement program

**Chiang Mai University, the University of Hohenheim and the Mae Rim Water Works MRWW are currently surveying water users' interests in the program "Drinkable Tap Water-Clean Stream".**

**What is the idea of the program?**

**The idea is that all MRWW customers should enjoy an uninterrupted supply of tap water which is also drinkable.**

**How can this idea be achieved, what needs to be done?**

**"Drinkable Tap Water-Clean Stream" consists of two main programs which are the improvement of the MRWW distribution system and an improvement of upstream water quality as the source of the MRWW water.**

**Why are these improvements necessary?**

**An improvement of the MRWW distribution system is necessary because of frequent pollution with biological pollutants in the area due to broken pipes in the distribution system. Biological pollutants might cause diarrhea or other diseases. The broken pipes are also responsible for frequent interruptions of water service which occur in some parts of Mae Rim.**

**An improvement of upstream water quality is necessary to ensure that MRWW receives good water for treatment and distribution to the households. There are two main problems regarding the upstream water quality: the first is the red color of the water which occurs often in the rainy season and the second is the contamination with pesticides which might lead to severe health damages like for example cancer. The red color of the water is caused by soil erosion in the uplands of the Mae Sa valley. Pesticides in the water are an immediate consequence of their high use in the uplands of the Mae Sa valley. As you can see from this map, your tap water originates exclusively from the rivers of the Mae Sa valley.**

**How is the program implemented?**

**The program "Drinkable Tap Water-Clean Stream" should be implemented in the following way: First, the pipe system should be mended and maintained so that biological pollution and interruption of water supply would stop. Second, an effective soil conservation program should be implemented so that soil erosion would be stopped in the uplands. Third, pesticide use in the uplands should be reduced for example by employing a more adapted and targeted pest control system.**

**Who will carry out the proposed measures?**

**MRWW will carry out the improvements of the water distribution system. Chiang Mai University will carry out the measures that lead to an improvement of upstream water quality. This will be done in cooperation with the upstream communities and farmers.**

*Box 4 continued:*

**Do only MRWW water users benefit from the program?**

**If these proposed measures were carried out benefits for the whole population of Mae Rim would result. For example, this program would also reduce the contamination of fruits and vegetables with pesticides. Also, the accumulation of pesticides in the surrounding ecosystems would be stopped so that future harm to plant and animal life will be prevented and the health of future generations will not be threatened by these pesticides. Therefore, from the proposed measures the whole population of Mae Rim and future generations in this area would benefit.**

**Who will guarantee that the program really works out?**

**MRWW will test the tap water quality regularly at the households and will post the test results immediately in each affected community of Mae Rim. There will be a responsible person at MRWW that you can contact for any questions and problems you might have regarding the tap water supply.**

The second part of the questionnaire contains the scenario description. Along with this verbal description respondents are shown a set of photographs illustrating the mentioned issues in order to provide a better visualization and perception of the scenario information. The exact scenario description as presented to the respondents by the interviewer is given in box 4-1. In order to be able to perceive the verbally described scenario elements respondents are subsequently asked to rate the eight scenario elements according to how important they are to them personally on a five-point Likert scale. For further reference, these eight scenario elements are: (1) no interruptions of water service, (2) no biological pollutants in the tap water, (3) no pesticides in the tap water, (4) no red color of the water, (5) less soil degradation in the uplands, (6) no accumulation of pesticides in the ecosystems, (7) less pesticides in fruits and vegetables, and (8) reduced health threats to future generations.

The third part of the questionnaire contains the description of the hypothetical payment scheme and finally the willingness-to-pay elicitation question, which is the core element of the CVM. In this part respondents are told that carrying out the measures proposed in the scenario description would involve costs the financing of which needed to be secured before the proposed program can be started in order to achieve the envisaged water quality improvement. As a means of financing the program people are told that it is intended to increase the water fees that MRWW customers have to pay for a specified period of 5 years. The English translation of the wording presented to the respondents in Thai language reads as follows: "**Since these measures are costly their financing has to be secured before such a program can be implemented. Therefore, it is intended to increase the water fee for the tap water supply for the next five years to get the program started.**" This formulation of the payment scheme stresses the fact that this program has not been decided on, yet. The subsequent WTP elicitation question is worded so that respondents should realize that the implementation of the program would somehow be influenced by their willingness to contribute to its financing.

As mentioned above, two different types of elicitation question formats were to be tested in this study, the dichotomous choice (DC) and the payment card (PC) format. For each format it was also intended to test whether procedural biases like the starting point bias or "yea"-saying in the DC format or the range and centering bias in the PC format occur since they would indicate boundedly rational behavior or limited information processing in response to heuristic cues included in the specific elicitation question design. For the DC version, therefore, a wide range of bids, i. e. starting bids well below and well above the expected range of the true WTP, should be used in the bid design in order to detect such distorting effects on response behavior. In pretests a first indication about the realistic range of bids was obtained which could be used for the bid design. For the PC version, at least two different ranges of specified bid intervals should be used so that the influence of the upper cut-off point on the bid chosen by the respondent can be determined. From these considerations a split-sample design following the scheme depicted in figure 4-4 was developed.

**Figure 4-4**: Split sample design of the WTP elicitation question

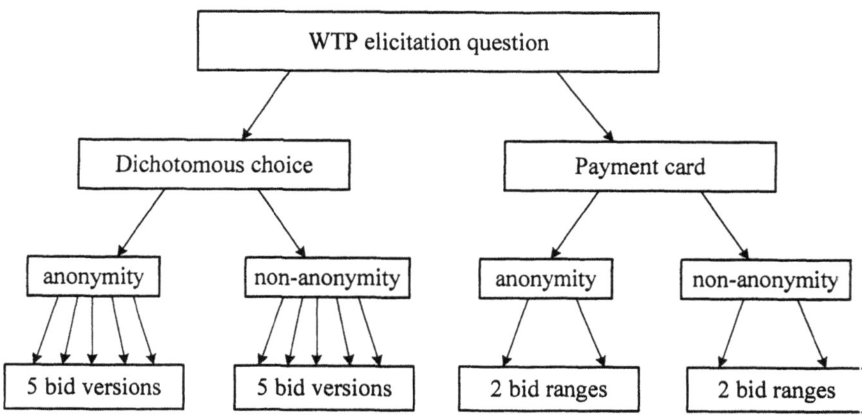


For the DC question the DeShazo format (see chapter 2) was selected due to findings in an earlier CVM study in the same problem context that responses to the double-bounded DC format were highly susceptible to anchoring effects. Table 4-4 compiles the bid design of the 5 questionnaire versions selected for the DC sample and the bounds of the two PC questionnaire versions where the cut-off bid signifies where the range of specified bid intervals ends and above which an open interval is left. The detailed specification of bid intervals of the payment card is given in the appendix.

After the description of the payment scheme (see above) respondents are asked the WTP elicitation question either in the DC version (anonymous or non-anonymous) or in the PC version (anonymous or non-anonymous). The non-anonymous question with the DC format for version 1 (see table 4-4) reads as follows: **"If, as a consequence, your water bill increased by altogether 25 Baht per month for the next five years, would you support this program?"** If the respondent answers "yes" the interview proceeds to the next question. If the respondent answers "no" a follow-up question using the lower follow-up bid (see table 4-4) is asked: **"If instead the monthly water bill increased by only 12 Baht, would you then be willing to support this program?"** After the response to the follow-up question the interview proceeds to the next question.

**Table 4-4:** Bid design of the DC and the PC elicitation question formats (monetary values in Thai Baht /month)

| Dichotomous choice | | | Payment card | | |
|---|---|---|---|---|---|
| version | first bid | follow-up bid | version | starting bid | cut-off range |
| 1 | 25 → | 12 | small | 0 | > 400 |
| 2 | 50 → | 25 | large | 0 | > 2000 |
| 3 | 100 → | 50 | | | |
| 4 | 200 → | 100 | | | |
| 5 | 400 → | 200 | | | |

In the anonymous version of the DC question the respondent is given a sheet containing the question with the first bid and is asked to check either the "yes" or the "no" box. Subsequently, the interviewer hands the respondent a second sheet with the follow-up question and is asked to check one of the boxes. Obviously, someone who has already checked "yes" on the first sheet would also check "yes" on the second. These sheets are then put into a "ballot box" indicating presumed anonymity of the response.

The formulation of the PC elicitation question reads as follows: "We would now like to ask you how much money your household would be willing to contribute to the program. Please, select from the following list the highest increase in your monthly water bill you would be willing to tolerate for the next five years if the improvements described above were realized." Here the respondent receives either the small or the large version as described in table 4-

4. In the anonymous version the respondent receives a separate sheet of paper containing the question and the respective payment card on which he could check the payment interval that contains his personal WTP. After the WTP elicitation question the respondent is asked how difficult it was to find an answer to this question. Subsequently, the respondent is asked to rate on a five-point Likert scale how important given statements were for his answer to the WTP question, i. e. these statements indicate the reasons for the stated WTP. The statements were formulated so that all respondents regardless of their response to the WTP question could answer them. The understandability of these formulations were tested in an extensive pretesting process.

In the fourth part of the questionnaire a number of questions concerning respondents' attitudes w. r. t. the environment, the role of government, the financing of public goods, the importance of money in their everyday lives and their donation behavior are asked. Further, respondents should rate their incomes and their households' economic situations in comparison to others and are asked how worried they are w. r. t. a number of personal and public aspects. This part of the questionnaire also contains the two questions forming the newly developed measurement scales of bounded rationality. Finally, in the fifth part the usual socio-economic and demographic questions are asked. This part also contains questions regarding households' indebtedness since it might be a determinant of stated WTP.

#### 4.4.2.3 The measurement scales of bounded rationality in northern Thailand – research implementation in the survey design

The scales of bounded rationality are implemented in the empirical design of this study in the form of two separate questions within the fourth part of the questionnaire. In order to maintain a suitable "choreography" of the interview the question containing the items for the task independent scale was positioned right after the respondents had given their response to the WTP elicitation question and had just rated the level of difficulty of responding to it. The general form of this question as presented in table 4-2 (see 4.3.2) was slightly adapted to fit the specific cultural context of Thai society. In this respect, item E " Doing quizzes and cross-word puzzles are a pleasant form of entertainment for me" was considered not to be applicable in Thailand since Thai people usually do not undertake such activities for entertainment that are well known in Western societies and e. g. even in Japan (just consider the Sudoku quizzes for that matter). Therefore, this item was changed and reformulated even in reverse sense to fit Thai people's liking of watching entertainment programs on television. Thus, the following formulation was chosen: "Documentary programs on TV annoy me so that I often switch to a different channel". The other items were considered suitable in the context of Thailand. In the questionnaire, respondents are asked to rate the degree to which these statements are true for them personally on a five-point Likert scale where "1" means "not true at all" and "5" means "fully true".

The task dependent scale of bounded rationality was placed separately from the question containing the items of the task independent scale with a number of other questions in between so that the respondents would not consider these two questions to be related to each other. Therefore, the question containing the items described in table 4-3 (see 4.3.2) forms the conclusion of part four of the questionnaire just before the standard socio-economic and demographic questions begin. All items of this questions were considered to fit the Thai context so the question was included into the questionnaire just as presented in table 4-3.

#### 4.4.2.4 Practical implementation of the survey

The sample for this survey was selected from the list of MRWW customers that receive their household tap water exclusively from the Mae Sa river. These households are located along 5 different water distribution lines which coincide quite well with particular neighborhoods of Mae Rim with a certain socio-economic structure. For example, one distribution line delivers water into a residential area that consists of houses and apartments built for housing athletes of the Southeast Asian Games in the year 1995 which are now predominantly used by government officials. Another distribution line exclusively serves the residential area of a military camp and so on. Therefore, the different questionnaire versions of the described split sample design were allocated to these neighborhoods according to their relative frequencies in the population of MRWW customers so that the selected households constitute a representative sample of the population under consideration.

The development of this survey and of the survey questionnaire followed a step-wise procedure that, apart from the usual expert interviews, in-depth interviews with households from the survey population and several waves of pretests where the questionnaire was tested on a limited selection of households and subsequently revised, also consisted of a participatory element of survey design. For this process, respondents of a previous CVM mail survey on the same project scenario were invited to join a series of group meetings with other respondents from the survey population in order to receive further information, discuss issues of the scenario of particular importance to them and comment on problematic issues of the questionnaire design. By means of these group discussions the researchers of this subproject intended to identify issues of conflict, resentments that respondents might have regarding certain aspects and questions, and taboos that respondents are reluctant to address. The mentioned aspects are considered to have the potential to distort the responses of CVM respondents and were attempted to be eliminated from the questionnaire. Details concerning the technique and the results of this participatory procedure are given in Ahlheim et al. (2007).

The survey was conducted from the end of July to the beginning of September 2005 by students of the Chiang Mai University who had been trained as interviewers for CVM surveys by the researchers of the project. Altogether, 55 interviewers were recruited, trained and employed. This large number of interviewers should result in a situation where effects caused by particular interviewers are negligible. Altogether, 823 households were interviewed from which 798 valid responses to the WTP elicitation questions were obtained. The distribution of interviewed households according to the split-sample design illustrated in figure 4-4 is given in table 4-5.

**Table 4-5:** Distribution of responses in the split-sample design

| Question format | Number of households interviewed (valid responses) | Response type | Number of households interviewed |
|---|---|---|---|
| Dichotomous choice | 467 (454) | anonymous | 190 |
| | | non-anonymous | 277 |
| Payment card | 356 (344) | anonymous | 153 |
| | | non-anonymous | 203 |
| Total | 823 (798) | | 823 |

### 4.4.3 Empirical results of the project

This section presents the empirical results of the research project. Before dealing with the results of the two scales of boundedly rational information processing and decision making, those general results obtained from this CVM study shall be highlighted that form the basis for the analysis of bounded rationality. First, the sample population shall be characterized by its socio-economic and demographic features in order to obtain an indication of the situation of the households under consideration. Second, the WTP results as assessed by the various procedures in the split-sample design shall be presented and discussed and the variables and factors that were found to systematically influence these WTP estimates shall be considered. Subsequently, the results of the scales of bounded rationality shall be analyzed in detail and their usefulness for explaining inconsistent response behavior shall be investigated.

#### 4.4.3.1 Socio-economic and demographic characteristics of the respondent population

Within the surveyed population of 823 household heads, male and female respondents were roughly equally represented with a percentage of 52% female and 48% male respondents. Exactly two thirds (66,4%) of the respondents had children or grandchildren. The values for the mean and standard deviation of household size, age and monthly household income are given in table 4-6.

**Table 4-6:** Values of household size, age and income

| Variable | Mean | Standard deviation |
|---|---|---|
| Household size | 3,07 | 1,45 |
| Age | 40,4 | 13,6 |
| Monthly income | 18760 Baht (≈ 375 €) | 14522 Baht (≈ 290 €) |

Household sizes ranged from 1 to 9 individuals per household, where 2-, 3- and 4-person households were the most frequent with ca. 23 % each. 15% of the households were single households and roughly another 15% of households had 5 or more members. Age of respondents ranged from 13 to 92 where those respondents below 18 years of age were excluded from the sample since they were considered not to be the household head in charge of economic decisions. The distribution of rough income classes is given in figure 4-5 which also contains the relative frequencies of the categorical variables of the sample population.

From b) in figure 4-5 it can be observed that while all classes of education are included in the survey, respondents holding a Bachelor degree are by far the most frequent. This evident overrepresentation of respondents with a Bachelor degree is obviously due to the very high frequency of officials in the sample, a peculiarity of the survey population chosen for this study. Since the survey sample is drawn from the list of MRWW customers for which no record of socio-economic and demographic variables exist the selected sample's representativeness can, unfortunately, not be verified by the usual comparison with the distribution of these variables within the general population.

**Figure 4-5:** Relative frequencies of categorical socio-economic and demographic variables

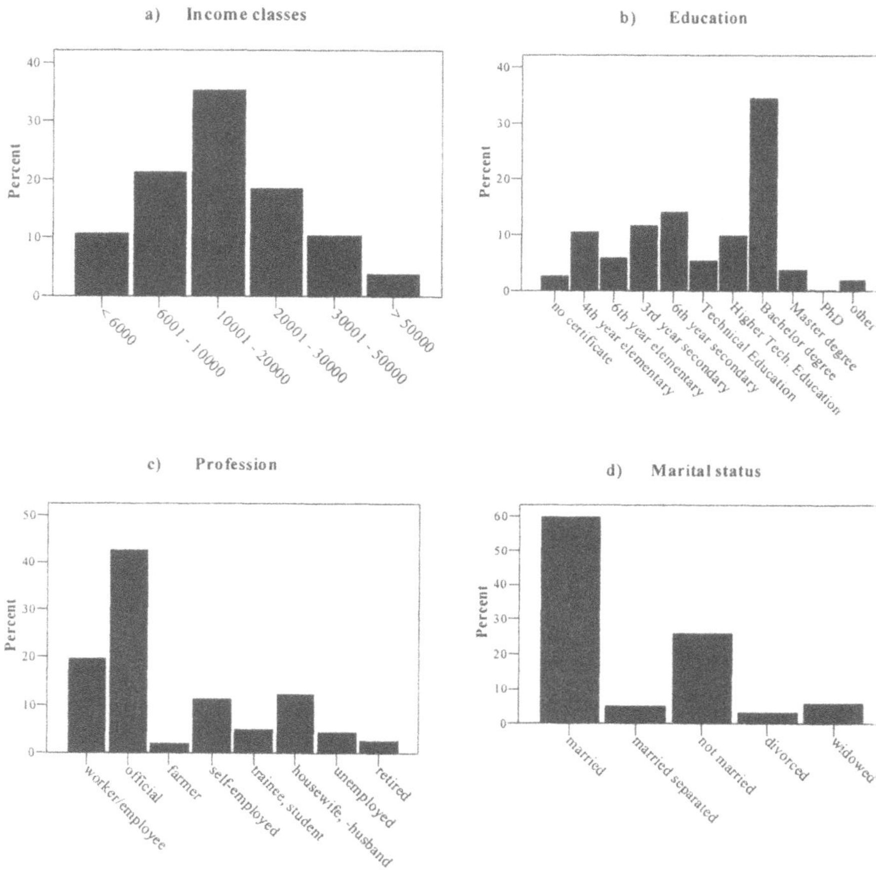


4.4.3.2 Estimates of willingness-to-pay for the tap water improvement program

The ultimate aim of a CVM survey is the assessment of the willingness-to-pay (WTP) of the survey population. The estimates of WTP of this survey scenario are given in table 4-7 where the two elicitation question formats DC and PC were evaluated separately using a variety of different data evaluation methods. First of all, the data were analyzed separately according to anonymity or non-anonymity of the elicitation question and jointly (last column). Second, for the

DC format two different types of data from the DC dataset were used for the evaluation: (1) single-bounded: only the responses to the first bid were used for the estimation of WTP since this estimate is free of anchoring effects introduced by a follow-up question, (2) DeShazo: the full set of responses to the elicitation question, i. e. the responses to the first bid as well as the responses to the (lower) follow-up bid in case of a rejection of the first bid were used for estimating WTP. The comparison of the DeShazo-based estimate with the single-bounded WTP estimate would reveal the existence of effects of the response to the follow-up bid anchoring on the response to the first bid. For the estimations using the Maximum-Likelihood estimator (see chapter 2) a probit model was used.

Third, the PC format was also analyzed in two different ways: (1) a probit model representing the probability of a respondent choosing a particular bid interval was used to generate WTP estimates, this represents the usual procedure for PC data, (2) WTP estimates were computed simply as the averages over the midpoints of the respective bid intervals that were chosen by the particular respondents. This latter method which is not as precise as the probit model in (1), however, is not dependent on any distributional assumptions, i. e. whether the error terms are distributed normally or in an extreme value kind etc. and is thus less prone to distortions emanating from wrong statistical assumptions. In table 4-7 all WTP estimates are given as averages (means) over the sample populations in Thai Baht per month, the 95%-confidence intervals are provided in parentheses underneath the WTP estimates. The computation of these confidence intervals follows the bootstrap procedure as described by Park et al. (1991).

From table 4-7 a number of interesting facts can be discerned and need to be interpreted. First, while there is a tendency of anonymous responses yielding a slightly lower WTP estimate the difference between these two forms of questioning is not significant as can be clearly seen from the 95%-confidence intervals. This applied both to the DC and the PC formats. The larger 95%-confidence intervals for the anonymous DC estimates is due to the sample size of anonymous being much smaller than the non-anonymous one. The difference in PC sample sizes is not as pronounced. Due to the non-significance of anonymous versus non-anonymous WTP responses the data can be pooled and an overall estimate for each question format is, thus, computed. Second, the comparison of the estimates based on the single-bounded data with those based on the DeShazo data confirms the expectation that the response to a lower follow-up bid is not prone to anchoring behavior on the first bid in contrast to a response to a higher follow-up (see chapter 2). From table 4-7 it can be seen that the 95%-confidence intervals of the DeShazo estimate are slightly narrower than those of the single-bounded estimate so that the DeShazo estimator is more efficient and should, thus, be employed for the analysis of the DC data here.

Third, the comparison of the WTP estimates for the PC question data show that the probit model and the model based on interval midpoints yield the same results for average (mean) WTP. Thus, the assumption of normally distributed error terms seems a sensible one although the probit model (and also the logit model) always implies that some households have a negative WTP for the proposed program which is counterintuitive since it is hard to imagine that anyone should experience a loss in utility if such an improvement program were realized, even at no cost. If WTP is to be strictly limited to the non-negative domain, other distributions like the log-normal or certain extreme value distributions (Weibull etc.) would have to be employed. However, as indicated by the WTP estimates of the PC format data normally distributed errors seem to be an appropriate assumption here. The smaller confidence intervals of the estimates of the midpoint method arise from the simplifying assumption that respondents have exactly this midpoint WTP while they actually have only chosen a more or less large interval in which their WTP lies. Again, anonymous answers exhibit a tendency to be lower than non-anonymous ones, however, this trend is not significant.

**Table 4-7:** Average household WTP for the tap water improvement scenario (Thai Baht per month)

| | | **Willingness-to-pay** (95%-confid. interval) | | |
|---|---|---|---|---|
| **Question format** | | **non-anonymous** | **anonymous** | **overall (non-anonymous and anonymous)** |
| **DC** | **Single-bounded** | **198** (159-239) | **198** (141-261) | **198** (167-232) |
| | **DeShazo** | **201** (176-227) | **193** (154-226) | **198** (176-219) |
| **PC** | **Probit** | **71** (46-94) | **66** (47-82) | **69** (53-83) |
| | **midpoints** | **72** (59-85) | **65** (54-76) | **69** (60-78) |

A fourth and very astonishing result from table 4-7 is that WTP estimates from the DC format are almost three times as high as those estimated from the PC format. However, this result is in line with the literature where many studies, though not all, have found the tendency of DC yielding higher WTP estimates than PC. As explained in chapter 2 this tendency is usually explained by "yea"-saying (Frew et al. 2003: 157) and cognitive dissonance (Blamey et al. 1999:

127, Akerlof and Dickens 1982) where respondents experience a conflict between the feeling to support the proposed program because they approve of it in general and the feeling to reject it due to the costs involved that they, in principle, perceive as too high. In case the first feeling wins the conflict the respondent will accept a bid that exceeds his "true" WTP. This discrepancy of WTP estimates between elicitation question formats will be discussed in more detail below in the context of the analysis of procedural biases and the role of bounded rationality.

#### 4.4.3.3 Determinants of willingness-to-pay

Apart from the figures of WTP for the particular tap water improvement program we were interested in those variables and factors systematically associated with the amount of WTP, i. e. which have the potential to explain the variation of WTP observed in the population. These variables and factors represent the determinants of WTP. They can be obtained from the responses to questions contained in the CVM questionnaire that are then used as explanatory variables in econometric regression models. Some of these variables can be directly taken from the questions, e. g. socio-economic and demographic variables like sex, age, education etc. In the case of many other questions, especially the attitudinal questions containing a large number of individual question items, it is necessary to perform some reduction of dimension of those items, i. e. to integrate question items with similar but slightly different meanings into one factor that can then be used as an explanatory variable in the regression model. Such dimension reduction is conveniently achieved by employing factor analysis. As already laid out in some more detail in section 4.3.1 this statistical method exploits the correlation structure among the various items of a question and groups those together that, among the respondent sample population, vary systematically. These groups of variables, the so-called factors, can then be interpreted to carry a common meaning where this meaning of the factor can only be indirectly inferred from the meanings of the constituent items. Subsequently, for each individual in the dataset a factor value is computed as an aggregation of the individual's responses to the single question items making up the factor. These factor values can then be used in the regression analysis where the factor serves as a regular explanatory variable.

Here, several explanatory variables and factors extracted from attitudinal questions are used. In the following, the expression in parentheses in capital letters refers to the name of the variables used in the model and listed in table 4-8. With respect to the socio-economic and demographic variables it is hypothesized that WTP systematically varies with the sex of the respondent (SEX), and positively with household income (INCOME), age (AGE), household size (HHSIZE), the education level (EDU), whether a respondent is married (MARRIED) and whether he or she has children / grandchildren or not (CHILD). Further, since officials are clearly over-represented in the sample a variable indicating whether the individual is an official or not is added (OFFICIAL). Further, it could be expected that WTP increases systematically with the actual water bill the household pays for MRWW water (MRWWBILL) since the more it uses this water the more it would benefit from an increased quality. Similarly, higher expenses for bottled drinking water (BOTTBILL) should increase WTP since more money is to be saved if the MRWW quality increases to potable water quality. However, WTP should decrease the better the quality of the MRWW water (MRWWQUAL) is perceived to be at the moment since the necessity of an improvement should be lower when the quality is already good. In contrast, the more water users worry about catching water-borne diseases (the factor WATERWORRIES) the more they are expected to be willing to pay for a quality improvement. Two factors were extracted from the question concerning the reasons for the stated WTP where the first (IMPROVEMENT) refers to the importance of an increase of private and public benefits resulting from the program and the second (COST REDUCTION) points to the importance of the possibilities of saving on bottled water and the increased convenience from not having to buy bottled water any more. Concerning the perception of difficulty of decision making (DIFFICULT) it is expected that stated WTP decreases with an increasing feeling of difficulty since the respondent becomes uncertain and aims at being on the safe side.

With respect to attitudinal variables a large number of question items and factors could be expected to systematically influence WTP. However, an exploratory statistical analysis revealed that only few significant effects exist so that only a limited number of factors was chosen to be included into the explanatory model. Among these factors is a factor indicating donation attitude (DONATION) constituted of the items "I find it difficult to say 'no' if a friend asks me a favor" and "It gives me a good feeling if I donate money". Two factors indicating the respondent's attitude about money were included where the first (SAVING) included the items "I build up savings because I want to have security for the future / because I want to leave something for my children" and would be expected to be negatively related with WTP in contrast to the second factor (HAPPINESS) consisting only of "Even with more money for myself I would not be happier than now" because such persons would care little about money and are, thus, expected to give it away more easily. In table 4-8 the parameter estimates and the statistical significance levels (p-values) are given for a probit model of the DeShazo-dataset for the DC sample and a probit model of the PC sample. Positive signs of the coefficients indicate a positive influence of the respective parameter on stated WTP, a p-value smaller or equal to 0.1 indicates statistical significance at 10%, a p-value smaller or equal to 0.05 significance at the 5%-level.

From table 4-8 it can be seen that only surprisingly few variables or factors seem to have a significant effect on stated WTP. This is especially the case for the PC model where the usual socio-economic and demographic variables are not at all significantly related to WTP. For the DC model those variables and factors that were found to have significant explanatory power show the expected sign: the higher the education level, the higher the MRWW water bill, and the more the improvements of private and public benefits were rated to be important reasons for WTP the higher the stated WTP. As well, respondents with children or grandchildren care more for this program than respondents without those. In contrast, the more difficult respondents perceived the valuation task to be and the more they strive to save money the lower the stated WTP. All these effects confirm the expectations. It is surprising, however, that household income shows no significant effect, although it carries a positive sign. Income is usually a strong and reliable variable to explain variations in WTP, but in this regression model its association with WTP is obviously lower than that of other explanatory variables so that no significant effect of income could be detected here.

Most of the socio-economic and demographic variables in the PC model, although not significantly, point into the same direction as those of the DC model, which is a reassuring fact. In the PC model it is surprising that DONATION exhibits a negative influence on WTP, opposite to what was expected. This finding is hard to explain, it may be argued, however, that respondents with a high DONATION score, i. e. rating high on its constituting items "I find it difficult to say no if a friend asks me a favor" and "It gives me a good feeling if I donate money", satisfy these feelings already by selecting some bid interval on the payment card, although it is low, and don't consider what this program is really worth to them. This interpretation is supported by regression results in 4.4.3.6 below. As expected, however, those respondents with a high score in the variable HAPPINESS which refers to respondents' feelings of not being happier even if they had more money exhibit a significant tendency to state higher WTP values in the payment card format.

These general data about the sample and the estimates of WTP and explanatory variables as well as factors provide an overview of the response behavior in this CVM study and form the basis for subsequent investigations concerning boundedly rational behavior and the employment of limited information processing in this study. In the following the responses will be evaluated w. r. t. the scales of bounded rationality developed in section 4.3.2.

**Table 4-8:** Parameter estimates of the explanatory variables (covariates) of WTP for the DC and for the PC samples*

| | Dichotomous choice | | Payment card | |
|---|---|---|---|---|
| Parameter | Coefficient | p-value | Coefficient | p-value |
| SEX | -16.97 | .9038 | 81.33 | .4787 |
| INCOME | 0.0435 | .4002 | 0.46 | .2757 |
| AGE | -2.19 | .7360 | -8.70 | .1466 |
| HHSIZE | -27.33 | .6171 | 15.40 | .7825 |
| EDU | 108.75** | .0077 | 57.36 | .1657 |
| MARRIED | 18.30 | .9211 | -255.41 | .1799 |
| CHILD | 619.53** | .0040 | 261.64 | .1916 |
| OFFICIAL | -262.77 | .1109 | -175.04 | .2981 |
| MRWWBILL | 0.53* | .0816 | 0.43 | .3234 |
| BOTTBILL | 0.087 | .9086 | 0.84 | .1308 |
| MRWWQUAL | -18.64 | .7944 | -10.97 | .8936 |
| WATERWORRIES | 0.015 | .8473 | 0.015 | .8614 |
| IMPROVEMENT | 233.98** | .0114 | 272.16** | .0106 |
| COST REDUCTION | 90.46 | .2755 | 149.53 | .1694 |
| DIFFICULT | -384.10** | .0000 | -47.17 | .5815 |
| DONATION | 108.01 | .3167 | -226.53** | .0111 |
| SAVING | -279.79** | .0016 | 41.02 | .6505 |
| HAPPINESS | 117.24 | .2658 | 213.80** | .0233 |

** means significance at the 5%-level, * significance at the 10%-level.

#### 4.4.3.4 The measurement scales of bounded rationality

At this point the focus of this study will now turn to the practical application of the bounded rationality scales developed above. First, the responses to the questions containing the items for the task independent and the task dependent scales of bounded rationality shall be evaluated using factor analysis as described in the previous section. The first objective is to be able, for both measures, to extract meaningful factors from the correlation structure of the responses to the question items. Interpretable and meaningful factors form the prerequisite for any further analysis using these developed scales. Next, the relationship between the task independent and the task dependent scales shall be investigated as it is expected that they correlate to a certain degree since individuals who show a general disposition for heuristic information processing might also exhibit a more pronounced use of such heuristics resulting in limited information processing in a specific task. Third, it will be attempted to find variables and characteristics within the dataset that could be used for explaining the observed individual differences in information processing, i. e. the determinants of the task independent and the task dependent information processing and decision types. Subsequently, the relationship between WTP and the two different scales shall be explored in detail. As mentioned above, while the a priori expectation that a higher level of boundedly rational information processing and decision making is negatively related to the amount of stated WTP is only tentative, it is expected that a systematic relationship between intuitive-heuristic processing and typical procedural biases of the CVM exists. It will be explored which of these biases mentioned in chapter 2 can be attributed to the bounded rationality of respondents. Finally, the results of this investigation shall be used to derive recommendations for the improvement of future CVM survey designs.

*The task independent scale*

In the questionnaire of the present CVM study (see appendix 7.1) the question containing the items of the task independent scale of bounded rationality was question number 9 (see page 224), whereas the task dependent items are contained in question number 18 (see page 228). This numbering shall be used as a shorthand reference for the two different scales from now on. As a first task, question 9 was subjected to a factor analytical evaluation as described above. From the various procedures that are available for such a task and that differ slightly in their methodology, for the present study the *principal components method* was used for factor extraction. This option represents the most frequently used standard in factor analysis. However, it was tested whether employing alternative options like e. g. the principal-axis method would lead to qualitatively different results which was not the case here. Furthermore, for the rotation of the extracted factors necessary to obtain interpretable factors the commonly-used *Varimax*-method was chosen. The Bartlett test of sphericity clearly shows that the correlation matrix of the question items is not an identity matrix ($p < 0.001$) so that the matrix contains enough systematic correlations between the items to allow an extraction of factors. Also, the Kaiser-Meyer-Olkin test (KMO) for sample adequacy yields a value for inter-item correlations of 0.6 which is sufficiently high, however not ideal. Four factors show an eigenvalue greater than 1 which indicates that each of these four factors can explain more of the variance in the data than any single variable by itself.[5] Altogether, the four extracted factors explain 59.5% of the variance. However, the item "Documentary programs on TV annoy me so that I often switch to a different channel" was excluded from the dataset since it was found to be not sufficiently related to one of the extracted factors. Recall that this item was adapted from the general formulation of the task independent measure in section 4.3.2 due to the fact that quizzes and crossword-puzzles are not common in Thailand.

Table 4-9 presents the 4 extracted factors from the items in question 9 except the "television"-item. The figures in the rows pertaining to each question item represent the respective item's factor loading on factors 1 to 4. The factor loading of an item can range between -1 and 1, it indicates the item's correlation with the respective factor, i. e. the degree to which the item "belongs" to the factor. It is desirable to extract factors from the dataset so that each item loads high on only one factor and low on all the others so that the meaning of each factor can easily be inferred by the question items. From this it follows that each item forms a constituting element of that factor on which it loads highest. In table 4-9 the factor loadings in the rotated factor matrix are ordered where the items between the vertical lines represent those items belonging to the respective factor. The last row in table 4-9 contains the consistency measures for each factor measured by Cronbach's alpha (cf. Janssen and Laatz 2003: 525). Cronbach's alpha measures the degree between 0 and 1 to which the items in one factor measure the same construct. It shows here that the first factor has the highest internal consistency, however, the value of 0.62 is still below the usually desired consistency level of 0.7. The consistencies of the other three factors are rather low which indicates that the respective factors represent a construct with quite a broad meaning.

From table 4-9 the semantic meanings of the four factors extracted from question 9 can be derived. The factors TIF1, TIF2 and TIF4 are relatively easy to interpret, TIF3 is more ambivalent and less clear cut. TIF1 obviously indicates intuition, i. e. the positive feelings toward intuitive reasoning and the trust in one's judgments. TIF2 is the systematic antipode of TIF1 indicating a liking of effortful cognitive processes, therefore TIF2 could reasonably be named "analytical-rational". TIF4 groups those kinds of information processes that indicate a minimum employment of cognitive effort for information processing and decision making. Those people who generally think that hard thinking is boring and who want to take decisions quickly and not waste much

[5] The criterion of eigenvalues greater than 1 is a common criterion for factor extraction and is used to determine the appropriate number of factors extracted. Eigenvalues smaller than 1 indicate that this factor has less explanatory power than the single variables in the set so it should not be extracted from the correlation matrix.

time on thorough thinking fit the picture of the "cognitive miser" rather well (see 3.3.4.2). This type of individuals thus bears close resemblance to the dominating view of human information processing under the "heuristics and biases" program described in chapter 3. Recall that this type of people was found to be prone to a wide variety of reasoning biases and use of simplifying heuristics. Thus, this factor must be considered promising for the detection of effects of boundedly rational decision making, i. e. the occurrence of procedural biases in CVM.

**Table 4-9**: Factor loadings of the task independent bounded rationality scale

| | Task Independent Factors (TIF) | | | |
|---|---|---|---|---|
| Items (abbreviated) | TIF1 "intuitive" | TIF2 "analytical-rational" | TIF3 "cautious" | TIF4 "cognitive miser" |
| Initial impressions are usually correct | .829 | .031 | .125 | -.051 |
| I trust my hunches | .803 | -.019 | .021 | .095 |
| I like challenges | .017 | .742 | -.086 | -.130 |
| Complex task is challenging | -.017 | .728 | .170 | .040 |
| I don't like time pressure | .096 | .038 | .719 | -.118 |
| I know it's right | .227 | .153 | .638 | .327 |
| I follow the group | .396 | .147 | -.533 | .181 |
| Thinking is boring | -.068 | -.233 | -.016 | .837 |
| Time is money so I take decisions quickly | .256 | .388 | -.079 | .502 |
| Consistency (Cronbach's alpha) | .62 | .36 | .23 | .14 |

The extraction of four factors with an eigenvalue greater than one thus also indicates that there is a systematic distinction between the intuitive type of TIF1 and the cognitive miser type of TIF4. This distinction can best be demonstrated by the factor loadings of the item "Thinking is boring". Not only does it load positively and highest on the "cognitive miser" factor indicating its strong association with this type, it also loads quite high negatively on the "analytical-rational" factor which indicates that those people who consider hard thinking boring definitely do not appreciate complex and challenging tasks. Since this item loads practically not at all on the first factor "intuitive" it can be seen that people who trust their intuitions and feel that these are actually correct are not of the cognitive miser type. The interpretation of TIF3 is not so straightforward. While its highest loading item "I hate to make important decisions under time pressure" suggests that this factor is associated with a high degree of reflection, the strong association with "Often, when I take decisions, I don't know why but I feel that I'm right" which is also to a considerable degree related to TIF1 "intuitive" and TIF4 "cognitive miser" reveals that TIF3 pertains to intuitive, however slow, information processing. Individuals loading high on this factor need their time to explore their intuitions, however, these stand in clear contrast to "initial impressions" or "hunches" as in TIF1 which seem to be a kind of fast intuitions. This slow processing is also documented by the negligible loading of "Time is money so I take decisions quickly", an item even considerably associated with the "analytical-rational" factor TIF2. Furthermore, their behavior in groups stands in clear contrast to the other factors' characteristics, especially those of TIF1, in that TIF3 is associated with a particularly low susceptibility to social or group influences. Considering that group leaders are often those who come up with persuasive thoughts or propositions quickly, TIF3 indicates a reluctance to get carried away by such behavior of others and rather stick to their own, albeit slower thought processes. In conclusion, this factor can, therefore, be named "cautious".

Since the items in question 9 are derived from existing items of the rational experiential inventory (REI) described above (cf. Epstein et al. 1996) where a few items have been reformulated and others have been added, it would be desirable to test whether the set of the REI items applied in this particular CVM study is able to replicate the same factor structure of the original REI. To this end, the responses to those five items taken from the original REI, i. e. items A, B, D, G and H in table 4-2, are evaluated separately using factor analysis. The results are listed in table 4-10.

As can be seen, only with the reduced items considered central to the original REI it is possible to replicate the two-factor structure distinguishing clearly between the two factors where the factor REI1 in table 4-10 corresponds to the "intuitive-experiential" factor called faith-in-intuition (FI) in Epstein et al (1996) and the factor REI2 corresponds to the "analytical-rational" factor derived from the need-for-cognition (NFC) scale based on Cacioppo and Petty (1982) as described above. The differentiation into the two factors is rather clear-cut as can be seen by the mostly very low factor loadings of the items not belonging to the respective factors in table 4-10. Again, this structure reveals that the cognitive miser type indicated here by the item "Thinking is boring" is hardly associated with the "intuitive-experiential" factor but is in fact the lower end of the "analytical-rational" factor as can be seen from its strong negative factor loading there. This correct replication of the original 31-item based REI factors by the simplified 5-item selection consisting of reformulated and slightly context-adapted REI items is reassuring and indicates that such measures of cognitive effort and information processing can also be applied in the cultural context of Thailand which has never been tried before.

**Table 4-10:** Factor analytical results of the REI items only

| | Rational Experiential Inventory (REI) Factors | |
|---|---|---|
| Items (abbreviated) | REI1 "intuitive-experiential" | REI2 "analytical-rational" |
| I trust my hunches | .850 | -.042 |
| Initial impressions are usually correct | .840 | .063 |
| I like challenges | .075 | .729 |
| Complex task is challenging | .119 | .697 |
| Thinking is boring | .153 | -.518 |
| Consistency (Cronbach's alpha) | .62 | .39 |

Regarding the more detailed TIF-scale, does the extraction of four factors in table 4-9 invalidate the assumption of the dual-process theories described in chapter 3 postulating only two fundamental types of information processing? I argue that this is not the case as indicated by the robust two-factor structure found for the items in table 4-10 where only the central items of the REI were used instead of the augmented and adapted set of question items in question 9. Rather, the three separate low-cognition factors found in table 4-9 represent three ways of employing such simplified information processing where TIF1 refers strongly to the concept of "ecological rationality" as defined by Todd and Gigerenzer (2003) since trust in those intuitions is expressed, TIF3 refers to slow and more consciously employed intuitive processing and TIF4 stands for personal cognitive limitations ("Thinking is boring") and impatience ("Time is money so I take decisions quickly"). Thus, these three separate factors stand as a whole for the wide variety of cognitive processes characterized by low effort and decision making based on intuition and simplified heuristics.

*The task dependent scale*

The second instrument for measuring and classifying the bounded rationality of CVM respondents, the task dependent scale, is based on the items contained in question 18. Before performing factor analysis on this question, it is useful to take a look at the responses to the single question items. These results are illustrated in table 4-11.

**Table 4-11:** Results of the single question items of question 18 (missing responses are neglected)

| | When you think about your decision whether and how much to contribute to the proposed project, are the following statements true? | % Yes | % No |
|---|---|---|---|
| A | I made my decision based on my first feeling about this program right after it was presented to me. | 81.1 | 18.0 |
| B | I really thought very hard about every single aspect of the program before making a decision of how much to pay. | 44.6 | 54.5 |
| C | The first impression that I had about this program changed on a second thought. | 24.7 | 74.2 |
| D | I would have liked to have more time for making a decision about my contribution to this program. | 62.6 | 35.6 |
| E | All aspects were equally important for my decision. | 84.7 | 14.2 |
| F | With the given information about the project I found it very hard to make a good decision. | 63.3 | 35.4 |
| G | There are so many aspects in this project but only a few of them were really relevant for my decision. | 57.7 | 40.9 |
| H | Even if I had had more time available for thinking about this program I don't think that my decision of how much to contribute to it would have been different. | 70.1 | 28.6 |

The percentages of "yes" and "no"-responses to the single question items already reveal a number of interesting points. First, respondents seem to be highly affected by intuitive and heuristic information processing and decision making as is indicated by the high percentage of "yes"-responses to items A, E and, to a lower degree, G. These three items correspond to the expected three different types of limited information processing laid out in section 4.2.2.2. Thus, the first research question, i. e. whether respondents in CVM surveys perform some "economy of cognition", can clearly be answered positively. The degree of such limited information processing is even surprisingly high, especially regarding items A and E. Further analysis of the influence of bounded rationality on response behavior in CVM surveys seems, therefore, highly relevant. Second, the percentage of "yes"-responses to items D and F concerning the available information on the scenario and the time for decision making indicates that more than 60% of the respondents felt a limitation in at least one of the two aspects during the interview. These two items could well be interpreted as an indirect assessment of respondents' uncertainties regarding their valuation of the proposed environmental change since limited time and information prevent them from evaluating the scenario sufficiently in the light of their preferences.

The data presented in table 4-11, however, do not show the combinations of responses to the single question items for each respondent. Certain combinations of responses may be considered inconsistent and should, therefore, be treated with reservation. Specifically, it would be expected that a respondent answering "yes" to item A chooses "no" for item C since a decision based on the first impression would be inconsistent with a change of this impression after having had a second thought about it. Equally, a respondent answering "yes" to item E would be expected to respond "no" to item G since plausibility suggests that either all aspects are equally important or only few aspects are relevant but not both. A substantial part of respondents was found not to conform to these strict plausibility requirements. Thus, respondents seemed to have trouble understanding the meaning of the question items correctly leading to inconsistent response patterns. This result sheds substantial doubt on the validity of the responses to the task dependent question items. Nevertheless, the data from these items shall be used for an analysis of limited information processing in the CVM, but the results need to be interpreted carefully.

However, in contrast to the analysis of the task independent scale, the responses to the task dependent question items are analyzed separately w. r. t. the WTP elicitation question format used. Such an approach appears necessary since it must be expected that information processing in the two elicitation formats will be different, at least during the part when respondents evaluate the proposed scenario in monetary terms. An indication that different reasoning processes are used is given by significant differences between the responses of the DC and the PC respondents regarding question items A, B and F. In the following, therefore, the results of the task dependent question items using factor analysis will be treated separately.

For the DC dataset the Bartlett test of sphericity ($p < 0.001$) and the Kaiser-Meyer-Olkin test (KMO = 0.649) indicate that the responses to this question are well suited for factor analysis, the KMO-value is even higher than the one for the responses to question 9. Three factors with an eigenvalue greater than 1 were extracted. In conjunction, they are able to explain 60.2 % of the variance in the dataset. For the extraction of factors item H was omitted from the analysis since it turned out not to be clearly related to any one of the extracted factors. An inclusion of item H would, therefore, have weakened the interpretation of the factors. Table 7-12 presents the respective items, factors and factor loadings for the DC dataset.

**Table 4-12**: Factor loadings of the task dependent bounded rationality scale (DC)

| | Task Dependent Factors (TDF_DC) | | |
|---|---|---|---|
| Items (abbreviated) | TDF1_DC "uncertain" | TDF2_DC "analytical" | TDF3_DC "elimination" |
| Would have liked more time for the decision | .750 | .148 | -.071 |
| Good decision is very hard with the given information | .697 | .133 | -.026 |
| All aspects were equally important | .618 | -.398 | .138 |
| Thought hard about every single aspect | .578 | .384 | .097 |
| First impression changed on a second thought | .018 | .746 | .127 |
| Decision is based on first feeling | -.228 | -.690 | .107 |
| Only few aspects were relevant for the decision | .013 | .031 | .978 |
| Consistency (Cronbach's alpha) | .60 | -.59 | - |

The grouping of the question items into three factors and the respective factor loadings provide interesting insights into the thought and decision processes of the respondents in this specific CVM task context. The first factor TDF1_DC contains as the two highest loading items those referring indirectly to respondents' uncertainties over their preferences (see above), TDF1_DC shall thus be termed "uncertain". It is interesting that item E "All aspects are equally important" is contained in this factor indicating that respondents in the DC question format exhibit a tendency to undifferentiated information processing when they feel uncertain due to information and time limitations. At the same time, item B "Thought hard about every single aspect" is clearly related to TDF1_DC as well, however to a lower degree. This item seems to contradict item E which suggests only superficial information processing. Item B, however, needs to be treated with reservation since it is rather prone to social desirability since respondents might be reluctant to admit to the interviewer (or to themselves) that they have not thought hard about every single aspect of the proposed scenario.

TDF2_DC refers to information processing and decision making based on thorough thoughts and considerations of the given scenario and the payment scheme. Respondents with a high factor score on this factor take into account all the given information and don't let themselves be guided by their first impressions as indicated by the negative factor loading of the item "Decision based on first feeling". They are even able to revise their first impression when they think more thoroughly about the program. This item indicates the corrective influence of the "analytical-rational" over the "intuitive-experiential" systems, a key feature of the dual-process models of reasoning. The high loading of the item "Thought hard about every single aspect", although not a primary element of TDF2_DC, underscores the analytical nature of this factor, however, as mentioned above, this item needs to be treated cautiously. Another item grouped primarily with TDF1_DC seems to play an important role here, too. With the high negative loading of "All aspects were equally important" this TDF2_DC indicates the ability to make trade-offs among the project's features where some are perceived more important than others. Thus, the limitations of time and information do not seem severe for TDF2-respondents.

Finally, TDF3_DC as a single-item factor stands for the third kind of limited information processing described in section 4.2.2.2 as indicated by the high loading on its constituting item "Only few aspects were relevant for the decision" and the very low loading of "Thought hard about every single aspect". Therefore, information processing and decision behavior as indicated by TDF3 is assumed to follow the most prominent elements of the scenario while eliminating the others from further consideration early in the process. Such a decision heuristic here could be called "elimination-of-aspects" (EOA) since entire elements of the valuation scenario are only "peripherally" processed and eliminated from consideration early on. In addition, the very low factor loadings of the "uncertainty" items show that TDF3_DC-respondents are quite certain regarding the outcome of such peripheral processing.

The PC-partition of question 18 is also well-suited for factor analysis as indicated by Bartlett's test of sphericity ($p < 0.001$) and the Kaiser-Meyer-Olkin test (KMO = 0.692). Here, question item H was also omitted from the analysis. For the PC-partition four separate factors were extracted which are able to explain more than 72 % of the variation in the data. Table 4-13 shows the result of the factor analysis of question 18 for the PC-dataset.

**Table 4-13:** Factor loadings of the task dependent bounded rationality scale (PC)

| | Task Dependent Factors (TDF_PC) | | | |
|---|---|---|---|---|
| Items (abbreviated) | TDF1_PC "uncertain" | TDF2_PC "analytical" | TDF3_PC "equal" | TDF4_PC "elimination" |
| Good decision is very hard with the given information | .827 | .035 | -.034 | .064 |
| Would have liked more time for the decision | .814 | .045 | .071 | .096 |
| Thought hard about every single aspect | .575 | .400 | .142 | -.050 |
| Decision is based on first feeling | .045 | -.824 | -.137 | -.084 |
| First impression changed on a second thought | .230 | .678 | -.123 | -.021 |
| All aspects were equally important | .083 | .025 | .976 | -.026 |
| Only few aspects were relevant for the decision | .098 | .045 | -.026 | .988 |
| Consistency (Cronbach's alpha) | .65 | -.55 | - | - |

The single question items are grouped into the factors in a similar way as in the DC-partition. However, here item E "All aspects were equally important" is extracted as a separate factor and, as can be seen from its low loading on TDF1_PC "uncertain", it is not at all related to preference uncertainty as was the case for the DC-partition of question 18. TDF3_PC is thus termed "equal". This slightly different grouping of the items by the factor analytical procedure suggests that PC respondents, on average, try harder to evaluate the given information even when they feel uncertain due to information and time limitations than DC respondents. This might be the result of being forced to select a WTP interval from a list in the payment card format rather than simply accept or reject a proposed bid in dichotomous choice. In the following, the relationships between the task independent and the task dependent scales shall be explored.

*Relationship between the two scales*

On the basis of the extracted factors respondents of the CVM survey can be classified as to the degree to which they are associated with each of the factors, i. e. the factor analytical method computes individual factor scores for each respondent signifying the degree to which he belongs to each factor. These factor scores represent the values of the variables to be used in further regression models where the extracted factors serve as explanatory variables. A similar employment of factor scores was described in the full regression model where factors of the attitudinal variables were used as explanatory variables in the model in section 4.4.3.3. These factor scores for each individual respondent can now be used for analyzing the relationship between the two measurement scales of bounded rationality.

As mentioned above, it would be expected that the two scales are correlated to some degree, i. e. that on average those respondents showing a tendency for behavior based on intuition as classified by the TIF scale also exhibit a tendency for limited information and heuristic behavior in the particular CVM task and vice versa. Table 4-14 shows the bivariate correlations using the Pearson correlation coefficient between the four factors pertaining to the task independent scale and the task dependent factors for the DC and the PC-partitions of the dataset.

On the whole, the correlations between the task independent and the task dependent factors are very weak and mostly insignificant. This finding clearly questions the expectation that, on average, the general cognitive disposition of individuals is systematically related to their use of limited information processing in specific tasks. Two significant correlations, however, are plausible and shall briefly be highlighted here. For the DC-partition TIF4 "cognitive miser" is significantly correlated to TDF3 "elimination" indicating that respondents who have a tendency to employ as little cognitive resources as possible try to reduce complex decision problems like the one to evaluate a CVM scenario to a much simpler task by concentrating only on a few important elements of that scenario. It is interesting, though, that PC respondents who were classified as cognitive misers show no such behavior. A cautious interpretation of this different behavior between the two question formats would be that whereas cognitive misers consider it sufficient in a DC format to process information superficially, i. e. concentrate on the most important aspects, the requirement to select a specific interval in the PC format activates more differentiated reasoning about the scenario. Consequently, a cognitively miserly

PC respondent feels forced to consider the proposed scenario more completely and thoroughly than if the DC elicitation format were used.

**Table 4-14:** Correlations among the task independent factors (TIF) and the task dependent factors (TDF), levels of significance are given in parentheses (p-values)

| Factors | TIF1 "intuitive" | TIF2 "analyt.-rational" | TIF3 "cautious" | TIF4 "cognitive miser" |
|---|---|---|---|---|
| TDF1_DC "uncertain" | .000 (.992) | -.006 (.893) | -.042 (.377) | -.065 (.171) |
| TDF2_DC "analytical" | .030 (.534) | .019 (.694) | .002 (.962) | .099 (.037) |
| TDF3_DC "elimination" | -.018 (.701) | .-045 (.342) | .038 (.422) | .096 (.044) |
| TDF1_PC "uncertain" | .157 (.004) | -.056 (.311) | .003 (.959) | .089 (.107) |
| TDF2_PC "analytical" | .048 (.389) | .000 (.999) | -.017 (.761) | .002 (.964) |
| TDF3_PC "equal" | -.099 (.071) | -.034 (.538) | .095 (.085) | -.005 (.928) |
| TDF4_PC "elimination" | -.053 (.341) | .103 (.061) | .026 (.640) | .059 (.281) |

Another difference between response behavior of PC and DC respondents is indicated by the significantly positive correlation between TIF1 "intuitive" and TDF1_PC "uncertain" whereas no such correlation was found for DC respondents. Here again respondents in the DC format, especially if classified as intuitive, seem to be at ease with their "yes" or "no" response to the proposed bid, the lack of information and time does not seem to limit their confidence in the given answer to the WTP question. In contrast, the task to select an appropriate interval in the PC format seems much more demanding for intuitive respondents where it is not sufficient to use intuition, or their hunches, to either accept or reject a proposed bid. As stated above, the selection of a specific interval from a list requires to use more cognitive resources than in the DC format resulting in a stronger feeling of uncertainty, here. Thus, the correlations between task independent and task dependent factors found here suggest that the PC format is more demanding for respondents, especially for those relying to a large extent on intuitive reasoning and limited information processing like the cognitive misers.

It is surprising, however, that a significantly positive correlation between TIF4 "cognitive miser" and TDF2_DC "analytical" was found since the two factors were expected to represent opposite concepts of information processing. Furthermore, no correlations could be detected between TIF2 and TDF2 so that the general cognitive disposition for effortful analytical reasoning is completely unrelated to analytical information processing in the task dependent case. These results shed considerable doubt on the validity of the responses to the question items A and C of the task dependent scale. As will be demonstrated in the further analysis below this doubt seems to be warranted.

#### 4.4.3.5 Characteristics of the task independent and task dependent types

In the following section, the systematic relationships between the socio-economic and attitudinal variables of the respondents and the two measures of bounded rationality will be investigated. The purpose of this analysis is to observe whether clear and interpretable pictures that might characterize the various information processing types emerge from the data of this survey. There are few clear a priori expectations regarding these relationships. However it can be hypothesized that, in general, the higher the disposition for analytical thinking the higher are the levels of education and income since most good positions in professional life require a sufficiently high level of analytical ability. At the same time it can be expected that cautious individuals have a higher tendency to save money for their children and for their personal security in the future. Cognitive misers, on the contrary, are expected to perform worse in terms of education levels and incomes and will probably save less money for the future. Concerning the "soft" attitudinal variables assessed in this survey like the perception of the role of government, the attitudes toward money and donations, their worries etc., no clear expectations exist so that no specific hypothesis shall be formulated here.

*The task independent type*

For the decision types as defined by the task independent scale of bounded rationality there exist a considerable number of relationships with attitudes and socio-economic characteristics that confirm the classification introduced above and explain their behavior through these characteristics. This analysis was conducted by computing the Pearson correlation coefficients between the individual factor scores of the task independent factors and a number of attitudinal and other variables that were assessed in part four and five of the CVM questionnaire. Here, a brief verbal description of the variables characterizing and, especially, distinguishing the four different types shall be given; the detailed correlation tables can be found in the appendix. In general, the factor scores of the TIF were correlated to some question items of donation attitude (question 11), the role of government in environmental regulation and management (question 12), the economic self-classification of the households (questions 13 – 15), attitude toward money (question 16), issues of worry (question 17), debts (question 19) and selected socio-economic items of question 20.

Of all the four task independent decision types the TIF1 "intuitive" type is the one that least stands out of the full dataset of respondents, so it can be considered the type occurring most frequently. However, in some attitudes this type significantly differs from the average respondent. Concerning his attitudes towards donations, for example, this factor rates significantly higher on almost all items, in particular his behavior in comparison to the other types seems to be influenced by donations being an established habit in society and an increase of his "boon", a kind of personal spiritual account in Buddhism, thus indicating that this type is particularly driven by social conventions. Furthermore, his tendency to make promises to others that he knows he will not keep in the end suggests a high degree of myopia, i. e. not taking future consequences of present actions sufficiently into account. When asked about the role of government in environmental protection and regulation he concedes that government should play an important role but that it is usually not effective and too late in regulation policies. In relation to personal and societal issues they might be worried about, respondents loading high on this factor seem to be particularly worried about their own economic situations and their health. From a socio-economic and demographic perspective slightly more women than men are associated with TIF1, they are slightly older and less educated. In conclusion, this type is closely associated to the average respondent but seems to be particularly adapted to the demands of society, probably because of a particular need for personal security as expressed by his high degree of worries concerning personal issues as compared to most of the other types.

Regarding the variables at hand, the TIF2 "analytical-rational" type can be clearly distinguished from the average respondent and from all other types, especially from the TIF4 "cognitive miser" type. In relation to their donation attitudes individuals of this type are particularly concerned of what others think of them, however, just as the cognitive miser they don't seem to be influenced by donations being a habit in society and by an increase of their "boon". Concerning the role of government they approve of raising taxes for environmental protection significantly more than all other respondent types. This is also reflected in their attitudes on public spending and financing of public goods since they approve significantly more of the public financing of libraries, swimming pools and theaters. In relation to other households they view their incomes and economic situations consistently as better and consider their incomes to be fair. This view is clearly due to their significantly higher levels of education and income. Therefore, money does not play such an important role in their lives. Although they spend most of it for personal consumption they don't view money to be as important for being happy as other types do and they also state to a significantly higher degree that they would not be happier if they had more money. This attitude is also reflected in their worries since they worry particularly little about their economic situations and the security of their incomes in the future. Instead, as TIF3 "cautious", they worry particularly about the environment and other political and social issues. From a demographic point of view, significantly more men than women in this sample belong to this type, especially unmarried ones. In conclusion, individuals of this type have a particularly positive feeling about themselves and feel that they are in control of things which seems to stem from their high levels of education and income and their greater independence from other people, e. g. family.

The TIF3 "cautious" type is even more distinct from the average respondent, overall he shows a more negative view of the world and is thus more careful. He is particularly concerned about keeping promises once made, an attitude that distinguishes him clearly from the other types. At the same time he is disillusioned about obtaining help from others when in need. His view of the role of government is even worse than that of TIF1 "intuitive" and TIF2 "analytical-rational", but in contrast to the latter he is particularly against raising more taxes to improve environmental protection. He is also particularly concerned that such goods as discotheques, the railroad, swimming pools, the water supply and the telephone system not be financed by public money. Concerning his economic situation in comparison to other households he usually classifies himself to be better off, which he actually is. This might be due to his attitude toward money which exhibits more care to save for the future and keep out of debts e. g. by avoiding instalment purchases or bank loans in comparison to the other types. While this type doesn't seem to worry much about issues relating to himself, he is particularly worried about the environment, world peace, the political situation of the country, the erosion of moral values, social justice, corruption and foreigners in the country, i. e. he shows a particularly high degree of worry in relation to public issues. This high level of worry might, therefore, also be the reason for the significantly higher rate of childlessness despite the significantly higher rate of being married. Overall, this type is characterized by a feeling of lack of control, i. e. fear of influences of the outside environment that are possibly harmful so that the individuals of this type seem to put more emphasis on precaution and provision for the future and always remain on the alert to do things correctly.

Finally, the TIF4 "cognitive miser" type was found to differ in particular from the TIF2 type. In his donation attitude he seems to care little about established habits in society, however he expects help in return when he is in need. In relation to the role of government he holds the view that it doesn't play an important role in environmental regulation and in contrast to the other types he does not perceive law enforcement as ineffective. It seems that his care for environmental issues is rather low which carries over to an uncritical opinion of the role of government there. Instead, he is more concerned with personal issues which is reflected in his worries about his own economic situation and the security of his income. This high level of worries concerning the personal situation seems to stem from the importance he attributes to money and his obvious inability to deal with it in a satisfactory way. He considers money to be highly important for being happy and therefore spends most of it. Individuals of the cognitive miser type have significantly more debts with money lenders, presumably at high interest rates and, as TIF3 "cautious", significantly worry more about their debt levels. Therefore, it is not surprising that they consider the economic situation of their households worse in comparison to others. It is noteworthy that TIF4 is significantly associated with approving of public financing of the water supply system, an aspect that might relate to their WTP for the current project. From a socio-economic and demographic point of view women are slightly more associated with TIF4 than men in this sample, as well as slightly larger household sizes (only moderately significant), lower levels of education and income (moderately significant). In conclusion, this "cognitive miser" type shows a high degree of myopia which can be seen from his attitude towards money and his spending and borrowing behavior. He cares much about private issues but not particularly about public ones which might be due to his significantly lower level of education, as well. Thus, this type stands in clear contrast to the other decision types, particularly to TIF2.

*The task dependent type*

For the task dependent types the analysis of correlations between factor scores and attitudinal and socio-economic variables does not reveal patterns that are as clearly interpretable as for the task independent types. This result could already be expected from the lack of systematic relationships between the TIF and TDF in table 4-14. However, a few insights can nevertheless be gained from such an analysis. TDF1_DC "uncertain" shows an interesting pattern in its donation attitude: this type is significantly associated with having difficulties to say "no" to a friend's request for a favor and with promises that are not intended to be fulfilled. Such attitudes could serve as an indicator for the social desirability effect in CVM interviews. TDF1-type people even like to buy things on installment more often than others while stating significantly more often that more money would not make them happier. Again, such attitudes w. r. t. money are problematic in the context of the CVM. TDF1_PC shows similar characteristics, however his particular difficulty to say "no" and his lower income levels are not significant (see appendix). Instead, TDF1_PC is significantly positively associated with stating that they cannot afford to pay more money, that government is responsible and that they have severe doubts regarding the scenario, i. e. attitudes that might indicate protest responses.

For the TDF2_DC "analytical-rational" type only very few significant correlations with personal attitudes were revealed. Decision makers of this type worry significantly less concerning public issues like the erosion of moral values and peace in the world than the other types. This tendency to be particularly little worried about public issues is even more pronounced for TDF2_PC than for the DC respondents. Also, TDF2_DC respondents consider incomes more often as unfair and save less for the future than the other types. Furthermore, this factor is significantly negatively correlated with the level of income. In addition, TDF2_PC respondents are significantly older and less educated than the other types.

Finally, TDF3_DC "elimination of aspects" shows an interesting pattern w. r. t. the attitudes regarding public spending. This type of decision making is significantly positively associated with approving of financing goods like electricity and water supply as well as the postal and telephone service with taxpayers' money. Since TDF3_DC is not significantly associated with a low social and economic status so that they could benefit from this public financing to a higher proportion than others, these attitudes on public spending indicate that TDF3_DC-type decision makers might exhibit a general tendency to eliminate important aspects from their considerations, just as they seem to have done in the present CVM interview. Regarding the PC-partition, respondents neither the "equal importance" nor the "elimination" types show any interpretable pattern of characteristics.

In summary, the analysis of the characteristics of the task independent and the task dependent types leads to the following conclusions: for the task independent factors, i. e. the factors regarding the general cognitive dispositions of individuals, rather clear patterns emerged from the correlation analysis with socio-economic and attitudinal variables assessed in the survey. The *a priori* expectations were confirmed in that the analytical-rational type TIF2 was significantly associated with higher levels of education and income, the cautious type was shown to save more money than the other types and the cognitive miser turned out to be poorer and less educated. For the task dependent factors describing types of information processing in specific decision situations the patterns were much weaker and harder to interpret or they were even non-existent. The characteristics of the "analytical" TDF2-type were rather counter-intuitive since, as opposed to the task independent TIF2 "analytical-rational", concerns toward public goods were particularly low. This result puts the validity of question items A and C of question 18, i. e. the items forming TDF2, in question.

These findings concerning the socio-economic and attitudinal characteristics of the two different measurement scales of bounded rationality lead to the question which of the two scales is better suited for a classification of bounded rationality in decision making: the one that classifies information processing and decision making types in general irrespective of the actual task at hand or the one that refers specifically to such a task, like e. g. the current CVM survey. This question shall be pursued in the following by analyzing to what extent each of these measurement scales can explain the observed variations of stated WTP and the occurrence of selected procedural biases.

#### 4.4.3.6 Bounded rationality and WTP

In 4.4.3.3 regression models for explaining the systematic variations of WTP as assessed by the DC and the PC format were presented, and from a number of variables and factors that were expected to affect stated WTP those showing a significant influence were detected. This section will build on those results and investigate whether the developed scales of bounded rationality show significant explanatory power in such regression models. However, the a priori expectations of the direction of such an influence on WTP are not as straightforward as was the case, for example, for the explanatory variables and factors in the models shown in table 4-8. For most of those variables, clear expectations existed, either from experience with previous CVM studies or from plausibility considerations. Since these bounded rationality scales have not been investigated yet, especially not in the context of the CVM, such hypotheses cannot be based on prior experience, thus, hypotheses need to be derived from theory.

In principle, there are two different reasons why stated WTP of respondents could be systematically related to their type of information processing and decision making. The first reason is that their preferences regarding the proposed water quality and environmental improvement differ systematically. Such differences might have arisen from different kinds of information processing of environmentally related information in their lives prior to the CVM survey potentially leading to different levels and kinds of general environmental problem awareness. This conjecture is warranted by significant differences between the various bounded rationality factors w. r. t. the rating of the importance of scenario elements in question 5 of the CVM questionnaire. TIF1 "intuitive" is significantly negatively related to the importance of less accumulation of pesticides in the ecosystem and clearer color of the water (see appendix for detailed correlation results), while TIF2 "analytical-rational" only rates interruptions of water service as significantly less important than the other types. TIF3 "cautious" is significantly positively related to the importance of all aspects of the scenario while TIF4 "cognitive miser" is significantly negatively related to the importance of most of the aspects. Just from this information it would be expected that both TIF1 and, especially, TIF4 show a negative association with WTP whereas TIF3 shows a positive association.

The second reason concerns the type of information processing during the CVM interview and is, therefore, based on the findings from the dual-process models of reasoning in chapter 3. As mentioned above, scenarios of environmental change are often quite complex and many consequences of environmental degradation, for example, are unfamiliar to the average respondent. Some elements of a scenario, e. g. in this case the lower contamination of ecosystems with pesticides, may not have conspicuous benefits to the respondent, at least not at first sight and thought. Consequently, such elements are attributed a lower value when the respective information is processed superficially as compared to when the respondent has taken some cognitive effort to scrutinize this element more thoroughly as to whether it might be of personal relevance to him or not. While during a CVM interview the possibility to obtain further information on the elements of the scenario is limited a respondent who thinks about the benefits of an element more thoroughly may remember prior information about the importance of this element, e. g. that pesticides kill aquatic organisms which, in turn, are necessary for an abundant fish population in a river. Limited information processors that are characterized by a superficial and selective evaluation of the given scenario information, therefore, can be expected to attribute less personal relevance to an environmental scenario as compared to more analytical respondents and might state a lower WTP as a consequence. This hypothesis shall be tested subsequently by employing the bounded rationality factors as explanatory variables in the WTP regression model.

Tables 4-15 and 4-16 present the results of the regression models including the various scales of bounded rationality for the DC and the PC datasets, respectively. For each dataset, only those explanatory variables and factors were included in the models that showed a significant association with WTP in table 4-8 (see section 4.4.3.3). In tables 4-15 and 4-16, model 1 contains these variables in conjunction with the task independent factors TIF1 to TIF4, model 2 uses the cognitive type factors based on the original REI items only (REI1 and REI2) and model 3 considers the task dependent factors TDF1_DC to TDF3_DC in the case of the dichotomous choice format and TDF1_PC to TDF4_PC in the case of the payment card format.

From table 4-15 it can be seen that some of the task independent factors of bounded rationality are statistically significant variables for explaining the variations of stated WTP across the DC respondents. In particular, as expected TIF1 "intuitive" shows a significantly negative effect on WTP, although slightly above the 5%-level, whereas TIF2 "analytical-rational" shows a strongly positive significant effect on WTP. The other two factors are not significant in this model, thus, against the expectation, the "cognitive miser" seems not to be significantly related to the amount of WTP. As expected, these influences are replicated in model 2 using the more aggregated REI-factors. REI1 which stands for the "intuitive-experiential" type shows a strongly negative significant association with WTP as does TIF1, and REI2 referring to the "analytical-rational" type exhibits a positive association with WTP, just as TIF2 with which it has most question items in common. The statistical significance is, however, not as strong. The first important result is, thus, that the task independent scale has explanatory power w. r. t. WTP on top of the existing significant explanatory variables that form the core of the regression models. That is, controlling for the effects of the variables education, children, amount of water bill, assessment of difficulty with the valuation task, reasons for the contribution and attitudes toward money the amount of WTP is significantly determined by the general type of information processing.

Second, the tentative hypothesis that more effortful analytical reasoning should lead to a higher WTP is supported here for the DC dataset. Third, the aggregated REI-measure of decision types seems to perform just as well as the four TIF, thus the disaggregation of the general "intuitive-experiential" factor into three separate factors related to effortless, intuitive information processing and decision making seems not to add to the explanatory power of the smaller 5-item REI measure in this study. However, the TIF might turn out to be useful for the identification of procedural biases, which will be investigated below. Surprisingly, none of the three factors of the task dependent scale turned out to be significantly related to WTP in the model specification of model 3, however TDF2 "analytical" and TDF3 "elimination" are not very far above the 10% level of significance. When the TDF were used as the only explanatory variables in the regression model, however, TDF2 "analytical" showed a significantly negative effect on WTP. This effect, thus, is already contained in the core explanatory variables, particularly in the highly significant positive effect of education (EDU) on WTP so that TDF2 does not add significant explanatory power to the model. This negative effect of TDF2 could have been anticipated by its significantly negative correlation with the level of education found above where it has been shown that processing according to TDF2 is not associated with the analytical-rational type of TIF2. Again, this negative association between TDF2 "analytical" and stated WTP is not plausible adding further doubt to the validity of this task dependent factor.

**Table 4-15:** Bounded rationality scales as explanatory factors of WTP for the DC dataset

| | Model 1 | | Model 2 | | Model 3 | |
|---|---|---|---|---|---|---|
| Variable / Factor | Coeff. | p-value | Coeff. | p-value | Coeff. | p-value |
| EDU | 89.59** | .0048 | 90.39** | .0039 | 108.54** | .0005 |
| CHILD | 621.95** | .0001 | 621.43** | .0001 | 592.50** | .0001 |
| MRWWBILL | .76** | .0014 | .76** | .0010 | .84** | .0002 |
| DIFFICULT | -380.1** | .0000 | -373.42** | .0000 | -371.53** | .0000 |
| IMPROVEMENT | 153.07** | .0153 | 155.90** | .0128 | 144.76** | .0153 |
| SAVING | -168.5** | .0195 | -175.11** | .0119 | -212.15** | .0023 |
| TIF1 "intuitive" | -132.07* | .0723 | - | - | - | - |
| TIF2 "analyt.-rational" | 144.67** | .0324 | - | - | - | - |
| TIF3 "cautious" | -19.01 | .7570 | - | - | - | - |
| TIF4 "cognitive miser" | 25.13 | .7138 | - | - | - | - |
| REI1 "intuitive-exp." | - | - | -164.74** | .0240 | - | - |
| REI2 "analyt.-rational" | - | - | 124.20* | .0562 | - | - |
| TDF1 "uncertain" | - | - | - | - | 10.07 | .8858 |
| TDF2 "analytical" | - | - | - | - | -89.95 | .1669 |
| TDF3 "elimination" | - | - | - | - | -89.11 | .1649 |
| Chi-square | 782 (df=12, p<0.01) | | 781 (df=10, p<0.01) | | 786 (df=11, p<0.01) | |

** means significance at the 5%-level, * significance at the 10%-level.

For the PC regression model the results are not as strong as for the DC model presented in table 4-15. While the signs of the coefficients are similar, now both TIF1 "intuitive" and TIF3 "cautious" exhibit a negative effect on WTP, albeit not highly significant. This result, however, confirms the expectations. In contrast to the DC dataset, TIF2 "analytical-rational" seems not to be significantly related to WTP. But in a reduced regression model excluding the factors DONATION, IMPROVEMENT and HAPPINESS as explanatory variables the analytical-rational factor TIF2 shows a positively significant relation with WTP and, at the same time, the significance of the negative effect of TIF1 "intuitive" is much higher. A number of interpretations can be considered from these results. First, the results of the task independent factors in the PC dataset support the interpretation of the DONATION factor in 4.4.3.3 since its surprising negative effect on WTP is strongly correlated ($p < 0.0001$) with the "intuitive-experiential" type. This means that these respondents seem to satisfy their need to do others a favor and to donate money by selecting some low bid interval on the payment card and stop considering the proposed program much further. Thus, the possibility to select a low amount while still being able to contribute could be regarded as facilitating heuristic behavior in the PC format leading to an incomplete evaluation of the entire program to be assessed. Second, the significantly negative association between TIF1 and stated WTP in addition to the effect of DONATION supports the hypothesis that limited information processing, i. e. following one's intuitions, results in a lower valuation of an environmental change scenario, at least in this CVM study. Since this effect occurs both in the DC and in the PC versions of the survey this seems to be a rather robust result.

Third, the missing statistical significance for TIF2 "analytical-rational" as opposed to the DC regression model in table 4-15 can be explained by its close correlation with the factor HAPPINESS ("Even with more money I would not be happier") which seems to have more explanatory power in this model. Thus, the effect that analytical respondents scrutinize the scenario elements more thoroughly than the other cognitive types and, consequently, state a higher WTP is much weaker when the PC elicitation format is used. Only if the factor HAPPINESS is excluded from the model does TIF2 show a significantly positive effect on stated WTP. Fourth, the significantly negative relation of TIF3 "cautious" with WTP in the PC dataset as opposed to the DC dataset indicates that in the PC question format slow but intuitive information processing leads respondents to "play safe" and select a significantly lower WTP interval on the payment card. It can, therefore, be hypothesized that this behavior constitutes one of the main reasons for the discrepancy of WTP between DC and PC question formats often found in the literature (see chapter 2 on the discussion of the different elicitation question formats).

**Table 4-16:** Bounded rationality scales as explanatory factors of WTP for the PC dataset

| | Model 1 | | Model 2 | | Model 3 | |
|---|---|---|---|---|---|---|
| Variable / Factor | Coeff. | p-value | Coeff. | p-value | Coeff. | p-value |
| DONATION | -181.66** | .0415 | -198.01** | .0177 | -135.44** | .0384 |
| IMPROVEMENT | 345.89** | .0002 | 337.22** | .0004 | 214.20** | .0095 |
| HAPPINESS | 198.42** | .0317 | 204.97** | .0254 | 121.00* | .0534 |
| TIF1 "intuitive" | -103.43* | .0795 | - | - | - | - |
| TIF2 "analyt.-rational" | 64.63 | .2868 | - | - | - | - |
| TIF3 "cautious" | -98.44* | .0864 | - | - | - | - |
| TIF4 "cognitive miser" | -21.63 | .6723 | - | - | - | - |
| REI1 "intuitive-exp." | - | - | -105.89** | .0477 | - | - |
| REI2 "analyt.-rational" | - | - | 54.20 | .3406 | - | - |
| TDF1 "uncertain" | - | - | - | - | -54.76 | .3767 |
| TDF2 "analytical" | - | - | - | - | -30.34 | .6039 |
| TDF3 "equal" | | | | | 54.38 | .3757 |
| TDF4 "elimination" | - | - | - | - | -27.13 | .6568 |
| Chi-square | 2408 (df=9, p<0.01) | | 2411 (df=7, p<0.01) | | 2412 (df=9, p<0.01) | |

** means significance at the 5%-level, * significance at the 10%-level.

Not surprisingly, the results for the REI-factors are similar to those of TIF1 and TIF2 for the PC responses. While TIF1 shows a negative relation with WTP indicating that also in the PC format heuristic information processing seems to have a negative effect on the stated contributions to the project proposed here, TIF2 is, again, not significant. In the reduced regression model, however, a strongly significant effect leading to higher contributions can be observed. In contrast to the DC dataset where the TIF-set did not generate insights not already observed from the much shorter REI, the TIF3 "cautious" factor seems to have additional explanatory power for responses to the PC question format. Just like in the DC regression models, no significant associations between the TDF scale and stated WTP could be found for the PC model, not even in the absence of any other explanatory variables or factors in the regression models. Thus, the bid intervals selected by respondents in the PC format seem, on average, not to be systematically influenced by the scores on the task dependent bounded rationality factors. In the following section it will be attempted to use the scales of bounded rationality for an analysis of the occurrence of procedural biases in CVM surveys in the light of cognitive factors of information processing and decision making.

#### 4.4.3.7 Detection of procedural biases and their relation to the measures of cognitive type

In section 4.2.2 a number of procedural biases that frequently and consistently occur in CVM studies are listed and discussed. In particular, these were the warm-glow effect and associated with it the embedding effect, the hypothetical bias, the social desirability effect, the starting point bias in the DC format, the range bias in the PC format and framing effects of the scenario description. It is one of the aims of this study to reassess and try to explain some of theses frequent biases in the light of bounded rationality and to attempt to find ways to mitigate them in future CVM designs. For the assessment of these biases the newly developed measurement scales of bounded rationality that are employed for the first time in a CVM study shall be used. Specifically, it shall be assessed whether there exist differences in the occurrence of these biases between the various groups of information processing types, i. e. between the task independent types TIF1 to TIF4, between the REI-based types and between the task dependent types (TDF) in the DC and the PC elicitation question formats.

A quantitative assessment of the occurrence of the mentioned procedural biases, however, can only be performed for those for which a suitable split sample design exists in this study. This is due to the fact that for such an assessment of procedural biases it is necessary to compare the WTP estimates for each split sample version, i. e. it is investigated whether statistically significant differences between these estimates occur for a certain cognitive type of the respondent group used for the WTP estimation or not. Therefore, only three out of the procedural biases mentioned above will be assessed in this study due to the limitation of the present split sample design: (1) the starting point bias in DC, (2) the range bias in PC, and (3) the social desirability effect via the anonymity / non-anonymity sample split. For an assessment of the remaining biases and effects a suitable split sample design would have to be developed which was not done in the CVM study underlying this research. In order to test for the occurrence of these three biases and their relationships with the measures of cognitive type the following procedure is employed:

*Classification of respondents into cognitive types*: each respondent of the dataset will be classified to belong primarily to one specific cognitive type, this is done for each of the three alternative scales, i. e. each respondent is classified according to the TIF, the REI and the TDF. The respondent will belong primarily to that type on which he has the highest factor score.

*Detection of the extent of procedural biases for the full dataset:* the full dataset of DC respondents will be subjected to a test of starting point bias and of the social desirability effect; equally, the full dataset of PC respondents will be subject to a test of range bias and of the social desirability effect.

*Detection of the extent of procedural biases for each cognitive type:* in analogy to the previous step the respondents of each cognitive type of each of the three bounded rationality scales will be subjected to the respective test of procedural biases. Finally, these results will be compared between the types of each scale.

**Table 4-17:** Number of respondents classified in each cognitive type factor (DC format)

| Factor | # of resp. | Factor | # of resp. | Factor | # of resp. |
|---|---|---|---|---|---|
| TIF1 | 122 | REI1 | 223 | TDF1_DC | 169 |
| TIF2 | 124 | REI2 | 238 | TDF2_DC | 131 |
| TIF3 | 105 | | | TDF3_DC | 160 |
| TIF4 | 108 | | | | |
| Total | 459 | | 461 | | 460 |

**Table 4-18:** Number of respondents classified in each cognitive type factor (PC format)

| Factor | # of resp. | Factor | # of resp. | Factor | # of resp. |
|---|---|---|---|---|---|
| TIF1 | 83 | REI1 | 165 | TDF1_PC | 98 |
| TIF2 | 77 | REI2 | 164 | TDF2_PC | 61 |
| TIF3 | 83 | | | TDF3_PC | 58 |
| TIF4 | 86 | | | TDF4_PC | 107 |
| Total | 329 | | 329 | | 324 |

Table 4-17 shows the classification of the respondents into the respective cognitive types for each bounded rationality scale for the DC dataset, table 4-18 shows the classification for the PC dataset.

The first procedural bias to be investigated using the bounded rationality scales is the starting point bias frequently observed in the DC format. As explained in chapter 2 this bias presumably stems from respondents' tendency to accept a proposed bid regardless of their true WTP, the classical "yea"-saying, or if the respondent feels that accepting the proposed bid is the only way of showing his support for the program although the bid is perceived as rather high (cognitive dissonance). It is argued here that the more people tend to rely on low-effort cognitive processes the more they are expected to be influenced in their response behavior by heuristic cues like a starting point. High-effort processes are, thus, necessary to override the influence of heuristic cues like e. g. the starting bid in that respondents reflect more deeply about their true WTP which they need to compare to the given starting bid. Therefore, the hypothesis can be formulated that such starting point bias in the DC format occurs more often or to a larger extent among respondents belonging primarily to the intuitive types like TIF1, TIF3, TIF4, or alternatively REI1 in the domain of the task independent scales and to TDF1 and TDF3 in the domain of the task dependent scales. In contrast, it would be expected that TIF2, REI2 and TDF2 are less susceptible to this kind of behavior so that no significant bias should be found here for these types.

In order to test for significant starting point biases, the following procedure shall be performed: the full bid range of five starting bids (25, 50, 100, 200 and 400 Baht, respectively) with their subsequent lower follow-up bids is divided into two separate but overlapping ranges. The lower range comprises the four lower bid versions, i. e. 25 to 200 Baht, and the upper range comprises the four upper bid versions, i. e. 50 to 400 Baht. Subsequently, average WTP is estimated separately for each of the partial datasets, i. e. in the lower range case all respondents having received a questionnaire with a starting bid of 400 Thai Baht are excluded from the estimation of WTP while in the upper range case those with a starting bid of 25 Baht are excluded. In case starting point bias exists in the full dataset the WTP estimated from the lower range should be significantly lower than the WTP estimated from the upper range because in the lower range the rather extreme bid of 400 Baht cannot distort the WTP estimates upwards by "yea"-saying or the above mentioned acceptance to show support (for a similar approach to detecting starting point bias in the single-bounded DC format cf. Boyle et al. 1998: 54).

In a simulation study where the true WTP of hypothetical respondents were known and responses to the proposed bids were generated by observing whether the bid was below or above this true WTP so that starting point bias is nonexistent by definition, it could be shown that the estimated average WTP should be the same regardless of the use of the upper or the lower range for estimation (simulation procedure and results are available from the author). Thus, it is expected that using the dataset of the CVM survey in Thailand no significant differences between the lower and the upper range estimates of WTP are found for the "analytical-rational" types TIF2 and REI2, as well as for the "analytical" type TDF2. The results of this procedure are listed in table 4-19. First for the full sample (all respondents) and then for each subsample of decision types (see table 4-17 and 4-18 above) the average WTP and the respective 95%-confidence intervals were estimated both for the lower and the upper ranges of bids. WTP estimates are considered to be significantly different between the two bid ranges at the 5%-level if the estimate of the lower range is not contained in the confidence interval of the upper range and vice versa. Therefore, if this condition is violated for at least one of the estimates the WTP estimates are not significantly different at the 5%-level.

From table 4-19 it can be seen that as expected there exists a significant starting point bias for the full dataset of "all respondents". However, the hypothesis stated above is not confirmed since all three "analytical-rational" decision types TIF2, REI2 and TDF2 show these significant differences of WTP estimates as well. Thus, those type of respondents seem not to be immune and should be considered to be as much susceptible to starting point biases as the other intuitive types. Instead, the intuitive type TIF3 "cautious" exhibits non-significant starting point bias.

The lack of significant starting point bias for TIF3, however, is not easily explained. The differences between the estimated WTPs for the lower and the upper range groups are still substantial (ca. 32%) so that the observed effect of the starting bids is obvious, however not significant at the 5%-level. It is also noteworthy that for the cognitive types TIF1, TIF2 and TIF4 the WTP-estimates using the upper ranges are between 45% and 55% higher than the lower range estimates. In the case of TIF3-type respondents the observed smaller influence of the starting bid on the WTP response could be attributed to their general carefulness and their uneasiness with tasks performed by government (see 4.4.3.5), of which MRWW is clearly considered to be a part due to its being publicly owned. Such attitudes could explain the much higher rejection rate of the high 400 Baht bid (ca. 60%) in comparison to the other types (only ca. 40%). Furthermore, since TIF3 is characterized by a particular aversion of following the group (see table 4-9) it can be hypothesized that TIF3-respondents regard the proposed bid as some kind of "consensus" figure which they must particularly scrutinize before accepting it for themselves. In conclusion, it seems, therefore, that these "cautious" respondents are most critical toward the starting bid which would explain that their WTP responses are less influenced by the particular value of the bid than the other types, including the ones considered "rational".

**Table 4-19:** Determination of the starting point bias for the DC format

| Cognitive type factor | starting bid range | WTP (95% confid. interval) | bias |
|---|---|---|---|
| all respondents | 25 - 200 | 132 (119 – 147) | yes |
| | 50 - 400 | 196 (172 – 220) | |
| TIF1 | 25 - 200 | 119 (95 – 141) | yes |
| | 50 - 400 | 181 (122 – 240) | |
| TIF2 | 25 - 200 | 148 (121 – 190) | yes |
| | 50 - 400 | 214 (158 – 271) | |
| TIF3 | 25 - 200 | 140 (110 – 193) | not significant |
| | 50 - 400 | 185 (128 – 240) | |
| TIF4 | 25 - 200 | 130 (103 – 162) | yes |
| | 50 - 400 | 202 (154 – 254) | |
| REI1 | 25 - 200 | 110 (95 – 126) | yes |
| | 50 - 400 | 159 (125 – 193) | |
| REI2 | 25 - 200 | 166 (141 – 207) | yes |
| | 50 - 400 | 234 (197 – 279) | |
| TDF1_DC | 25 - 200 | 117 (96 – 143) | yes |
| | 50 - 400 | 182 (132 – 225) | |
| TDF2_DC | 25 - 200 | 108 (87 – 130) | yes |
| | 50 - 400 | 167 (117 – 213) | |
| TDF3_DC | 25 - 200 | 163 (138 – 200) | yes |
| | 50 - 400 | 220 (183 – 262) | |

The tests for the social desirability effect and for the range bias follow a different concept from the one for the starting point bias. Here, dummy variables can be used in the WTP regression model for indicating a particular treatment of the split sample design. In the case of the social desirability effect a split sample between an anonymous WTP question and a non-anonymous WTP question is used in the survey where it is expected that anonymous responses are free of social desirability effects, thus forming a point of reference against which the regular, i. e. non-anonymous, response can be compared. The dummy variable assumes a value of 1 in case of anonymity and a value of 0 in the regular non-anonymous case. Table 4-20 shows the coefficient estimates of this dummy variable in regression models for each cognitive type. A negative coefficient indicates a lower WTP estimate for anonymous responses versus non-anonymous responses, thus, if the coefficient is found to be significantly negative a significant social desirability effect is indicated.

**Table 4-20:** Determination of the anonymity and range biases

| | DC Anonymity | | PC Anonymity | | PC Range | |
|---|---|---|---|---|---|---|
| | Coeff. | p-value | Coeff. | p-value | Coeff. | p-value |
| all respond. | -.06 | .6087 | -.07 | .5719 | .11 | .3660 |
| TIF1 | -.17 | .4531 | -.17 | .4820 | .21 | .4320 |
| TIF2 | .05 | .8555 | -.40 | .1822 | .02 | .9364 |
| TIF3 | .20 | .4341 | -.35 | .1026 | .25 | .3543 |
| TIF4 | -.27 | .2992 | -.02 | .9333 | -.03 | .8822 |
| REI1 | -.12 | .4731 | -.03 | .8522 | .17 | .3355 |
| REI2 | .03 | .8424 | -.12 | .4836 | .03 | .8265 |
| TDF1_DC | -.03 | .8901 | - | - | - | - |
| TDF2_DC | .29 | .1780 | - | - | - | - |
| TDF3_DC | -.46* | .0504 | - | - | - | - |
| TDF1_PC | - | - | -.13 | .6835 | -.07 | .7695 |
| TDF2_PC | - | - | .35 | .2740 | .08 | .7364 |
| TDF3_PC | - | - | .21 | .4574 | -.02 | .2656 |
| TDF4_PC | - | - | -.46* | .0604 | -.07 | .7695 |

Variables marked * are significant at the 10%-level.

For testing the PC responses w. r. t. the range bias sometimes postulated in the literature a dummy variable indicating the two different PC designs was used. A value of 0 for this dummy variable indicates a cut-off value of 400 Baht (small range) and a value of 1 stands for a cut-off value of 2000 Baht (large range) on the payment card. The results of this test are shown in table 4-20 in the last two columns titled "PC Range". Here, a positive sign of the coefficient stands for a higher estimated WTP in case the PC design with a cut-off value of 2000 Baht was used, thus, a significantly positive coefficient of the PC range dummy variable indicates a significant range bias for the particular cognitive type.

According to the results listed in table 4-20 only two significant effects of anonymity in the WTP elicitation question were observed from the data in this study. While in the domain of the task independent information processing and cognitive types no significant effects of anonymity on stated WTP could detected neither for the DC format nor for the PC format, a clearly negative and significant effect of anonymity was found for the respondents belonging primarily to the task dependent factor "elimination" (TDF3_DC and TDF4_PC), i. e. those respondents who answered "yes" to the question whether only few aspects of the scenario were relevant for their decision. Those respondents seem to be guided by social desirability in their responses in that they state a significantly higher WTP both in the DC and in the PC format in case an interviewer is present in person. However, the significance of this effect is not as strong for the PC format as for the DC format. Consequently, the respondents considering only few aspects of the scenario appear to have the tendency to follow the desirability cue and answer on the basis of their urge to state what the interviewers would most likely want to hear from them.

However, the question remains whether the responses of the other types, including REI and TIF, where no significant differences between regular and anonymous WTP responses were detected are free from the social desirability effect so that social desirability plays no role, at least not a significant one, for these types. Alternatively, it could be argued that the reason why no differences were detected is that these types simply did not believe that their answers would remain unknown to the interviewer. This would, indeed, have been the correct guess since the interviewer was instructed to open the box containing only one completed questionnaire together with some blank sheets of paper right after the interview and then to transfer the secret responses into the respondent's questionnaire. So, did those respondents anticipate this fake anonymity and thus state socially desirable responses in both cases? In this study, there is no possibilities to clarify this question so that it may be assumed that no social desirability effects exist in the responses of these other types.

Concerning the results for the PC format table 4-20 is rather clear: no social desirability effects and no range bias were found on the level of all respondents where all cognitive types are lumped together. On the specific level of the task dependent types, however, it emerges that TDF4_PC "elimination" is significantly influenced by the presence of an interviewer. Contrary to a number of empirical CVM studies where significant range biases were found, the respondents in this study in northern Thailand seem hardly to be influenced by the range of the payment card intervals. In the PC case, therefore, only few additional insights into response behavior could be obtained by analyzing the responses of the different cognitive types separately. Overall, in the case of the starting point bias and the social desirability effect the separate analysis revealed significant differences regarding the cognitive types' response behaviors in this study so that additional insights for explaining the occurrence of these biases could be gained.

## 4.5 Discussion and implications of the empirical results of the study

This study represents the first application of bounded rationality scales in the context of the contingent valuation method. The empirical results presented so far are suited to give clear answers to the first three research questions laid out in section 4.2.2.3. The fourth question regarding the implications of the results of this study for the design of future CVM surveys remains to be discussed in this section. However, first the main results concerning research questions (1) to (3) shall be highlighted in the following.

The first research question concerning the existence of an "economy of cognition" in CVM surveys is to be confirmed. This result is derived from the responses to the items to the task dependent scale of bounded rationality. A substantial number of respondents confirmed that they made use of some of the simplifying heuristics postulated in section 4.2.2.2, namely following their intuitions ("gut feelings"), giving equal weight to the elements of the scenario or considering only the most important or prominent ones while neglecting others. The results given in table 4-11 demonstrate that between almost 60% to more than 80% of respondents made use of these heuristics at least to some extent. Consequently, a further analysis of the consequences of such an "economy of cognition" for the benefit estimates and for the occurrence of procedural biases in CVM is warranted.

The second research question dealt in greater detail with the issue of detecting such intuitive and heuristic response behavior in CVM interviews and measuring the extent to which it is used in order to enable an analysis of its consequences for WTP responses. To this end two separate approaches were undertaken. The first approach focused on the individual differences in people's general cognitive dispositions, i. e. their personal tendencies to process information more intuitively using effortless heuristic reasoning or more analytically using more effortful cognitive processes. The empirical instrument for classifying and measuring these dispositions was based on well-validated cognitive psychological scales, the Need-for-Cognition scale (cf. Cacioppo and Petty 1982) and the Faith-in-Intuition scale (cf. Epstein et al. 1996). In order to be applicable in CVM interviews these scales were shortened by selecting only the most important question items for the empirical instrument used here. For the second approach a new empirical instrument aiming at the direct elicitation of respondents' types of information processing used in the specific task of evaluating a CVM scenario was developed. The question items of this instrument are based specifically on the expected heuristics that CVM respondents might use when considering and valuing the proposed scenario. This instrument included also question items focusing at the indirect elicitation of respondents' uncertainties since it was argued before that preference uncertainty may be a prerequisite for the use of heuristic behavior and the occurrence of procedural biases (see 4.2.1).

Concerning the validity of the scales it was shown that both approaches, i. e. the task independent approach focusing on the general cognitive dispositions as well as the task dependent approach, produced a meaningful factor structure when subjected to a factor analytical procedure. This means that it was possible to interpret the extracted factors as representing the common concepts, e. g. intuitive and analytical information processing, made up by their constituting single question items. The task independent scale was subdivided into the more comprehensive TIF-scale consisting of 10 items and the narrower REI-scale that consisted only of the 5 most important items from the original NFC and FI-scales. It was found that each of the three scales considered divided into one or more intuitive factors and a rational factor, where the TIF separates the intuitive factor of the narrower REI into three more disaggregated factors due to the addition of five further question items. Thus, as already indicated by the dual-process theories in chapter 3 it was demonstrated that "intuitive-experiential" information processing and decision making is not a homogeneous way of thinking but comes in different facets each of which applies to a special aspect of intuition.

The TIF-scale *per se* produced coherent results and interpretations of the cognitive types in general, as was demonstrated by the emergence of clear and interpretable pictures of these types by correlating them to the socio-economic and attitudinal characteristics assessed in the survey. The task dependent scale was shown to be more problematic since the dataset contained a high degree of contradictory responses so that the validity of some of the question items of that scale is highly questionable. This seems to be particularly true for the three question items B "I really thought very hard about every single aspect of the program before making a decision of how much to pay", A "I made my decision based on my first feeling about this program right after it was presented to me" and C "The first impression that I had about this program changed on a second thought". The strong association of item B with the uncertainty items seems counterintuitive so that it is suspected that respondents answering this question were influenced by social desirability. While items A and C are, as expected, strongly negatively correlated and, thus, contained with opposite signs in the same factor TDF2 interpreted as "analytical", the response behavior of this factor and its correlation with other personal characteristics of the respondents contradict this interpretation. Thus, the question items of the task dependent scale need to be improved if this scale is to be used to analyze cognitive aspects of response behavior in CVM surveys in the future.

Concerning the third research question several interesting results were obtained from which new insights into different kinds of information processing and response behavior stemming from individual differences in cognitive characteristics of respondents can be gained. First, for the DC elicitation question format the tentative hypothesis that the higher the tendency of respondents toward analytical-rational information processing the higher their WTP and the higher the tendency toward intuitive reasoning the lower their WTP was supported. For the PC elicitation format significantly negative effects on stated WTP could only be found for the two factors TIF1 "intuitive" and TIF3 "cautious", TIF2 "analytical-rational" was found to be positive but not significant in the regression model. The task dependent factors had no significant association with WTP in neither of the question formats. These results show that the different kinds of information processing and reasoning can be significant determinants of WTP. In particular, they underscore the necessity that respondents be given the opportunity and be encouraged to process and evaluate the scenario information thoroughly. As expected here, superficial intuitive evaluation of the scenario results in a significant tendency to underestimate the social value of environmental improvement scenarios.

Second, new insights were gained concerning two of the three procedural biases analyzed: (1) the starting point bias in the DC elicitation question format and (2) the social desirability effect both in the DC and in the PC formats. While the responses to the DC question on the whole showed a significant starting point bias, the occurrence of this bias seems to depend on the type of respondents' general cognitive disposition. No significant starting point bias was detected for the group of respondents who are classified as belonging primarily to the TIF3 "cautious" type indicating that such a general cognitive disposition, i. e. a particular aversion to time pressure and group decisions, facilitates the thorough and critical scrutiny of the starting bid in a DC elicitation question. This finding is in contrast, however, to the *a priori* hypothesis that the more analytical-rational factor TIF2 would be less susceptible to the starting bid. It was shown that TIF2-type respondents are influenced just as much by the starting bid in a DC question as the intuitive respondents and the cognitive misers who were thought to be particularly vulnerable to this bias. Since analytical or rational information processing is not a solution for the problem of the general occurrence of starting point bias in the DC format the results of the present study further add to the strong reservations regarding the use of this format in CVM surveys.

The analysis of the social desirability effect was the only instance where the task dependent scale produced any meaningful results. In a comparison of WTP responses between settings where these responses were given either anonymously or in the regular, i. e. non-anonymous, way no significant differences between the two treatments were found for the DC or the PC format. A disaggregated analysis differentiating between the cognitive characteristics of respondents revealed, however, that those respondents belonging primarily to the task dependent "elimination" type stated a significantly higher WTP in case they gave their answer directly to the interviewer, i. e. non-anonymously. While the exact reason for this anonymity effect needs to be investigated further it can already be deduced here that the presence of an interviewer who they want to please with their response seems to be a decisive element of the CVM setting for respondents considering only a few elements of a scenario and neglecting others. The differentiated analysis also shows that while no over-all social desirability effect is detected a particular subset characterized by its type of task specific information processing may be significantly influenced by social desirability nevertheless.

While it was expected that in analogy to the starting point bias in the DC format respondents would be influenced by the particular range of specified WTP intervals on a payment card no such range bias, not even for certain subsets of respondents classified according to their cognitive characteristics, was found in this study. This result underscores the suitability of the payment card format in contrast to the dichotomous choice format in CVM surveys. The classification of respondents regarding their cognitive characteristics, both in a task independent way focusing on their general cognitive dispositions and in a task dependent way, forms, therefore, a suitable basis for a more thorough analysis of the occurrence of biases in CVM surveys and for the development of improved survey designs.

On the whole, the analysis of CVM response behavior using the cognitive characterization of respondents lead to the following conclusions regarding the suitability and practicability of the three measurement scales employed. The task independent approach proved to be well suited for the analysis of CVM responses w. r. t. the influence of cognitive factors. The characterization of respondents according to their general cognitive dispositions contributed to an explanation of both the amount of WTP and the occurrence of the starting point bias in the DC format. Here, the more comprehensive scale TIF including a number of question items not contained in the original NFC and FI scales from which the more aggregated REI factors were derived proved to be particularly useful. In the TIF scale the general intuitive reasoning processes were further disaggregated into "intuitive", "cautious" and "cognitive miserly" types where especially the "cautious" type was less susceptible to the starting point bias. Thus, it is recommended that the more comprehensive TIF scale is preferable to the more aggregated REI scale.

In contrast to the task independent approach, the performance of the task dependent type approach was not very successful. This result is rather surprising since it was expected that this kind of measure that is built to fit the information processing and decision context of the CVM more closely would provide a number of additional insights into CVM response behavior. While the decision types that could be extracted from the responses to the question items seemed to be meaningful at first sight, almost all further analyses employing this measure did not yield conclusive or plausible results. Especially, almost no correlations were found between the TIF and the TDF scales. The most surprising result in this respect was the analysis of the determinants of TDF2 which was classified as the "analytical" processing type. It would have been expected that this factor is rather closely related to the "analytical-rational" factor TIF2. However, this was not the case which was obvious from a lack of correlation between the respective factor scores (see table 4-14) and from entirely different socio-economic and attitudinal determinants. TDF2-type respondents are less concerned of public issues, have lower levels of education and rate their households' economic situations as worse in comparison to others. This is in sharp contrast to the determinants of TIF2, the "analytical-rational" type in the TIF-framework. Furthermore, in the DC-partition TDF2 correlates weakly but significantly with TIF4, the cognitive miser, which is also rather counterintuitive. Furthermore, none of the TDF-types exhibited significant effects on WTP in any of the regression models of the DC or the PC format. The only useful result obtained from the task dependent framework was that those respondents who seemed to base their valuation decisions on only few aspects of the scenario showed to be particularly susceptible to the presence of an interviewer which was detected by the significantly negative effect on WTP of the anonymity dummy variable (see table 4-20).

Therefore, the present empirical study of bounded rationality measures supports the use of the task independent approach for measuring information processing and decision making types whereas the task dependent approach, however close it may be to the context of the CVM, cannot be recommended for further use, at least not on the basis of the results of this study in Thailand. The rather general task independent measures were shown to be well suited for analyzing the effects of different types of information processing on stated WTP and, in at least a few instances, were found to be useful for detecting problematic issues of CVM design. Thus, this approach should be pursued further in future CVM surveys.

Finally, concerning the fourth research question, the results discussed above lead to a number of recommendations for future CVM surveys. The first recommendation is to abandon the dichotomous choice elicitation question format and use the payment card format, instead. This recommendation results from the finding of the almost ubiquitous starting point bias where even those respondents classified as primarily analytical-rational were significantly susceptible to the proposed starting bid. The high degree of respondent uncertainty as measured by the proportion of "yes"-responses to items D and F of the task dependent scales might be a reason for this susceptibility. The DC format, therefore, should only be used if it can be assured that respondents are sufficiently certain of their preferences toward the environmental good and of their evaluation of it. Here, the mentioned question items D and F of the task dependent scale could provide a useful guidance.

Second, the finding that intuitive and superficial information processing when evaluating a CVM scenario was significantly associated with lower WTP leads to the recommendation that more emphasis must be laid on the investigation of possibilities to enable and encourage respondents to process the scenario information more thoroughly. This recommendation is not meant as an advertisement of the scenario since it is not the purpose of environmental valuation to obtain the highest valuation possible. Rather, it accounts for the suspicion that the benefits of elements of an environmental change scenario that are unfamiliar to the respondent are often not obvious at first sight and, as a result, are easily neglected in the evaluation of the scenario. It is certainly difficult to devise new ways of increasing the information processing depth during a CVM interview. Clearly, it is no solution to simply provide more information to the respondent since the average CVM scenario is already quite complex and contains a lot of information to be processed. However, it is important to provide this information in a way that is on the one hand easy to digest for the respondent and on the other focused on aspects that were found to illustrate the benefits, i. e. the personal relevance of the scenario to the respondent. One promising way to find such appropriate ways of information presentation is certainly to base the scenario preparation and formulation more on participatory group processes like focus groups or group meetings with respondents who have already been interviewed in a pretest round. Such group processes where individuals can interact, exchange information and points of view and from which insights regarding the aspects of personal relevance can be gained lie at the core of the PVM briefly described in chapter 2.

The third recommendation follows from the result that a significant social desirability effect of respondents of the "elimination" type was observed both in the DC and the PC formats. Hence, for the response to the WTP elicitation question the interviewer should provide the respondent with the possibility to state his willingness-to-pay anonymously, e. g. by the possibility to indicate the payment interval on a payment card on a separate sheet of paper which is then deposited into some kind of ballot box. While this procedure is certainly just an illusion of anonymity, it has proven to be quite suitable in practice so that it should be employed as a simple way to eliminate or at least reduce effects of social desirability during CVM interviews.

The fourth and final recommendation following from the research in this study is to use the scales of bounded rationality developed here as a tool for analyzing datasets of CVM responses regarding respondents' depth of information processing and the occurrence of procedural biases. So far the significantly negative association between intuitive cognitive factors and stated WTP is only a preliminary result and it cannot yet be generalized that it is a characteristic feature of respondents employing strategies of limited information processing like intuition or neglect of information. Therefore, this hypothesis should be tested in CVM studies using different kinds of valuation scenarios and it should also be tested in different countries to account for cultural differences. The lack of such significant effects, however, could serve as a criterion for the rationality of CVM responses. While the use of the task independent approach can be recommended here due to the demonstration of its plausible factor structure and explanatory power only selected items of the task dependent approach, e. g. the items for an indirect assessment of respondents' uncertainty and the items regarding the specific use of limited information processing like equal weighting or elimination of aspects, should be used. The task dependent approach must, therefore, be subject to further investigation in the future.

# 5 Summary and conclusions

The main objective of this study is to scrutinize economic concepts of rationality in the context of environmental economic valuation. Continuing methodological and procedural concerns toward one of the most widely used valuation methods, the survey-based contingent valuation method (CVM), make an analysis of the rationality of response behavior in such surveys necessary. Using the concept of full rationality commonly adopted in economics as a reference point, an alternative rationality concept based on a less normative but instead more realistic perspective on human information processing and decision making is applied in this study to analyze the rationality of responses in CVM surveys. Such a concept based on modern cognitive psychological research has already been developed and was widely analyzed in the recent decades in the fields of economic psychology and behavioral economics under the name of bounded rationality. As the name already suggests the basic premise of bounded rationality is that economic agents in real world decision environments are characterized by limitations of their cognitive capacities that prevent them from acting fully rational in the normative sense of standard economic models.

As it turns out, however, such cognitive limitations may result in decision making that is quite well adapted to the structure of decision environments in the real world. But how should and how do respondents behave in environmental valuation surveys that are just simulations of real-world decisions and what are the consequences of bounded rationality for the validity of such survey results? Almost 50 years have passed since 1978 Nobel laureate in economics Herbert A. Simon first coined the expression "bounded rationality" setting off a wide variety of research in the disciplines of economics and psychology. This study aims at an exploration of how this conceptual framework can contribute to better understand respondents' behavior in CVM surveys in order to recommend changes of the design of such surveys leading to more rational responses and, consequently, to better benefit estimates of environmental change scenarios.

After the presentation of the main theme of this study in the introductory first chapter, the second chapter presents the theoretical foundations of environmental economic valuation and summarizes the state-of-the-art of environmental valuation methods. The welfare theoretic foundations of the valuation of environmental changes are described from which the direct valuation methods are derived as suitable approaches to capture use values as well as non-use values of environmental goods so that, in principle, the total economic value of an environmental change can be assessed. Among these direct methods the contingent valuation method (CVM) is the most prominent and most widely applied method. Hence, the subsequent analysis focuses on this particular valuation procedure. The basic idea of the CVM as a direct valuation method is to create a hypothetical market for the environmental good under consideration on which the households of a particular study area are given the possibility to purchase that good, just as they generally do for market goods in their everyday lives. However, since this simulated market involves household interviews asking people their willingness-to-pay (WTP) for an improvement of the environmental good no real transactions are observed to reveal the households' true preferences. Such hypothetical decisions are problematic, consequently, the CVM approach creates a number of theoretical and procedural concerns that put its validity for an assessment of environmental values in question.

Despite decade-long empirical research a multitude of methodological issues remain open and call for a further investigation to which the present study aims to contribute. One core question still open to debate is the most suitable format of the WTP elicitation question. While in the early days of the CVM an open-ended WTP question asking respondents the maximum amount they would be willing to pay for an improvement of an environmental good was very popular due to simplicity of the statistical methods required for its evaluation a shift to closed-ended questions has occurred in the 1980s. In these questions respondents are presented a payment proposal (a bid) which they can either accept or reject to pay. On the basis of these dichotomous choices which were thought to better resemble every day purchase decisions an average WTP of the population can be estimated by making use of quite complicated statistical methods relying on idealized assumptions. An alternative to this dichotomous choice format (DC) is the payment card (PC) resembling open-ended questions where respondents are given a list of payment intervals from which they can choose the one containing their WTP. While better resembling purchase decisions in the store, DC responses were found to be significantly and quite strongly influenced by the amount of the payment proposal in that respondents anchor their responses on that amount initially presented to them.

This observation called the rationality of CVM responses fundamentally into question since it indicated that respondents were not simply giving their "true" WTP but a response that constituted some mix of preference evaluation, uncertainty effect and possibly psychologically determined biases. It has been argued for example that respondents are influenced by the presence of the interviewer in that they are motivated to please him or her with their answer to the WTP question. Thus, the reasons for such anchoring behavior in the DC format, and possibly other biasing effects in the PC format as well, might be found in the specific perception of the WTP question. Other biasing effects like the influence of the hypothetical nature of the purchase, the embedding of the specific environmental good to be valued into a larger or symbolic environmental good, the budget constraint of the households and related income heterogeneities or varying household sizes have been addressed in the literature, however, they have not been conclusively solved. All these effects of inconsistent and unexpected responses to CVM questions represent violations to the commonly assumed postulate of fully rational decision making. It is, therefore, promising to analyze these biases from the perspective of the rationality of respondents by making use of the more realistic concept of bounded rationality mentioned above.

An important candidate for the explanation of the mentioned procedural biases of CVM estimates is the issue of preference uncertainty. Some authors argue that respondents in a CVM interview do not hold clear and retrievable preferences for environmental goods in relation to market goods. This stems from a lack of experience with using a novel environmental good or with the monetary valuation task as such. These authors have developed *ad hoc* valuation procedures aiming at accounting for respondents' preference uncertainty. All of the approaches found in the literature rely on some kind of self-reported response certainty or confidence measure either given after responding to the WTP question (post-decisional certainty measure) or while considering their answers to various payment card intervals (multiple-bounded dichotomous choice). The results of the latter approach reveal that "yes"-responses to ordinary DC questions contain a considerable degree of uncertainty as to whether the respondents would actually pay that amount whereas open-ended and PC questions seem to induce significantly more cautious response behavior. Preference uncertainty, therefore, seems to play an important role for boundedly rational responses in CVM so that this issue is analyzed jointly with the effects of cognitive limitations mentioned above.

Chapter 3 deals with rationality concepts in economics and as such forms the conceptual core of the present study. In order to provide a suitable starting point for the further analysis of rationality an overview of rationality concepts in economics is given. It is shown how the currently prevalent assumption of full rationality in economics developed from Adam Smith's postulate that economic agents act in pursuit of their own self-interest. Starting with Alfred Marshall, rational economic action is subsequently described by a formal set of axioms where the well-known preference theoretic axioms of reflexivity, completeness and transitivity form the basis of most microeconomic models today. These sets of rationality axioms constitute the normative basis for rational economic choice behavior from which the normative objective of optimization, in the case of households the maximization of utility (or expected utility in the case of risk and uncertainty), is directly derived.

This normative rationality concept has been, however, widely criticized as being unrealistic since economic agents were shown to consistently violate some of the underlying axioms in experiments or even in real world economic decisions. Based on these findings the normative rationality concept with its set of axioms is contrasted to a number of alternative, more descriptive concepts of rationality that have emerged in the literature. As an antipode to full or instrumental rationality, the concept of procedural rationality focuses not on the rationality of the final outcome of an economic decision but on the way, i. e. the procedure, economic decisions are taken. Here, the cognitive limitations of decision makers play the decisive role and, consequently, have to be taken into account for explaining decision making. Although procedurally rational decisions may not lead to optimal outcomes from the perspective of full rationality, the way they were taken, i. e. the procedure, is considered rational when considering the limitations of real-world decision makers.

Two rationality concepts that contain elements both of full or perfect rationality and of procedural rationality are the concepts of institutional rationality and evolutionary rationality. Institutional rationality distinguishes between two modes of behavior, a rule-following and a purpose-seeking one. In this concept it is argued that rule-following behavior has developed from purpose-seeking behavior that has proven to be successful in certain situations and has, therefore, formed an institution to which a large part of individuals in a society adhere. Such institutional rule-following behavior is rational in the sense that scarce cognitive resources are saved for those purposes for which no successful institutions have yet been found. Vernon Smith's concept of evolutionary rationality resembles institutional rationality. However, Smith perceives institutions as the outcome of an evolutionary process where economic actions that have proven successful and robust courses of action need not have developed from a conscious, purposeful and thoughtful behavior but may be the results of random variations of rather naïve reasoning. All these alternative rationality concepts have in common that they perceive economic decisions to be embedded in a context, either of simple cognitive limitations or of a historical process of development of rules, where Adam Smith's notion of self-interest is not strictly interpreted as optimization but as a weaker form of utility-generating behavior. Therefore, these three concepts shall be subsumed under the common name of bounded rationality in this study.

The bounded rationality concept and the economic models building on it have developed largely in parallel to the research and modeling of standard neoclassical economics with its normative view of full rationality for the past 50 years. Bounded rationality forms the basic assumption of behavioral economics which combines research approaches from the neighboring fields of economics and psychology in order to obtain models of economic decision making that can account for the numerous violations of full rationality observed in practice. Thus, bounded rationality rests on empirical findings in economics and psychology that a multitude of judgment and decision making situations exist in which people were shown not to adhere to the rationality axioms mentioned above so that their behavior does not conform to the predictions of full rationality. Rather, people were found to exhibit reproducible systematic biases in their behavior which seemed to result from making use of a variety of strategies of limited information processing resulting in so-called heuristic procedures preventing well-reflected and fully rational judgments and decisions.

Explanations for such systematically biased behavior can be found in research findings from the field of cognitive psychology which investigates the mechanisms of perception, information processing and decision making of the human mind. Cognitive psychology, therefore, provides a suitable framework for analyzing boundedly rational behavior in CVM surveys. The observed behavior seems to be rooted in the dual-process nature of information processing in the brain. Various cognitive psychological models claim that scarce cognitive resources for information processing are allocated to two fundamentally different systems of reasoning resulting in a kind of "economy of cognition". One system often called *heuristic* or *intuitive-experiential* performs relatively effortless information processing relying on stored situational rules and mental shortcuts while a second system called *analytical* or *systematic* is occupied with effortful reasoning processes requiring conscious thought and largely serial processing. It is argued that such a dual-process system is the result of an evolutionary process of the human mind so that a maximum of information processing can occur with the given limitations of cognitive resources. While in some situations effortless heuristic processing may lead to systematic reasoning errors a number of authors demonstrate the ecological rationality, i. e. the adaptivity, of such behavior in many real world judgment and decision situations. Thus, the cognitive psychological models of dual-process reasoning conform well to the institutional and evolutionary rationality concepts mentioned earlier.

In chapter 4, then, the role of bounded rationality is analyzed specifically in the context of environmental valuation employing the CVM. Earlier, two separate issues were identified to contribute to the observed inconsistencies in CVM responses: preference uncertainty and strategies of limited information processing. In chapter 2 a number of *ad hoc* approaches for dealing with preference uncertainty and deriving adjusted estimates of benefits were presented. However, those approaches do not rest on a well-defined theory of preference uncertainty. Therefore, it is investigated here whether the concept of fuzzy preferences might be suited for taking preference uncertainty into account more appropriately. In the fuzzy preference approach the assertion that one good x is at least as good as a different good y is not necessarily made with certainty but on a continuous scale between 0 and 1 where 0 represents certainty that x is not at least as good as y and 1 represents certainty that x is indeed at least as good as y. Any degree in between represents uncertainty and allows for the case that, instead, y could to some degree be also at least as good as x. Thus, the approach of fuzzy preference relations represents a generalization of the case of full certainty of preferences where the assertions of preference can only carry the values of 0 or 1, i. e. are either true or false.

For fuzzy preferences a set of rationality axioms in analogy to the reflexivity, completeness and transitivity axioms mentioned above exists that allows to describe preference uncertainty by a fuzzy preference ordering. However, the fuzzy preference approach precludes the concept of a utility function and also of the expenditure function from which the traditional measures of economic welfare changes like the Hicksian Compensating Variation (CV) are derived. It was found, therefore, that preference uncertainty cannot be suitably taken into account in environmental valuation by generalizing the preference ordering to be fuzzy. The direct assessment of the degree of preference uncertainty as performed by the *ad hoc* procedures described in chapter 2 is not suited, either, since such statements can hardly be considered to be valid. Instead, an approach to take uncertainty into account more indirectly is suggested here by asking questions that are expected to be closely related to uncertainty but that do prevent respondents from having to admit that they are uncertain. These questions form part of the approach to assess the bounded rationality of respondents.

The empirical part of this study focuses on the investigation of four fundamental research questions relating to the rationality of response behavior in the context of the CVM. First, and most generally, it is to be determined whether a response behavior exhibiting an "economy of cognition", i. e. the use of strategies of limited information processing, is actually observed in CVM responses. In order to answer this question, a suitable instrument for measuring such behavior is needed. Hence, the second research question focuses on the development of empirical instruments to classify strategies of limited information processing and measure the degree to which respondents employ these strategies. Third, the relationship between the use of these strategies and the responses to the WTP elicitation question in a CVM survey is to be analyzed. In this context the tentative hypothesis is made that WTP is positively related to the degree of analytical information processing. This hypothesis is motivated by the fact that often environmental benefits pertain to non-use values and are, thus, not always obvious to average people. Discovering the relevance of such benefits for people's living situations may require rather deep thought processes. Also, it is hypothesized that respondents classified as analytical information processors are less susceptible to produce biased responses since they may be more aware of their preferences. The fourth and final research question aims at deriving recommendations for the improvement of future CVM survey designs based on the results of this empirical survey.

The development of the empirical instruments for measuring the degree of bounded rationality in the practical CVM survey conducted here is based on existing and validated psychological scales regarding individual differences in people's cognitive characteristics. Various psychologists have found individual differences in information processing styles in empirical studies and have developed instruments for an assessment of such differences. One of these instruments, the rational experiential inventory (REI) developed by Epstein et al. (1996) is adopted here from which suitable survey instruments to be included in CVM questionnaires are developed. In the study conducted here, two different but related approaches to measure these cognitive characteristics are taken: the first instrument focuses on the determinations of people's general cognitive dispositions, i. e. their tendencies to employ more intuitive versus more analytical information processing, the second instrument elicits directly whether respondents in the survey have made use of specific strategies of information processing. This instrument also includes two indirect questions concerning preference uncertainty. In order to investigate the hypotheses stated above, therefore, two separate questions are constructed: the task independent question based on the REI for the assessment of cognitive dispositions and the task dependent question for the assessment of specific information processing strategies.

These two separate sets of question items were included in a broad empirical CVM study aiming at an assessment of the economic value of an improvement of tap water and environmental quality in a suburban area in northern Thailand (cf. Ahlheim et al. 2007). The study was conducted in the subproject F1.2 of the Collaborative Research Center (SFB) 564 "Research for Sustainable Land Use and Rural Development in Mountainous Regions of Southeast Asia". Using factor analytical procedures it is found that the respondents of this CVM survey can indeed be classified into different cognitive types of information processing and decision making both on the levels of general cognitive dispositions and of the specific strategies used. It is further shown using the first set of questions developed from the REI and adapted to the context of CVM studies that in addition to the two processing types postulated by the dual-process models the heuristic thinking style can be further divided into three categories: (1) respondents feeling comfortable with relying on their intuitions and experiences (*intuitive-experiential* type), (2) respondents being cautious and feeling uncomfortable when under time pressure (*cautious* type) and (3) respondents with an aversion of effortful information processing in general (*cognitive miser* type). A shortened version of this task independent question based on only 5 items of the original 31-item REI is able to replicate the two-factor structure distinguishing between *intuitive-experiential* and *analytical-rational* information processing styles.

The task dependent set of question items was analyzed separately for the respondents answering the dichotomous choice (DC) question format and for those answering the payment card (PC) format. For the DC respondents a three-factor structure is revealed where the first type of processing and decision making is characterized by feeling uncertain due to limited information and time (*uncertain* type), the second shows a clear tendency for effortful processing making use of the full set of the available scenario information (*analytical* type) and the third seems to rely only on particular pieces of information considered crucial while ignoring the other aspects (*elimination of aspects* type). The dataset of the PC respondents generated a four-factor structure where in addition to the types mentioned above one separate and independent strategy of limited information processing seems to be to attribute equal importance to all elements of the CVM scenario.

As expected a number of systematic relationships between the types of information processing and responses to the WTP question are found, both for the DC and the PC question formats. The *intuitive-experiential* types exhibited a significantly negative effect on stated WTP for both question formats whereas the *analytical-rational* type is significantly positively related with WTP only for the DC format. This finding confirms the expectation stated above. Moreover, the response to the PC elicitation question is significantly negatively related with the *cautious* type which confirms the expectation that respondents feeling uncertain to some extent in a CVM interview tend to choose a lower interval on the payment card. It is rather surprising, however, that no systematic relationships with WTP are found for the task dependent information processing types. It would at least have been expected that an increased feeling of uncertainty as measured by the respective question items would result in lower WTP statements for both question formats. This lack of explanatory power of the task dependent factors is, therefore, rather unexpected and sheds doubt on the validity of those factors.

From these results it can be concluded that the cognitive dispositions of respondents as measured by the measurement instrument of bounded rationality developed here have explanatory power for WTP in addition to the usual socio-economic and attitudinal characteristics of the sample respondents and, therefore, play an important role in this CVM study. A first explanation of the observed significant relationships is that preferences for water quality and environmental goods in this CVM scenario are systematically lower for respondents relying primarily on their intuitions and higher for those approaching decision problems more analytically. The important question, however, is why these preferences regarding environmental goods as assessed by the monetary welfare measure WTP (as an empirically observable approximation of the Hicksian CV) should be lower than average for the intuitive information processors and higher than average for the analytical-rational information processors. This question cannot be answered here conclusively but the observed significant relationships between the cognitive factors and WTP and the lack of significance for many other personal variables that characterize these types of respondents indicates that it is indeed the type of information processing that is responsible for the differences in WTP in this study.

As could be shown, analytical-rational information processing was significantly related to higher levels of education and income, higher approval of tax financing of public goods, also for the environment, a low importance of money and to relatively high degrees of worries regarding public goods. All of these characteristics are expected to be potentially related to an increased WTP, while in this study only the level of education was shown to have significant explanatory power as a single variable. It remains open for debate, however, whether people are better educated and have a higher income, for example, because they show a higher level of analytical skills or vice versa. Nevertheless, a respondent's tendency for analytical information processing seems to subsume all these personal characteristics and, at the same time, shows to be the most powerful explanatory factor for the observed higher WTP. The same argument, albeit pointing to the opposite direction, is true for the intuitive-experiential cognitive factor. Therefore, the *a priori* hypothesis that in this study analytical information processing leads to an increased consciousness of personal relevance of the scenario elements as opposed to more intuitive and thus superficial processing still seems to be a good candidate for explaining the systematic differences in stated WTP between those cognitive types. Further research, however, is needed for a confirmation of this hypothesis in other valuation studies.

Finally, it was investigated whether certain types of information processing are particularly susceptible to procedural biases in CVM like the social desirability effect or the starting point and range biases. However, the prior expectation that higher degrees of dispositions of analytical-rational processing exhibit lower tendencies for the mentioned biases are not confirmed. Instead, it is observed that the more respondents are cautious as classified by the respective factor scale of TIF3 the lower the tendency for a starting point bias in the DC format. This finding provides evidence that the widely found starting point bias in the DC format should not be considered a genuine feature of this question format but that it depends crucially on the cognitive disposition of the respondents. At the same time, however, the hope must be abandoned that the starting point bias in the DC format could be overcome by encouraging respondents to employ more analytical information processing. Respondents' susceptibility to take the starting bid as an anchor point for their WTP response seems, therefore, deeply rooted in their minds. The analogous effect in the PC format, the range bias, could not be detected in this study, not even for the less analytical respondents. These results, therefore, lead to the first recommendation for future CVM surveys to be very careful in using the dichotomous choice elicitation format and only to employ it if it can be assured that respondents are sufficiently certain regarding their preferences for environmental goods. In practice, however, this will rarely be the case so that the payment card format clearly appears to be the format of choice for future CVM surveys.

Furthermore, it is shown that within the task dependent factors the "elimination" type who bases his WTP statement only on the most important pieces of information and neglects the others is particularly susceptible to the social desirability effect, both for the DC and the PC formats. This result is interesting since, as opposed to the starting point bias, the full dataset of DC or PC responses did not show this effect so that the significantly biasing influence of the presence of an interviewer would not have been detected. Analyzing CVM responses w. r. t. cognitive factors, therefore, provides additional information for testing the validity of the responses. From these findings it can be recommended that, whenever possible, the opportunity to provide the WTP statement confidentially should be provided.

In **conclusion**, the research conducted in this study has developed a detailed methodology to analyze respondents' rationality in CVM surveys where the central focus is the type of information processing used in the course of the interviews. This focus which is based on a conceptual framework of modern cognitive psychology allows to assume a more comprehensive perspective on response behavior in environmental valuation interviews than the often adopted concentration on the numerous procedural biases. The systematic relationships between the main cognitive characteristics of respondents and stated WTP highlight the explanatory power of this perspective in this particular empirical CVM study. It is recommended, therefore, that future surveys adopt this methodology for an analysis of boundedly rational information processing. However, for the time being future surveys should focus on the task independent framework for the analysis of bounded rationality of respondents since it was shown that respondents' general cognitive dispositions are decisive for their response behavior. The current version of the task dependent framework, in contrast, produced mostly no or implausible results and needs further refinement in order to be applicable in standard CVM surveys.

The results of this survey in northern Thailand demonstrate that a large part of the respondents conform to the basic assumptions of bounded rationality since strategies of limited information processing were widely adopted for the evaluation of the CVM scenario. It can be concluded, therefore, that full rationality of respondents is mostly not assured in practice. Rather, the results highlight the necessity to take greater efforts to induce respondents to invest more cognitive resources and process the provided information more analytically when evaluating the personal relevance of a CVM scenario. In order to achieve such a deeper evaluation it is proposed here to employ methods of participatory questionnaire design using focus groups or participatory respondent groups. It has already been demonstrated by Ahlheim et al. (2007) that the interaction among respondents of a survey during group sessions lead to an intensive process of information acquisition and evaluation from which highly useful insights for the design of an appropriate valuation scenario can be gained. The results of the present study and the first experiences obtained from the participatory groups stress the necessity to adopt a perspective on rationality that is more in line with the limited way humans actually process information and take decisions. For the design of CVM surveys, especially of the proposed environmental change scenario, more effort must be made to take into account that respondents search for ways to economize on cognitive resources during such interviews. The results obtained using this newly developed methodology for analyzing the consequences of bounded rationality in CVM interviews have pinpointed the key factors that are responsible for the observed shortcomings of CVM response behavior and have shown some first guidelines for their reduction in future environmental valuation surveys.

# 6 References


Abdalla, C.W., Roach, B.A., Epp, D.J. (1992): Valuing environmental quality changes using averting expenditures: An application to groundwater contamination. Land Economics 86, 163-169

Adamowicz, W., Boxall, P., Williams, M., Louviere, J. (1998): Stated preference approaches for measuring passive use values: choice experiments and contingent valuation. American Journal of Agricultural Economics 80, 64-75

Ahlheim, M. (2003): Zur ökonomischen Bewertung von Umweltveränderungen. In: Genser, B. (ed.): Finanzpolitik und Umwelt. Berlin, 9-71

Ahlheim, M. (1998): Contingent valuation and the budget constraint. Ecological Economics 27 (2), 205-211

Ahlheim, M., Buchholz, W. (2000): WTP or WTA - Is that the question? Reflections on the difference between "willingness to pay" and "willingness to accept". Zeitschrift für Umweltpolitik und Umweltrecht, 2/2000, 253-271

Ahlheim, M., Ekasingh, B., Frör, O., Kitchaicharoen, J., Neef, A., Sangkapitux, D., Sinphurmsukskul, N. (2007): Using citizen expert groups in environmental valuation – Lessons from a CVM study in Northern Thailand. Hohenheimer Diskussionsbeiträge 283/2007

Ahlheim, M., Frör, O. (2003): Valuing the non-market production of agriculture. Agrarwirtschaft 52(8), 356-369

Ahlheim, M., Lehr, U. (2001): Household equivalence scales and the assessment of environmental benefits. Discussion paper 1/2001, Faculty of Environmental Sciences and Engineering, Brandenburg Technical University Cottbus

Ahlheim, M., Rose, M. (1989): Messung individueller Wohlfahrt. Springer-Verlag, Berlin

Ahlheim, M., Wagenhals, G. (1988): Exakte Wohlfahrtsmaße in der Nutzen-Kosten-Analyse. Zeitschrift für Wirtschafts- und Sozialwissenschaften 108: 169-193

Akerlof, G.A., Dickens, W.T. (1982): The economic consequences of cognitive dissonance. American Economic Review 72(3), 307-319

Alberini, C., Boyle, K., Welsh, M. (2003): Analysis of contingent valuation data with multiple bids and response options allowing respondents to express uncertainty. Journal of Environmental Economics and Management 45, 40-62

Alberini, A., Chiabai, A. (2005): Urban environmental health and sensitive populations: how much are the Italians willing to pay to reduce their risks? Fondazione Eni Enrico Mattei, Working Papers: 2005:105

Alberini, A., Kanninen, B., Carson, R.T. (1997): Modeling response incentive effects in dichotomous choice contingent valuation data. Land Economics 73(3), 309-324

Allais, M. (1953): Le comportement de l'homme rationnel devant le risque: critique des postulats et axiomes de l'école américaine. Econometrica 21, 502-546

Allport, G. (1954): The nature of prejudice. Addison-Wesley, Reading

Almond, G.A. (1945): The political attitudes of wealth. Journal of Politics 7(3), 213-255

Alvarez-Farizo, B., Hanley, N. (2006): Improving the Process of Valuing Non-market Benefits: Combining Citizens' Juries with Choice Modelling. Land Economics 82(3), 465-478

Anderson, J.R. (2001): Kognitive Psychology. 3rd edition, Spektrum

Anderson, J.R., Lebiere, C. (1998)(eds.): Atomic components of thought. Erlbaum, Mahwah, NJ, USA

Andreoni, J. (1990): Impure altruism and donations to public goods: a theory og warm-glow giving. The Economic Journal 100, 464-477

Andreoni, J. (1989): Giving with impure altruism: applications to charity and ricardian equivalence. Journal of Political Economy 97(6), 447-460

Ariely, D., Loewenstein, G., Prelec, D. (2003): "Coherent arbitrariness": stable demand curves without stable preferences. The Quarterly Journal of Economics, February, 73-105

Arrow, K.J. (1950): A difficulty in the concept of social welfare. Journal of Political Economy 58, 328-346

Arrow, K.J., Fisher, A.C. (1974): Environmental preservation, uncertainty, and irreversibility. Quarterly Journal of Economics 88, 312-319

Arrow, K., Solow, R., Portney, P., Leamer, E., Radner, R., Schuman, H. (1993): Report on the NOAA panel on contingent valuation: natural resource damage assessment under the oil pollution act of 1990, Federal Register 58, 4601-14

Baddeley, A.D. (1986): Working memory. Oxford University Press, Oxford

Baddeley, A.D., Thompson, N., Buchanan, M. (1975): Word length and the structure of short-term memory. Journal of Verbal Learning and Verbal Behavior 14, 575-589

Barbier, E. (1994): Valuing environmental functions: tropical wetlands. Land Economics 70(2), 155-173

Baron, J., Greene, J. (1996): Determinants of insensitivity to quantity in valuations of public goods: contribution, warm glow, budget constraints, availability and prominence. Journal of Experimental Psychology: Applied 2, 107-125

Barreiro, J., Sánchez, M., Viladrich-Grau, M. (2005): How much are people willing to pay for silence? A contingent valuation study. Applied Economics 37, 1233-1246

Barret, C.R., Pattanaik, P.K., Salles, M. (1990): On choosing rationally when preferences are fuzzy. Fuzzy Sets and Systems 34, 197-212

Bartlik, T.J., Smith, V.K. (1987): Urban amenities and public policy. In: Mills, E.S. (ed.): Handbook of Regional and Urban Economics, North-Holland, Amsterdam

Bateman, I.J., Brouwer, R., Georgiou, S., Hanley, N., Machado, F., Mourato, S, Saunders, C. (2005): A 'natural experiment' approach to contingent valuation of private and public UV health risk reduction strategies in low and high risk countries. Environmental and Resource Economics 31, 47-72

Bateman, I.J., Cole, M., Cooper, P., Georgiou, S., Hadley, D., Poe, G.L. (2004a): On visible choice sets and scope sensitivity. Journal of Environmental Economics and Management 47(1), 71-93

Bateman, I.J., Day, B.H., Dupont, D., Georgiou, S., Noceda-Matias, N., Subramanian, L. (2004b): OOH la la: testing the one-and-one-half bound dichotomous choice elicitation method for robustness to anomalies. Applied Environmental Economics Conference 2004, The Royal Society

Bateman, I.J., Willis, K.G. (eds.) (2001): valuing environmental preferences. theory and practice of the contingent valuation method in the US, EU, and developing countries. Oxford University Press, Oxford

Beattie, J., Covey, J., Dolan, P., Hopkins, L., Jones-Lee, M., Loomes, G., Pidgeon, N., Robinson, A., Spencer, A. (1998): On the contingent valuation of safety and the safety of contingent valuation: part 1 – caveat investigator. Journal of Risk and Uncertainty 17, 5-25

Berrens, R.P., Jenkins-Smith, H., Bohara, A.K., Silva, C.L. (2002): Further investigation of voluntary contribution contingent valuation: fair share, time of contribution, and respondent uncertainty. Journal of Environmental Economics and Management 44, 144-168

Bettman, J.R., Luce, A.F., Payne, J.W. (1998): Constructive consumer choice processes. Journal of Consumer Research 25, 187-217

Bishop, R.C., Heberlein, T.A. (1979): Measuring values of extra-market goods: Are indirect measures biased? American Journal of Agricultural Economics 61, 926-930

Blamey, R.K., Bennett, J.W., Morrison, M.D. (1999): Yea-saying in contingent valuation surveys. Land Economics 75(1), 126-141

Blumenschein, K., Johannesson, M., Blomquist, G.C., Liljas, B., O'Conor, R.M. (1998): Experimental results on expressed certainty and hypothetical bias in continent valuation. Southern Economic Journal 65(1), 169-177

Bohm, P. (1972): Estimating demand for public goods: An experiment. European Economic Review 3, 111-130

Boyle, K.J., Johnson, F.R., McCollum, D.W., Desvousges, W.H., Dunford, R.W., Hudson, S.P. (1996): Valuing public goods: discrete versus continuous contingent-valuation responses. Land Economics 72(3), 381-396

Boyle, K.J., MacDonald, H.F., Cheng, H.T., McCollum, D.W. (1998): Bid design and yea saying in single-bounded, dichotomous-choice questions. Land Economics 74 (1), 49-64

Broadbent, D.E. (1958): Perception and communication. Pergamon, New York

Brookshire, D.S., Randall, R., Stoll, J.R. (1980): Valuing increments and decrements in natural resource service flows. American Journal of Agricultural Economics 62, 478-488

Bush, P. (1987): The theory of institutional change. Journal of Economic Issues 21, 1075-1116

Cacioppo, J.T., Petty, R.E., Feinstein, J., Jarvin, W.B.G. (1996): Dispositional differences in cognitive motivation: The life and times of individuals varying in need for cognition. Psychological Bulletin 119, 197-253

Cacioppo, J.T., Petty, R.E. (1982): The Need for Cognition. Journal of Personality and Social Psychology 42(1), 116-131

Cameron, T.A. (2006): Directional heterogeneity in distance profiles in hedonic property value models. Journal of Environmental Economics and Management 51, 26-45

Cameron, T.A.; Shaw, W.D.; Ragland, S.R. (1999): Nonresponse Bias in Mail Survey Data: Salience vs. Endogenous Survey Complexity. In: Herriges, J.A., Kling, C. (eds.): Valuing recreation and the environment: Revealed preference methods in theory and practice, 217-251

Capen, E.C., Clapp, R.V., Campbell, W.M. (1971): Competitive bidding in high-risk situations. Journal of Petroleum Technology 23, 641-653

Carson, R.T. (1997): Contingent Valuation: Theoretical Advances and Empirical Tests since the NOAA Panel. American Agricultural Economics Association 79(5), 1501-1507

Carson, R.T., Flores, N.E., Martin, K.M., Wright, J.L. (1996a): Contingent valuation and revealed preference methodologies: comparing the estimates for quasi-public goods. Land Economics 72, 80-99

Carson, R.T., Hanemann, W.M., Kopp, R.J., Krosnick, J.A., Mitchell, R.C., Presser, S., Ruud, P.A., Smith, V.K. (1996b): Referendum Design and Contingent Valuation: The NOAA Panel's No-Vote Recommendation. Discussion Paper 96-05, Resources for the Future, Washington D.C.

Carthy, T., Chilton, S., Covey, J., Hopkins, L., Jones-Lee, M., Loomes, G., Pidgeon, N., Spencer, A. (1999): On the contingent valuation of safety and the safety of contingent valuation: part 2 – the CV/SG chained approach. Journal of Risk and Uncertainty 17, 187-213

Chaiken, S. (1980): Heuristic versus systematic information processing and the use of source versus message cues in persuasion. Journal of Personality and Social Psychology 39, 752-766

Chaiken, S., Maheswaran, D. (1994): Heuristic processing can bias systematic processing: effects of source credibility, argument ambiguity, and task importance on attitude judgment. Journal of Personality and Social Psychology 66, 460-473

Chaiken, S., Trope, Y. (1999): Dual-process theories in social psychology. Guilfold Press, New York

Champ, P.A., Bishop, R.C. (2006): Is Willingness to Pay for a Public Good Sensitive to the Elicitation Format? Land Economics 82(2), 162-173

Champ, P.A., Bishop, R.C., Brown, T.C., McCollum, D.W. (1997): Using donation mechanisms to value nonuse benefits from public goods. Journal of Environmental Economics and Management 33, 151-162

Chen, S., Chaiken, S. (1999): The Heuristic-Systematic Model in its broader context. In: Chaiken, S., Trope, Y. (eds.): Dual-process theories in social psychology. Guilfold Press, New York, 73-96

Chen, S., Shechter, D., Chaiken, S. (1996): Getting at the truth or getting along: accuracy- vs. impression-motivated heuristic and systematic information processing. Journal of Personality and Social Psychology 71, 262-275

Cherry, T., Shogren, J., Crocker, T.T. (2003): Rationality spillovers. Journal of Environmental Economics and Management 45, 63-84

Ciriacy-Wantrup, S. V. (1947): Capital returns from soil-conservation practices. Journal of Farm Economics 29, 1181-1196

Clawson, M. (1959): Methods of measuring the demand for and value of outdoor recreation. Washington D.C.

Conlisk, J. (1996): Why bounded rationality? Journal of Economic Literature 34, 669-700

Cooper, J.C. (1994): A comparison of approaches to calculating confidence intervals for benefit measures for dichotomous choice contingent valuation surveys. Land Economics 70(1), 111-122

Cooper, J.., Hanemann, M., Signorello, G. (2002): One-and-one-half-bound dichotomous choice contingent valuation. The Review of Economics and Statistics 84(4), 742-750

Cooper, J., Loomis, J. (1993): Sensitivity of willingness-to-pay estimates to bid design in dichotomous choice contingent valuation models: reply. Land Economics 69, 203-208

Cooper, J., Loomis, J. (1992): Sensitivity of willingness-to-pay estimates to bid design in dichotomous choice contingent valuation models. Land Economics 68, 211-224

Costanza, R., d'Arge, R., de Groot, R., Farber, S., Grasso, M., Hannon, B., Limburg, K., Naeem, S., O'Neill, R.V., Paruelo, J., Raskin, R.G., Sutton, P., van den Belt, M. (1998): The value of the world's ecosystem services and natural capital. Ecological Economics 25, 3-15

Craik, G.I.M., Lockhart, R.S. (1972): Levels of processing: a framework for memory research. Journal of Verbal Learning and Verbal Behavior 11, 671-684

Cullis, J., Jones, P. (1998): Public finance and public choice. 2nd edition, Oxford University Press, Oxford

Cummings, R., Brookshire, D., Schulze, W. (1986): Valuing environmental goods: an assessment of the contingent valuation method. Rowman and Allanheld, Totowa

Cummings, R., Taylor, L. (1999): Unbiased value estimates for environmental goods: a cheap talk design for the contingent valuation method. American Economic Review 89, 649-665

Cutler, D.M., Poterba, J.M., Summers, L. (1991): Speculative dynamics. Review of Economic Studies 58(3), 529-546

Dasgupta, M., Deb, R. (1996): Transitivity and fuzzy preferences. Social Choice and Welfare 13, 305-318

Daubert, J.T., Young, R.A. (1981): Recreational Demands for maintaining instream flows: a contingent valuation approach. American Journal of Agricultural Economics 63, 667-676

De Wilde, P. (2003): Fuzzy utility and equilibria. IEEE transactions on systems, man and cybernetics – Part B: Cybernetics

Desvousges, W. H., Johnson, F. R., Dunford, R. W., Boyle, K. J., Hudson, S. P., Wilson, K. N. (1993): Measuring natural resource damages with contingent valuation: tests of validity and reliability. In: Hausman, J. A. (ed.): Contingent valuation: a critical assessment, Amsterdam

DeShazo, J.R. (2002): Designing transactions without framing effects in iterative question formats. Journal of Environmental Economics and Management 43, 360-385

Diamond, P.A., Hausman, J.A., Leonard, G.K., Denning, M.A. (1993): Does contingent valuation measure presferences? In: Hausman, J. A. (ed.): Contingent valuation: a critical assessment, Amsterdam

Dillman, D.A. (1978): Mail and telephone surveys: The Total Design Method. New York

Eichenberger, R. (1992): Verhaltensanomalien und Wirtschaftswissenschaft. Deutscher Universitätsverlag, Wiesbaden

Ellsberg, D. (1961): Risk, ambiguity, and the savage axioms. Quarterly Journal of Economics 75, 528-556

Endres, A., Holm-Müller, K. (1998): Die Bewertung von Umweltschäden. Theorie und Praxis sozioökonomischer Verfahren. Kohlhammer, Stuttgart

Epstein, S. (1985): The implications of cognitive-experiential self-theory for research in social psychology and personality. Journal for the Theory of Social Behaviour 15, 283-310

Epstein, S., Pacini, R. (1999): Some basic issues regarding dual-process theories from the perspective of cognitive-experiential self-theory. In: Chaiken, S., Trope, Y. (eds.): Dual-process theories in social psychology. Guilfold Press, New York, 462-482

Epstein, S., Pacini, R., Denes-Raj, V., Heier, H. (1996): Individual differences in intuitive-experiential and analytical-rational thinking styles. Journal of Personality and Social Psychology 71(2), 390-405

Ethier, R.T., Poe, G.L., Schulze, W.D., Clark, J. (2000): A comparison of hypothetical phone and mail contingent valuation responses for green-pricing electricity programs. Land Economics 76(1), 54-67

Fishburn, P.C. (1991): Nontransitive preferences in decision theory. Journal of Risk and Uncertainty 4, 113-124

Foster, V., Bateman, I., Harley, D. (1997): Real and hypothetical WTP for environmental protection: a non-experimental comparison. Journal of Agricultural Economics 48, 123-138

Foster, V., Mouato, S. (2000): Valuing the multiple impacts of pesticide use in the UK: a contingent ranking approach. Journal of Agricultural Economics 51(1), 1-21

Fox, J., Shogren, J., Hayes, D., Kliebenstein, J. (1998): CVM-X: Calibrating contingent valuations with experimental markets. American Journal of Agricultural Economics 80, 455-465

Frederick, S. (2005): Cognitive reflection and decision making. Journal of Economic Perspectives 19(4), 25-42

Freeman III, A.M. (1993): The measurement of environmental and resource values. Resources for the future, Washington, D.C.

Frew, E.J., Whynes, D.K., Wolstenholme, J.L. (2003): Eliciting willingness to pay: comparing closed-ended with open-ended and payment scale formats. Medical Decision Making, March-April, 150-159

Friedman, M. (1953): Essays in positive economics. University of Chicago Press, Chicago

Fromm, O. (2000): Ecological structure and functions of biodiversity as elements of its total economic value. Environmental and Resource Economics 16, 329-341

Frykblom, P., Shogren, J.F. (2000): An experimental testing of anchoring effects in discrete choice questions. Environmental and Resource Economics 16, 329-341

Garrod, G.D., Willis, K.G. (1997): The non-use benefits of enhancing forest biodiversity: A contingent ranking study. Ecological Economics 21, 45-61

Gilbert, D.T. (1999): What the mind's not. In: Chaiken, S., Trope, Y. (eds.): Dual-process theories in social psychology. Guilfold Press, New York, 3-11

Gilovich, T., Griffin, D., Kahneman, D. (2002): Heuristics and biases. the psychology of intuitive judgment. Cambridge University Press, Cambridge

Glenberg, A.M., Smith, S.M., Green, C. (1977): Type I rehearsal: maintenance and more. Journal of Verbal Learning and Verbal Behavior 16, 339-352

Greene, W.H. (2002): LIMDEP™ Version 8.0 Reference Guide, Econometric Software Inc., Plainview, New York

Grether, D.M. (1992): Testing Bayes rule and the representativeness heuristic: some experimental evidence. Journal of Economic Behavior and Organization 17(1), 31-57

Griffiths, W.E., Hill, R.C., Judge, G.G. (1993): Learning and practicing econometrics. John Wiley & Sons, New York

Haab, T.C., McConnell, K.E. (2002): Valuing environmental and natural resources. Edward Elgar, Cheltenham

Haefele, M.A., Loomis, J.B. (2001): Using the conjoint analysis technique for the estimation of passive use values of forest health. Journal of Forest Economics 7(1), 9-27

Halstead, J.M., Lindsay, B.E., Brown, C.M. (1991): Use of the tobit model in contingent valuation: experimental evidence from the pemigewasset wilderness Area. Journal of Environmental Management 33, 79-89

Handgraaf, M.J.J., van Raaij, W.F. (2005): Fear and loathing no more: The emergence of collaboration between economists and psychologists. Journal of Economic Psychology 26, 387-391

Hanemann, W.M. (1984): Welfare evaluations in contingent valuation experiments with discrete responses. American Journal of Agricultural Economics 66, 332-341

Hanemann, W.M., Kanninen, B. (1999): The statistical analysis of discrete response CV data. In: Bateman, I.J., Willis, K.G. (eds.): Valuing Environmental preferences. theory and practice of the contingent valuation method in the US, EU, and developing countries. Oxford University Press, Oxford, 302-441

Hanemann W.M., Loomis, J., Kanninen B. (1991): Statistical efficiency of double-bounded dichotomus choce contingent valuation. American Journal of Agricultural Economics 73, 1255-1263

Hanley, N., Mourato, S., Wright, R.E. (2001): Choice modelling approaches: a superior alternative for environmental valuation?. Journal of Economic Surveys 15(3), 435-459

Hanley, N., Shogren, J.F. (2005): Is cost-benefit analysis anomaly-proof? Environmental and Resource Economics 32, 13-34

Hanusch, H. (1994): Nutzen-Kosten-Analyse, 2nd edition. Vahlen, München

Hargreaves Heap, S. (1989): Rationality in economics. Blackwell, Oxford

Harrison, G.W. (1992): Valuing public goods with the contingent valuation method: a critique of Kahneman and Knetsch. Journal of Environmental Economics and Management 23, 248-257

Harrison, G., Rutström, E. (1999): Experimental evidence of hypothetical bias in value elicitation methods. Working paper, University of South Carolina

Hausman, J. A. (1993): Contingent valuation: A critical assessment, Amsterdam

Heberlein, T.A., Wilson, M.A., Bishop, R.C., Schaeffer, N.C. (2005): Rethinking the scope test as a criterion for validity in contingent valuation. Journal of Environmental Economics and Management 50, 1-22

Hendricks, K., Porter, R.H., Boudreau, B. (1987): Information, returns, and bidding behavior in OCS auctions: 1954-1969. Journal of Industrial Economics 35, 517-542

Herriges, J.A., Shogren, J.F. (1996): Starting point bias in dichotomous choice valuation with follow-up questioning. Journal of environmental economics and management 30, 112-131

Hicks, J. R. (1942): Consumer's surplus and index numbers.Review of Economic Studies 9, 126-137

Hicks, J. R. (1939): The foundations of welfare economics. Economic Journal 49, 696-712

Hodgson, G. (1994): The return of institutional economics. In: Smelser, N., Swedberg, R. (eds.): The handbook of economic sociology. Princeton University Press, Princeton

Holland, J.H. (1996): The rationality of adaptive agents. In: Arrow, K.J., Colombatto, E., Perlman, M., Schmidt, C. (eds.): The rational foundations of economic behaviour. Proceedings of the IEA conference held in Turin, Italy. St. Martins_ Press, New York, 281-301

Holm-Müller, K. (2003): Bewertung nicht-marktfähiger Leistungen der Landwirtschaft - eine Herausforderung für die Forschung. Agrarwirtschaft 52,353-355

Holmes, T.P., Kramer, R.A. (1995): An independent sample test of yea-saying and starting point bias in dichotomous-choice contingent valuation. Journal of environmental economics and management 29, 121-132

Horowitz, J.L. (1984): Estimating compensating and equivalent income variations from hedonic price models. Economic Letters 14(4), 303-308

Irwin, J.R., Slovic, P., Lichtenstein, S., McClelland, G.H. (1993): Preference reversals and the measurement of environmental values. Journal of Risk and Uncertainty 6, 5-18

Janssen, J., Laatz, W. (2003): Statistische Datenanalyse mit SPSS für Windows. 4th edition, Springer, Heidelberg

Johannesson, M., Liljas, B., Johansson, P.-O. (1998): An experimental comparison of dichotomous choice contingent valuation questions and real purchase decisions. Applied Economics 30, 643-647

Johansson, P.-O. (1994): Valuation and aggregation. In: Pethig, R. (ed.): Valuing the environment: methodological and measurement issues. Kluwer, Dordrecht

Jones-Lee, M., Loomes, G. (1997): Valuing health and safety: some economic and psychological issues. In: Nau, R., Gronn, E., Machina, M., Bergland, O. (eds.): Economic and environmental risk and uncertainty: new models and methods, KluwerAcademic Publishers, Dordrecht

Jones-Lee, M., Loomes, G., O'Reilly, D., Philips, P.R. (1993): The value of preventing non-fatal road injuries: findings of a willingness-to-pay national sample survey. Working Paper WP/SRC/, Transport Research Laboratory, Crowthorne

Kahneman, D., Knetsch, J. (1992): Valuing Public Goods. The Purchase of Moral Satisfaction. Journal of Environmental Economics and Management 22, 57-70

Kahneman, D., Slovic, P., Tversky, A. (1982): Judgment under uncertainty: heuristics and biases. Cambridge University Press, Cambridge

Kahneman, D., Tversky, A. (1979): Prospect theory: an analysis of decision making under risk. Econometrica 47 (2), 263-291

Kanninen, J. (1995): Bias in discrete response contingent valuation. Journal of Environmental Economics and Management 28, 114-125

Kanninen, J. (1993): Optimal experimental design for double-bounded dichotomous choice contingent valuation. Land Economics 69, 138-146

Kanninen, J., Kriström, B. (1993): Sensitivity of willingness-to-pay estimates to bid design in dichotomous choice valuation models: comment. Land Economics 69, 199-202

Karlin, L., Kestenbaum, R. (1968): Effects of the number of alternatives on the psychological refractory period. Quarterly Journal of Experimental Psychology 20, 167-178

Klaes, M., Sent, E.-M. (2005): The emergence of bounded rationality. History of Political Economy 37(1), 27-59

Klir, G.J., Yuan, B. (1995): Fuzzy sets and fuzzy logic: theory and applications. Prentice Hall, Upper Saddle River

Kohlhase, J.E. (1991): The impact of toxic-waste sites on housing values. Journal of Urban Economics 30, 1-26

Kolstad, C.D., Guzman, R.M. (1999): Information and the divergence between willingness to accept and willingness to pay. Journal Environmental Economics and Management 38, 66-80

Krutilla, J. (1967): Conservation reconsidered. American Economics Review 56: 777-786

Krysan, M., Schuman, H., Scott, L.J., Beatty, P. (1994): Response rates and response content in mail versus face-to face surveys. Public Opinion Quarterly 58, 381-399

Lagueux, M. (2004): The forgotten role of the rationality principle in economics. Journal of Economic Methodology 11(1), 31-51

Lancaster, K.J. (1966): A new approach to consumer theory. Journal of Political Economy 74(2), 132-157

Leggett, C.G., Kleckner, N.S., Boyle, K.J., Duffield, J.W., Mitchell, R.C. (2003): Social desirability bias in contingent valuation surveys administered through in-person interviews. Land Economics 79(4), 561-575

Lewbel, A. (1989): Household equivalence scales and welfare comparisons. Journal of Public Economics 39, 377-392

Li, C.-Z., Mattsson, L. (1995): Discrete choice under preference uncertainty: an improved structural model for contingent valuation. Journal of Environmental Economics and Management 28, 256-269

Lichtenstein, S., Slovic, P. (1971): Reversals of preferences between bids and choices in gambling decisions. Journal of Experimental Psychology 101, 16-20

Lipman, B.L. (1991): How to decide how to decide how to...: modeling limited rationality. Econometrica 59(4), 1105-1125

List, J.A. (2002): Preference reversals of a different kind: the "more is less" phenomenon. American Economic Review 92(5), 1636-1643

List, J.A., Shogren, J.F. (2002): Calibration of willingness-to-accept. Journal of Environmental Economics and Management 43, 219-233

Loomis, J., Ekstrand, E. (1998): Alternative approaches for incorporating respondent uncertainty when estimating willingness to pay: the case of the Mexican spotted owl. Ecological Economics 27, 29-41

Loreau, M., Naeem, S., Inchausti, P. (2002): Biodiversity and ecosystem functioning – synthesis and perspectives. Oxford University Press, Oxford

Machina, M. (1987): Choice under uncertainty: problems solved and unsolved. Journal of Economic Perspectives 1, 121-154

Macmillan, D.C., Philip, L., Hanley, N., Alvarez-Farizo, B. (2002): Valuing the non-market benefits of wild goose conservation: a comparison of interview and group-based approaches. Ecological Economics 43, 49-59

Madariaga, B., McConnell, K.E. (1987): Exploring existence value. Water Resources Research 23, 936-942

Maddala, G.S. (1983): Limited dependent and qualitative variables in econometrics. Cambridge

Mäler, K.-G. (1974): Environmental economics: a theoretical inquiry. Baltimore

Marshall, A., (1890): Principles of economics. Macmillan and Company, New York

Mas-Colell, A., Whinston, M.D., Green, J.R. (1995): Microeconomic theory. Oxford University Press, New York

Matthews, S., O'Connor, R., Platinga, A.J. (2002): Quantifying the impacts on biodiversity of policies for carbon sequestration in forests. Ecological Economics 40, 71-87

May, K. (1954): Intransitivity, utility, and the aggregation of preference patterns. Econometrica 22(1), 1-13

McClelland, J.L., Rumelhart, D.E., Hinton, G.E. (1986): The appeal of distributed processing. In: Rumelhart, D.E., McClelland (eds.): Parallel distributed processing: explorations in the microstructure of cognition (vol. 1). MIT Press, Cambridge

McFadden, D. (1974): Conditional logit analysis of qualitative choice behavior. In: Zarembka, P. (ed.): Frontiers in econometrics, economic theory and mathematical economics. Academic Press, New York, 105-142

McFadden, D., Leonard, G.K. (1993): Methodologies for data collection and analysis. In: Hausman, J. A. (ed.): Contingent valuation: A critical assessment, Amsterdam

Medin, D.L., Ross, B.H., Markman, A.B. (2005): Cognitive psychology. Fourth edition. John Wiley & Sons, Hoboken

Menges, R., Schröder, C, Traub, S. (2005): Altruism, warm glow and the willingness to donate for green electricity: an artefactual field experiment. Environmental and Resource Economics 31(4), 431-458

Mitchell, R.C., Carson, R.T. (1989): Using surveys to value public goods: the contingent valuation method. Resources for the Future, Washington, D.C.

Mongin, P., Walliser, B. (1988): Infinite regressions in the optimizing theory of decision. In: Munier, B.R. (ed.): Risk, Decision and Rationality. D. Reidel Publishing, 435-457

Morrison, G.C. (1997): Resolving differences in willingness to pay and willingness to accept: comment. American Economic Review 87(1), 236-240

Moskowitz, G.B., Skurnik, I., Galinsky, A.D. (1999): The history of dual-process notions, and the future of preconscious control. In: Chaiken, S., Trope, Y. (eds.): Dual-process theories in social psychology. Guilfold Press, New York, 12-36

National Oceanic and Atmospheric Administration (NOAA) (1994): Natural resource damage assessments, proposed rules. Federal Register 59, 1062

Neisser, U. (1967): Cognitive psychology. Appleton, New York

Nunes, P.A.L.D. (2002): The contingent valuation of natural parks. assessing the warm-glow propensity factor. Edward Elgar, Cheltenham

Nunes, P.A.L.D., Schokkaert, E. (2003): Identifying the warm glow effect in contingent valuation. Journal of Environmental Economics and Management 45, 231-245

Oakley, H.D. (1922): On the meaning of value. Philosophical Review 31(5), 431-448

Ott, N. (2001): Unsicherheit, Unschärfe und rationales Entscheiden: die Anwendung von Fuzzy-Methoden in der Entscheidungstheorie. Physica-Verlag, Heidelberg

Ovchinnikov, S. (1981): Structure of fuzzy binary relations. Fuzzy Sets and Systems 6, 169-195

Ovchinnikov, S., Roubens, M. (1992): On fuzzy strict preference, indifference, and incomparability relations. Fuzzy Sets and Systems 49, 15-20

Paivio, A. (1986): Mental representations: a dual coding approach. Oxford University Press, New York

Palmquist, R.B. (2004): Property value models. In: Maler, K.-G., Vincent, J. (eds.): Handbook of environmental economics, vol. 2, valuing environmental changes, North-Holland, Elsevier

Palmquist, R.B. (1991): Hedonic methods In: Braden, J.B., Kolstad, C.D. (eds.): Measuring the demand for environmental quality. Amsterdam, 77-120

Park, T., Loomis, J., Creel, M. (1991): Confidence intervals for evaluating benefits estimates from dichotomous choice contingent valuation studies. Land Economics 67 (1), 64-73

Pashler, H.E. (1998): The psychology of attention. MIT, Cambridge

Payne, J.W., Bettman, J.R., Johnson, E.J. (1993): The adaptive decision maker. Cambridge University Press, Cambridge

Payne, J.W., Bettman, J.R., Johnson, E.J. (1992): Behavioral decision research: a constructive processing perspective. Annual Reviews Psychology 43, 87-131

Payne, J.W., Schkade, D.A. (1999): Measuring constructed preferences: towards a building code. Journal of Risk and Uncertainty 19(1-3), 243-270

Petty, R.E. (1977): A cognitive response analysis of the temporal persistence of attitude changes induces by persuasive communications. Unpublished doctoral dissertation. Ohio State University

Petty, R.E., Wegener, D.T. (1999): The Elaboration Likelihood Model: current status and controversies. In: Chaiken, S., Trope, Y. (eds.): Dual-process theories in social psychology. Guilfold Press, New York, 41-72

Philip, L.J., Macmillan, D.C. (2005): Exploring values, context and perceptions in contingent valuation studies: The CV market stall technique and willingness to pay for wildlife conservation. Journal of Environmental Planning and Management 48(2), 257-274

Pingle, M., Day, R.H. (1996): Modes of economizing behavior: experimental evidence. Journal of Economic Behavior and Organization 29, 191-209

Polome, P., van der Veen, A., Geurts, P. (2006): Is Referendum the Same as Dichotomous Choice Contingent Valuation? Land Economics 82(2), 174-188

Powe, N. A., Garrod, G.D., McMahon, P.L. (2005): Mixing Methods within Stated Preference Environmental Valuation: Choice Experiments and Post-Questionnaire Qualitative Analysis. Ecological Economics 52(4), 513-526

Ramirez, O.A., Carpio, C.E., Ortiz, R., Finnegan, B. (2002): Economic value of the carbon sink services of tropical secondary forests and its management implications. Environmental and Resource Economics 21, 23-46

Randall, A., Hoehn, J.P. (1996): Embedding in market demand systems. Journal of Environmental Economics and Management 30, 369-380

Ready, R.C., Buzby, J.C., Hu, D. (1996): Differences between continuous and discrete contingent value estimates. Land Economics 72(3), 397-411

Ready, R.C., Whitehead, J.C., Blomquist, G.C. (1995): Contingent valuation when respondents are ambivalent. Journal of Environmental Economics and Management 29, 181-196

Redmond, W.H. (2004): On institutional rationality. Journal of Economic Issues 38(1), 173-188

Rieskamp, J., Busemeyer, J.R., Mellers, B.A. (2006): Extending the bounds of rationality: evidence and theories of preferential choice. Journal of Economic Literature XLIV, 631-661

Ridker, R.G. (1967): Economic costs of air pollution: studies in measurement. Praeger, New York

Rohracher, H. (1984): Einführung in die Psychologie. 12th edition. Urban & Schwarzenberg, Munich

Rosen, H.S. (1974): Hedonic prices and implicit markets: product differentiation in pure competition. Journal of Political Economy 82, 34-55

Rosenberg, A. (1992): Economics – Mathematical politics or science of diminishing returns? The University of Chicago Press, Chicago

Rowe, R.D., Schulze, W.D., Breffle, W.S. (1996): A test for payment card biases. Journal of Environmental Economics and Management 31, 178-185

Ryan, M., Scott, D.A., Donaldson, C. (2004): Valuing health care using willingness to pay: a comparison of the payment card and dichotomous choice methods. Journal of Health Economics 23, 237-258

Safra, Z., Segal, U., Spivak, A.A. (1990): Preference reversal and nonexpected utility behavior. American Economic Review 80(4), 922-930

Salles, M. (1998): Fuzzy utility. In: Barberà, S.; Hammond, P.J.; Seidl, C.(eds.): Handbook of utility theory, Volume 1. Kluwer, Boston, 321-343

Samnaliev, M., Stevens, T.H., More, T. (2006): A comparison of alternative certainty calibration techniques in contingent valuation. Ecological Economics 57, 507-519

Schkade, D.A., Payne, J.W. (1994): How people respond to contingent valuation questions: a verbal protocol analysis of willingness to pay for an environmental regulation. Journal of Environmental Economics and Management 26, 88-109

Schmidt, U., Stramer, C., Sugden, R. (forthcoming): Prospect theory can explain preference reversal. Discussion paper, University of Hannover

Seidl, C. (2001): Preference reversal. Journal of Economic Surveys 16(5), 621-655

Shanks, D.R., Tunney, R.J., McCarthy, J.D. (2002): A re-examination of probability matching and rational choice. Journal of Behavioral Decision Making 15, 233-250

Shephard, R.N. (1967): Recognition memory for words, sentences, and pictures. Journal of Verbal Learning and Verbal Behavior 6, 156-163

Shogren, J.F., Shin, S.Y., Hayes, D.J., Kliebenstein, J.B. (1994): Resolving differences in willingness to pay and willingness to accept. American Economic Review 84(1), 255-270

Silberberg, E. (1990): The structure of economics. A mathematical analysis. McGraw-Hill, New York

Simon, H.A. (1999): Interview with Herbert A. Simon. Working paper, CISTEMA, Copenhagen Business School

Simon, H.A. (1997): Rationality in decision making. Herbert A. Simon, an empirically based microeconomics. Raffaele Mattioli Lectures, Cambridge University Press

Simon, H.A. (1987): Bounded rationality. In: Eatwell, J., Milgate, M., Newman, P. (eds.): The New Palgrave Dictionary of Economics. Macmillan, London

Simon, H.A. (1957): Models of man. Social and rational. Fifth printing 1967. Wiley and Sons, New York

Simon, H.A. (1955): A behavioral model of rational choice. Quarterly Journal of Economics 69, 99-118

Sloman, S.A. (2002): Two systems of reasoning. In: Gilovich, T., Griffin, D., Kahneman, D. (eds.): Heuristics and biases. the psychology of intuitive judgment, 379-396. Cambridge University Press, Cambridge

Slonim, R. (1994): Learning in a search-for-the-best-alternative experiment. Journal of Economic Behavior and Organization 25(2), 141-165

Smith, A. (1993): An inquiry into the nature and causes of the wealth of nations. A selected edition, original publication in 1776. Oxford University Press, Oxford

Smith, V.K., Desvousges, W.H., McGivney, M.P. (1983): Estimating water quality benefits: an econometric analysis. Southern Economic Journal 50(2), 422-437

Smith, V.L. (2003): Constructivist and ecological rationality in economics. American Economic Review 93(3), 465-508

Standing, L. (1973): Learning 10,000 pictures. Quarterly Journal of Experimental Psychology 25, 207-222

Stephan, G., Ahlheim , M. (1996): Ökonomische Ökologie. Springer, Berlin

Sternberg, S. (1966): High-speed scanning in human memory. Science 153, 652-654

Stevens, T.H., Barrett, C., Willis, C.E. (1997): Conjoint analysis of groundwater protection programs. Agricultural and Resource Economics Review 26(2), 229-236

Sugden, R. (2005): Anomalies and stated preference techniques: a framework for a discussion of coping strategies. Environmental and Resource Economics 32, 1-12

Sugden, R. (1999): Alternatives to the neo-classical theory of choice. In: Bateman, I.J., Willis, K. (eds.): Valuing Environmental preferences: theory and practice of the contingent valuation method. Oxford University Press, Oxford

Sunstein, C. (2002): Risk and reason. Cambridge University Press, New York

Taylor, S.E. (1981): The interface of cognitive and social psychology. In: Harvey, J.H. (ed.): Cognition, social behavior, and the environment, 189-211. Erlbaum, Hillsdale

Thaler, R.H. (1992): The winner's curse. paradoxes and anomalies of economic life. Princeton University Press, Princeton

Tetlock, P.E. (1985): Accountability: the neglected social context of judgment and choice. Research in Organizational Behavior 7, 297-332

Tobin, J. (1958): Estimation of relationships for limited dependent variables. Econometrica 26, 24-36

Todd, P.M., Gigerenzer, G. (2003): Bounding rationality to the world. Journal of Economic Psychology 24, 143-165

Tversky, A. (1969): Intransitivity of preferences. Psychological Review 76, 31-48

Tversky, A., Kahneman, D. (1974): Judgment under uncertainty: heuristics and biases. Science 185, 1124-1131

Ulich, D., Bösel, R.M. (2005): Einführung in die Psychologie. Grundriss der Psychologie Bd. 2, 4th edition, Kohlhammer Urban, Stuttgart

Um, M.J., Kwak, S.J., Kim, T.Y. (2002): Estimating willingness to pay for improved drinking water quality using averting behavior method with perception measures. Environmental and Resource Economics 21, 287-302

Vanberg, V.J. (2004): The Rationality Postulate in Economics: its Ambiguity, its Deficiency and its Evolutionary Alternative. Journal of Economic Methodology, 11(1), 1-29

Vartia, Y.O. (1983): Efficient methods of measuring welfare changes and compensated income in terms of ordinary demand functions. Econometrica 51, 79-98

Veisten, K, Hoen, H.F., Strand, J. (2004): Sequencing and the adding-up property in contingent valuation of endangered species: are contingent non-use values economic values? Environmental and Resource Economics 29, 419-433

von Hayek, F. (1973): Law, legislation, and liberty. University of Chicago Press, Chicago

von Hayek, F. (1967): Studies in philosophy, politics and economics. University of Chicago Press, Chicago

Wang, H. (1997): Treatment of "Don't -Know" Responses in Contingent Valuation Surveys: A Random Valuation Model. Journal of Environmental Economics and Management 32, 219-232

Watson, J.B. (1968): Behaviorismus. Kipenheuer & Witsch, Köln

Waugh, N.C., Norman, D.A. (1965): Primary memory. Psychological Review 72, 89-104

Weisbrod, B.A. (1964): Collective-consumption services of individual-consumption goods. Quarterly Journal of Economics 78, 471-477

Welsh, M.P., Poe, G.L. (1998): Elicitation effects in contingent valuation: comparisons to a multiple bounded discrete choice approach. Journal of Environmental Economics and Management 36, 170-185

Wertheimer, M. (1971): Kurze Geschichte der Psychologie. Piper, München

Winter, S.G. (1971): Satisficing, selection, and the innovating remnant. Quarterly Journal of Economics 85(2), 237-261

Whitehead, J.C., Groothuis, P.A., Blomquist, G.C. (1993): Testing for non-response and sample selection bias in contingent valuation. Economics Letters 41, 215-220

Whynes, D.K., Wolstenholme, J.L., Frew, E. (2004): Evidence of range bias in contingent valuation payment scales. Health Economics 13, 183-190

Zadeh, L.A. (1965): Fuzzy sets. Information and Control 8, 338-358

Zaichkowsky, J.L. (1985) Measuring the involvement construct. Journal of Consumer Research 12, 341-352

Zimmermann, H.-J. (1996): Fuzzy set theory – and its applications. 3rd edition. Kluwer Academic Publishers, Boston

# 7 Appendix

## 7.1 Survey questionnaire

**Economic benefits of an improvement of the Mae Rim tap water supply**

**Sawwadee krab/kah!**

*INT: Please start the interview with an open conversation with the respondent. In this conversation, please introduce yourself and, at the appropriate situation in the conversation, mention all the information given in the following text to the respondent. You may either read the text exactly as given to the respondent, or you may use this information in an open conversation:*

*"Chiang Mai University and the University of Hohenheim in Germany are doing research together with the Mae Rim Water Works to examine the possibilities for an improvement of the water supply in Mae Rim. This survey serves to explore the possibilities and the wishes of the population regarding such an improvement. Your household has been randomly selected out of all the customers of the Water Works. We kindly ask you to answer the following questions so that your opinion can contribute to build a better tap water supply system in this region. This interview will last approximately 20 minutes."*

| | | | | | *Next* |
|---|---|---|---|---|---|
| | **First, we would like to ask you some general questions regarding your daily water use.** | | | | |
| 1-1 | **For which purposes do you use the water from the Mae Rim Water Works?** | | | | |
| | *INT.: Please check one number per line.* | | Yes | No | |
| | A | Bathing | 01 | 02 | |
| | B | Dish washing | 01 | 02 | |
| | C | Laundering | 01 | 02 | |
| | D | House-cleaning | 01 | 02 | |
| | E | Gardening | 01 | 02 | |
| | F | Car washing | 01 | 02 | |
| | G | Cooking | 01 | 02 | |
| | H | Drinking | 01 | 02 | if "no": 1-2 |
| | I | Do you treat the water before drinking? | 01 | 02 | if "no": 1-2 |
| | How do you treat it? | | | | |

| | | | | | |
|---|---|---|---|---|---|
| | J | By filtering | 01 | 02 | |
| | K | By boiling | 01 | 02 | |
| | L | By adding chemicals | 01 | 02 | |

| | | |
|---|---|---|
| 1-2 | **For how many years have you been connected to the water system of the Mae Rim Water Works?** [ ][ ] years | |
| 1-3 | **Do you experience problems with the MRWW system like e. g. low pressure, interruption of water supply for several hours per day or for entire days? Please specify with the help of the scale how frequently each of these problems occurs.** | |

| | *INT.: Please present the scale and check one number per line.* | never 1 | rarely 2 | some-times 3 | often 4 | very often 5 |
|---|---|---|---|---|---|---|
| A | Low pressure | 1 | 2 | 3 | 4 | 5 |
| B | Interruption of water supply for several hours per day | 1 | 2 | 3 | 4 | 5 |
| C | Interruption of water supply for entire days | 1 | 2 | 3 | 4 | 5 |

| | | | |
|---|---|---|---|
| 1-4 | **What is your average monthly water bill for the water delivered by the Mae Rim Water Works?** | [ ][ ][ ][ ] Baht | |
| 1-5 | **Do you also have a village water system in your village?** | Yes .......... 01<br>No .......... 02 | <br>1-10 |
| 1-6 | **Are you connected to this village water system?** | Yes ........... 01<br>No ........... 02 | <br>1-10 |
| 1-7 | **For which purposes do you use the water from the village water system?** | | |

| | *INT.: Please check one number per line.* | Yes | No | |
|---|---|---|---|---|
| A | Bathing | 01 | 02 | |
| B | Dish washing | 01 | 02 | |
| C | Laundering | 01 | 02 | |
| D | House-cleaning | 01 | 02 | |
| E | Gardening | 01 | 02 | |
| F | Car washing | 01 | 02 | |
| G | Cooking | 01 | 02 | |
| H | Drinking | 01 | 02 | if "no": 1-8 |

| | | | | | |
|---|---|---|---|---|---|
| | I | Do you treat the water before drinking? | 01 | 02 | if "no" : 1-8 |
| | How do you treat it? | | | | |
| | J | By filtering | 01 | 02 | |
| | K | By boiling | 01 | 02 | |
| | L | By adding chemicals | 01 | 02 | |
| 1-8 | **What is your average monthly water bill for the village water system?** | | ☐☐☐☐ Baht | | |
| 1-9 | **For how many years have you been connected to the village water system?** | | ☐☐ years | | |
| 1-10 | **Do you have installed a water supply system of your own which you use, for example a ground water well or pump etc.** | | Yes ......... 01<br>No ......... 02 | | 1-13 |
| 1-11 | **For which purposes do you use the water from your own water system?** | | | | |
| | *INT.: Please check one number per line.* | | Yes | No | |
| | A | Bathing | 01 | 02 | |
| | B | Dish washing | 01 | 02 | |
| | C | Laundering | 01 | 02 | |
| | D | House-cleaning | 01 | 02 | |
| | E | Gardening | 01 | 02 | |
| | F | Car washing | 01 | 02 | |
| | G | Cooking | 01 | 02 | |
| | H | Drinking | 01 | 02 | if "no": 1-12 |
| | I | Do you treat the water before drinking? | 01 | 02 | if "no": 1-12 |
| | How do you treat it? | | | | |
| | J | By filtering | 01 | 02 | |
| | K | By boiling | 01 | 02 | |
| | L | By adding chemicals | 01 | 02 | |
| 1-12 | **How many years ago have you established your own water system?** | | ☐☐ years ago | | |

| | | | |
|---|---|---|---|
| 1-13 | **Do you have installed a water storage tank system?** | Yes ..................... 01<br>No ..................... 02 | |
| 2 | **Now let's talk about your drinking water.** | | |
| 2-1 | **Which is the primary source of drinking water in your house or apartment?**<br><br>*INT: Please check only one of the possibilities.* | MRWW water.................................. 01<br>Village water system ....................... 02<br>Own system ................................. 03<br>Bottled water delivered to your house/apt. ..................................... 04<br>Bottled water bought in the store ....... 05<br>Other ............................................ 06<br><br>Which?________________ | <br>3-1<br>3-1<br>3-1<br>3-1<br>3-1 |
| 2-2 | **What are the reasons for choosing your primary source of drinking water? Please select up to three most important reasons for your choice.** | | 3-3 |

| | *INT.: Please present list and check the stated reasons, three at most!.* | X |
|---|---|---|
| A | All other sources are hazardous to my health. | |
| B | It has the best quality. | |
| C | It tastes better than the others. | |
| D | It is the cheapest source. | |
| E | It is more convenient than the other sources. | |
| F | I have always used this source. | |

| | | | |
|---|---|---|---|
| 3-1 | **How would you characterize the quality of the drinking water from your primary source? Please specify with the help of the scale.**<br><br>*INT: if the respondent doesn't know, circle "6"* | very poor ................... 01<br>poor ........................ 02<br>just o.k. ................... 03<br>good ........................ 04<br>excellent ................... 05<br>do not know............. 06 | |

| | | | |
|---|---|---|---|
| 3-2 | **What are the reasons for choosing your primary source of drinking water? Please select up to three most important reasons for your choice.** *INT.: Please present list and check the stated reasons, three at most!.* | X | |
| | A All other sources are hazardous to my health. | | |
| | B It has the best quality. | | |
| | C It tastes better than the others. | | |
| | D It is the cheapest source. | | |
| | E It is more convenient than the other sources. | | |
| | F I have always used this source. | | |
| 3-3 | **How much money do you spend on average per month on bottled drinking water?** | [ ][ ][ ][ ] Baht | |
| 4 | **Now we would like to talk about the MRWW service and the water quality** | | |
| 4-1 | **How would you characterize the service of the MRWW, for example the response to complaints and problems, promptness of repairs and so on? Please specify with the help of the scale.** | very poor .................. 01<br>poor ........................ 02<br>just o.k. .................. 03<br>good ........................ 04<br>excellent .................. 05 | |
| 4-2 | **How would you characterize the overall quality of the water of the MRWW water system? Please specify with the help of the scale.** *INT.: if the respondent doesn't know, circle "6"* | very poor .................. 01<br>poor ........................ 02<br>just o.k. .................. 03<br>good ........................ 04<br>excellent .................. 05<br>do not know .............. 06 | |
| 4-3 | **Have you ever drunk the MRWW water?** | Yes ......................... 01<br>No .......................... 02 | |

| | | | | | | | | |
|---|---|---|---|---|---|---|---|---|
| 4-4 | **We would like to know your opinion regarding some specific characteristics of MRWW water. When you currently think about drinking the MRWW water how worried are you about these characteristics using the following scale?** | | | | | | | |
| | *INT.: Please present the scale and check one number per line.* | | not worried at all<br>1 | little worried<br>2 | some-times worried<br>3 | quite worried<br>4 | very worried<br>5 | |
| | A | Taste | 1 | 2 | 3 | 4 | 5 | |
| | B | Color | 1 | 2 | 3 | 4 | 5 | |
| | C | Odor | 1 | 2 | 3 | 4 | 5 | |
| 4-5 | **When you currently think about drinking the MRWW water how worried are you about getting the following diseases?** | | | | | | | |
| | *INT.: Please present the scale and check one number per line.* | | not worried at all<br>1 | little worried<br>2 | some-times worried<br>3 | quite worried<br>4 | very worried<br>5 | |
| | A | Diarrhea | 1 | 2 | 3 | 4 | 5 | |
| | B | Kidney stones | 1 | 2 | 3 | 4 | 5 | |
| | C | Cancer | 1 | 2 | 3 | 4 | 5 | |
| 4-6 | **Have you or has somebody in your family ever become ill from the MRWW water?** | | | | | Yes ..................... 01<br>No ..................... 02 | | |

Chiang Mai University, the University of Hohenheim and the Mae Rim Water Works MRWW are currently surveying water users' interests in the program "Drinkable Tap Water-Clean Stream".

What is the idea of the program?

The idea is that all MRWW customers should enjoy an uninterrupted supply of tap water which is also drinkable.

How can this idea be achieved, what needs to be done?

"Drinkable Tap Water-Clean Stream" consists of two main programs which are the improvement of the MRWW distribution system and an improvement of upstream water quality as the source of the MRWW water. *INT.: Show photograph card (see below)*

Why are these improvements necessary?

An improvement of the MRWW distribution system is necessary because of frequent pollution with biological pollutants in the area due to broken pipes in the distribution system. Biological pollutants might cause diarrhea or other diseases. The broken pipes are also responsible for frequent interruptions of water service which occur in some parts of Mae Rim.

An improvement of upstream water quality is necessary to ensure that MRWW receives good water for treatment and distribution to the households. There are two main problems regarding the upstream water quality: the first is the red color of the water which occurs often in the rainy season and the second is the contamination with pesticides which might lead to severe health damages like for example cancer. The red color of the water is caused by soil erosion in the uplands of the Mae Sa valley. Pesticides in the water are an immediate consequence of their high use in the uplands of the Mae Sa valley. As you can see from this map, your tap water originates exclusively from the rivers of the Mae Sa valley. *INT.: Show map of the watershed (see below)*

How is the program implemented?

The program "Drinkable Tap Water-Clean Stream" should be implemented in the following way: First, the pipe system should be mended and maintained so that biological pollution and interruption of water supply would stop. Second, an effective soil conservation program should be implemented so that soil erosion would be stopped in the uplands. Third, pesticide use in the uplands should be reduced for example by employing a more adapted and targeted pest control system.

Who will carry out the proposed measures?

MRWW will carry out the improvements of the water distribution system. Chiang Mai University will carry out the measures that lead to an improvement of upstream water quality. This will be done in cooperation with the upstream communities and farmers.

Do only MRWW water users benefit from the program?

If these proposed measures were carried out benefits for the whole population of Mae Rim would result. For example, this program would also reduce the contamination of fruits and vegetables with pesticides. Also, the accumulation of pesticides in the surrounding ecosystems would be stopped so that future harm to plant and animal life will be prevented and the health of future generations will not be threatened by these pesticides. Therefore, from the proposed measures the whole population of Mae Rim and future generations in this area would benefit.

Who will guarantee that the program really works out?

MRWW will test the tap water quality regularly at the households and will post the test results immediately in each affected community of Mae Rim. There will be a responsible person at MRWW that you can contact for any questions and problems you might have regarding the tap water supply.

**Scenario brochure:** **photograph card given to respondents during scenario presentation, translation from Thai language**

## Drinkable Tap Water - Clean Stream

Broken pipes in the MRWW water distribution system frequently cause pollution with biological pollutants in the area. Biological pollutants can cause diarrhea or other diseases. The broken pipes are also responsible for frequent interruptions of water service which occur in some parts of Mae Rim. Therefore, it is necessary to **repair and improve the MRWW water distribution system.**

The red color of the tap water often occurs in the rainy season. It is caused by soil erosion in the uplands of the Mae Sa valley. The Mae Sa river transports the red soil particles in the water to Mae Rim where it affects the color of your tap water. Therefore, it is necessary to reduce soil erosion in order to **improve upstream water quality** so that a good quality of tap water in the downstream areas of Mae Rim is ensured.

Pesticides in the water are an immediate consequence of their high use in the uplands of the Mae Sa valley. Contamination of the tap water with pesticides might lead to severe health damages like for example cancer. **An improvement of upstream water quality** will also ensure the reduction of pesticide contamination in the tap water.

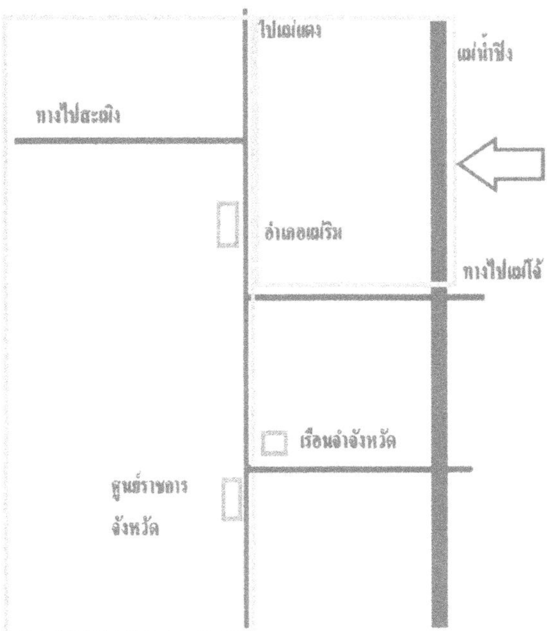


On this map the area marked with light gray lines are those areas where water from the Mae Sa river is used for household tap water. As you can see your household's tap water **originates exclusively from the rivers of the Mae Sa valley** and, therefore, your tap water is influenced by the effects of soil erosion and pesticide application mentioned above.

| 5 | Now we would like to know how important the elements of the described program are for yourself. Please answer the following questions using the scale. | | | | | | |
|---|---|---|---|---|---|---|---|
| | *INT.: Please present the scale and check one number per line.* | | not important at all<br>1 | not so important<br>2 | fairly important<br>3 | important<br>4 | very important<br>5 |
| | A | no interruptions of water service | 1 | 2 | 3 | 4 | 5 |
| | B | no biological pollutants in the tap water | 1 | 2 | 3 | 4 | 5 |
| | C | no pesticides in the tap water | 1 | 2 | 3 | 4 | 5 |
| | D | clear color of the water | 1 | 2 | 3 | 4 | 5 |
| | E | less soil degradation in the uplands | 1 | 2 | 3 | 4 | 5 |
| | F | no accumulation of pesticides in the ecosystems | 1 | 2 | 3 | 4 | 5 |
| | G | less pesticides in fruits and vegetables | 1 | 2 | 3 | 4 | 5 |
| | H | reduced health threats for future generations | 1 | 2 | 3 | 4 | 5 |

**WTP Elicitation question**

**Note:** Four different versions of the WTP elicitation question are presented here, the versions are used alternatively in the interviews. For the bid design in the DC question format and the two different PC bid ranges see table 7-1.

**Version 1: Dichotomous Choice question format (non-anonymous)**

| | | | |
|---|---|---|---|
| 6a | **Since these measures are costly their financing has to be secured before such a program can be implemented. Therefore, it is intended to increase the water fee for the tap water supply for the next five years to get the program started.**<br>**If, as a consequence, your water bill increased by altogether 50 Baht per month for the next five years, would you support this program?** | Yes ............ 01<br>No ............. 02<br>.................. *(other)* | 7<br>6b<br>7 |

| | | | |
|---|---|---|---|
| 6b | **If instead the monthly water bill increased by only 25 Baht, would you then be willing to support this program?** | Yes ............ 01<br>No ............. 02 | |

## Version 2: Dichotomous Choice question format (anonymous)

| | | |
|---|---|---|
| 6a | **Since these measures are costly their financing has to be secured before such a program can be implemented. Therefore, it is intended to increase the water fee for the tap water supply for the next five years to get the program started.**<br>**I will now give you a sheet of paper so that you can answer the following question anonymously, just like in an election. When you have marked your answer, please fold it and put it into this box.**<br>*(INT: Hand the respondent sheet for question 6a)*<br>**The question reads as follows: If, as a consequence, your water bill increased by altogether 50 Baht per month for the next five years, would you support this program?** | Y<br>N |
| 6b | **Here is a second sheet with another question that I am supposed to give you.**<br>*(INT: Hand the respondent sheet for question 6b)*<br>**The question you are asked to answer is:**<br>**If instead the monthly water bill increased by only 25 Baht, would you then be willing to support this program? Please check "Yes" or "No" and put the sheet into this box.**<br>**Of course, if you have already answered "Yes" in the previous question, then just check "Yes" again.** | Y<br>N |

## Version 3: Payment Card question format (non-anonymous)

| | | |
|---|---|---|
| 6 | **Since these measures are costly their financing has to be secured before such a program can be implemented. Therefore, it is intended to increase the water fee for the tap water supply for the next five years to get the program started.**<br>**We would now like to ask you how much money your household would be willing to contribute to the program. Please, select from the following list the highest increase in your monthly water bill you would be willing to tolerate for the next five years if the improvements described above were realized.** | |

### Version 4: Payment Card question format (anonymous)

| | | |
|---|---|---|
| 6 | **Since these measures are costly their financing has to be secured before such a program can be implemented. Therefore, it is intended to increase the water fee for the tap water supply for the next five years to get the program started.**<br><br>**We would now like to ask you how much money your household would be willing to contribute to the program. I will now give you a sheet of paper so that your choice is kept completely confidential.**<br><br>**Please, select from the list on the sheet the highest increase in your monthly water bill you would be willing to tolerate for the next five years if the described improvements were realized.**<br><br>**When you have marked your answer, please fold it and put it into this box.** | |

### Payment Card bid intervals (large version)

| | | | | | |
|---|---|---|---|---|---|
| A | 0 Baht | J | 61 – 70 Baht | S | 281 – 340 Baht |
| B | 1 – 5 Baht | K | 71 – 85 Baht | T | 341 – 400 Baht |
| C | 6 – 10 Baht | L | 86 – 100 Baht | U | 401 – 470 Baht |
| D | 11 – 15 Baht | M | 101 – 120 Baht | V | 471 – 550 Baht |
| E | 16 – 20 Baht | N | 121 – 150 Baht | W | 551 – 700 Baht |
| F | 21 – 35 Baht | O | 151 – 180 Baht | X | 701 – 1000 Baht |
| G | 36 – 40 Baht | P | 181 – 210 Baht | Y | 1001 – 1400 Baht |
| H | 41 – 50 Baht | Q | 211 – 240 Baht | Z | 1401 – 2000 Baht |
| I | 51 – 60 Baht | R | 241 – 280 Baht | AA | greater 2000 Baht |

| | | | |
|---|---|---|---|
| 7 | **Did you find it difficult to make a decision about your contribution to the improvements?**<br><br>**Please give your answers using the following scale.**<br><br>*INT.: Please present the scale.* | very easy .......................... 01<br>quite easy ........................ 02<br>neutral ............................ 03<br>difficult ........................... 04<br>very difficult ..................... 05 | |

| 8 | **How true are the following considerations with respect to your decision on the amount to contribute to the improvements of tap water supply? Please give your answer using the scale.** | | | | | | |
|---|---|---|---|---|---|---|---|
| | *INT.: Please present the scale and check one number per line.* | | not true at all<br>1 | mostly not true<br>2 | partly true<br>3 | mostly true<br>4 | fully true<br>5 |
| | A | I will be able to save money since I don't have to buy bottled water or to use the water filter any more. | 1 | 2 | 3 | 4 | 5 |
| | B | It is more convenient to get all my water from the tap. | 1 | 2 | 3 | 4 | 5 |
| | C | My household will not run the risk of becoming ill from the tap water any more. | 1 | 2 | 3 | 4 | 5 |
| | D | I want to contribute to reduced the health risk to the whole population of Mae Rim. | 1 | 2 | 3 | 4 | 5 |
| | E | I never felt at ease with the red color of the tap water and want to contribute to stop it. | 1 | 2 | 3 | 4 | 5 |
| | F | It gives me a good feeling to know that future generations will live in a healthier environment. | 1 | 2 | 3 | 4 | 5 |
| | G | I would like to pay more for this improvement but I cannot afford it. | 1 | 2 | 3 | 4 | 5 |
| | H | I have severe doubts that these improvements can be realized as described. | 1 | 2 | 3 | 4 | 5 |
| | I | I think government is responsible for such a program and should pay for it. | 1 | 2 | 3 | 4 | 5 |
| | J | My water costs are already high enough. We should receive the good quality service without additional costs. | 1 | 2 | 3 | 4 | 5 |

| 9 | **We would like to know how you reached your decision. How true are the following statements regarding your personal attitude? Please give your answers using the following scale.** | | | | | | |
|---|---|---|---|---|---|---|---|
| | *INT.: Please present the scale and check one number per line.* | | not true at all<br>1 | mostly not true<br>2 | partly true<br>3 | mostly true<br>4 | fully true<br>5 |
| | A | A complex problem is a challenge to me rather than a nuisance. | 1 | 2 | 3 | 4 | 5 |
| | B | Thinking hard and for a long time about something bores me. | 1 | 2 | 3 | 4 | 5 |
| | C | I enjoy doing something that challenges my thinking abilities like for example playing chess (*or some other typical Thai game that requires strategic thinking*). | 1 | 2 | 3 | 4 | 5 |
| | D | In a group of friends I generally trust the arguments of others without always questioning where they come from. | 1 | 2 | 3 | 4 | 5 |
| | E | Documentary programs on TV annoy me so that I often switch to a different channel. | 1 | 2 | 3 | 4 | 5 |
| | F | Time is money, so I take decisions quickly. | 1 | 2 | 3 | 4 | 5 |
| | G | I believe in trusting my hunches. | 1 | 2 | 3 | 4 | 5 |
| | H | My initial impressions of people are almost always right. | 1 | 2 | 3 | 4 | 5 |
| | I | I hate to make important decisions under time pressure. | 1 | 2 | 3 | 4 | 5 |
| | J | Often, when I take decisions, I don't know why but I feel that I'm right. | 1 | 2 | 3 | 4 | 5 |

| 10 | **Do you think that the following facilities and institutions should be financed by taxes? Please be aware of the fact that all government spending require the imposition of taxes to raise the necessary funds.** | | | |
|---|---|---|---|---|
| | *INT.: These facilities and institutions could be used free of charge if financed by taxes.* | | Yes | No |
| | A | Libraries | 01 | 02 |
| | B | Discotheques | 01 | 02 |
| | C | State Railway of Thailand | 01 | 02 |
| | D | Swimming-pools, gyms, sports fields | 01 | 02 |
| | E | Schools | 01 | 02 |

| | | | | | |
|---|---|---|---|---|---|
| | F | Provincial Electricity Authority | 01 | 02 | |
| | G | Theaters | 01 | 02 | |
| | H | Provincial Water Authority | 01 | 02 | |
| | I | Mass Transit Authority | 01 | 02 | |
| | J | Thailand Post | 01 | 02 | |
| | K | Telephone of Thailand | 01 | 02 | |

**We would now like to ask you some more questions about yourself. Since we can only ask these questions a small number of households we need these socio-economic data in order to generalize the results of these interviews to the whole population of Mae Rim.**

| | | | | | | | | |
|---|---|---|---|---|---|---|---|---|
| 11 | **To what extent do the following statements apply to you?** | | | | | | | |
| | **Please answer the following questions using the scale.** | | never<br>1 | rarely<br>2 | some-times<br>3 | mostly<br>4 | always<br>5 | |
| | A | I find it difficult to say "no" if a friend asks me a favor. | 1 | 2 | 3 | 4 | 5 | |
| | B | It gives me a good feeling if I donate money for people I do not know personally, for example for old people, disabled people or orphans | 1 | 2 | 3 | 4 | 5 | |
| | C | The increase of my "boon" associated with the donation is very important to me. | 1 | 2 | 3 | 4 | 5 | |
| | D | I help other people because they will help me when I am in need. | 1 | 2 | 3 | 4 | 5 | |
| | E | I donate money because "giving" is an established habit in our society. | 1 | 2 | 3 | 4 | 5 | |
| | F | I promise to do something although I do not want to do it. | 1 | 2 | 3 | 4 | 5 | |
| | G | I give promises and then I do not keep them. | 1 | 2 | 3 | 4 | 5 | |
| | H | I am concerned what other people might think of me. | 1 | 2 | 3 | 4 | 5 | |

| | | | | | | | | |
|---|---|---|---|---|---|---|---|---|
| 12 | **To what extent do you agree with the following statements? Please answer the following questions using the scale.** | | | | | | | |
| | *INT.: Please present the scale and check one number per line.* | | do not agree at all<br>1 | do not agree<br>2 | quite agree<br>3 | agree<br>4 | fully agree<br>5 | |
| | A | Taking care of environmental protection is an important task of government. | 1 | 2 | 3 | 4 | 5 | |
| | B | Law enforcement concerning environmental management is usually not effective. | 1 | 2 | 3 | 4 | 5 | |
| | C | Usually, government's action concerning environmental protection is 'too late'. | 1 | 2 | 3 | 4 | 5 | |
| | D | Government should collect more taxes to increase the budget for environmental management. | 1 | 2 | 3 | 4 | 5 | |

| | | | |
|---|---|---|---|
| 13 | **How would you classify the economic situation of your household?**<br>**Please give your answers using the scale.**<br>*INT.: Please present the scale.* | very poor ..................... 01<br>poor ............................. 02<br>neither rich, nor poor...... 03<br>rich .............................. 04<br>very rich ...................... 05 | |
| 14 | **How do you judge the economic situation of your household in comparison with the average households in Mae Rim?**<br>**Please give your answers using the scale.**<br>*INT.: Please present the scale.* | much worse.................. 01<br>a little worse ............... 02<br>average ........................ 03<br>a little better ................ 04<br>much better ................. 05 | |
| 15 | **How fair do you consider your household income in comparison with other households' incomes?**<br>**Please give your answers using the scale".**<br>*INT.: Please present the scale.* | not fair at all ................ 01<br>not so fair..................... 02<br>somewhat fair ............... 03<br>basically fair.................. 04<br>very fair ....................... 05 | |

| 16 | **To what extent are the following statements true regarding your personal situation? Please answer the following questions using the scale.** | | | | | |
|---|---|---|---|---|---|---|
| | *INT.: Please present the scale and check one number per line.* | not true at all<br>1 | not so true<br>2 | fairly true<br>3 | mostly true<br>4 | complete ly true<br>5 |
| A | I need money to be happy. | 1 | 2 | 3 | 4 | 5 |
| B | I usually spend all my income because buying things makes me happy. | 1 | 2 | 3 | 4 | 5 |
| C | I like to buy things on installment. | 1 | 2 | 3 | 4 | 5 |
| D | I build up savings because I want to have security for the future. | 1 | 2 | 3 | 4 | 5 |
| E | I build up savings because I want to leave something for my children. | 1 | 2 | 3 | 4 | 5 |
| F | Even with more money for myself I would not be happier than now. | 1 | 2 | 3 | 4 | 5 |

| 17 | **To what extent are you worried about the following issues? Please give your answer using the scale.** | | | | | |
|---|---|---|---|---|---|---|
| | *INT.: Please present the scale and check one number per line.* | not worried at all<br>1 | little worried<br>2 | some-what worried<br>3 | quite worried<br>4 | very worried<br>5 |
| A | About your own economic situation | 1 | 2 | 3 | 4 | 5 |
| B | About your health | 1 | 2 | 3 | 4 | 5 |
| C | About the progressive degradation of the environment | 1 | 2 | 3 | 4 | 5 |
| D | About peace in the world | 1 | 2 | 3 | 4 | 5 |
| E | About the political situation in our country. | 1 | 2 | 3 | 4 | 5 |
| F | About the security of your income | 1 | 2 | 3 | 4 | 5 |
| G | About the erosion of moral values among young people | 1 | 2 | 3 | 4 | 5 |
| H | About the decrease in social justice in our country | 1 | 2 | 3 | 4 | 5 |
| I | About corruption | 1 | 2 | 3 | 4 | 5 |
| J | About too many foreigners living in Thailand | 1 | 2 | 3 | 4 | 5 |

| | | | | |
|---|---|---|---|---|
| 18 | **When you think about your decision whether and how much to contribute to the proposed tap water improvement program, are the following statements true?** | | | |
| | *INT.: Please check one number per line.* | | Yes | No |
| | A | I made my decision based on my first feeling about this program right after it was presented to me. | 01 | 02 |
| | B | I really thought very hard about every single aspect of the program before making a decision of how much to pay. | 01 | 02 |
| | C | The first impression that I had about this program changed on a second thought. | 01 | 02 |
| | D | I would have liked to have more time for making a decision about my contribution to this program. | 01 | 02 |
| | E | All aspects were equally important for my decision. | 01 | 02 |
| | F | With the given information about the project I found it very hard to make a good decision. | 01 | 02 |
| | G | There are so many aspects in this project but only a few of them were really relevant for my decision. | 01 | 02 |
| | H | Even if I had had more time available for thinking about this program I don't think that my decision of how much to contribute to it would have been different. | 01 | 02 |
| | **Now we would like to ask you some personal questions.** | | | |
| 19-1 | **Do you have at the moment any debts from...** | | | |
| | *INT.: Please check one number per line.* | | Yes | No |
| | A | ... the bank or the BAAC? | 01 | 02 |
| | B | ... your friends or your family? | 01 | 02 |
| | C | ... private money lenders? | 01 | 02 |
| | D | ... others such as cooperative or village fund? | 01 | 02 |
| | E | ... delayed payments or installment payments? | 01 | 02 |
| 19-2 | *INT: if at least one of the questions in 19-1 was "yes" ask:*<br>**What is the level of your indebtedness? Please include also installment debts. Please select from the given brackets.**<br>*otherwise continue with question 20-1.* | less than 20000 Baht .......................... A<br>20000 up to less than 50000 Baht ......... B<br>50000 up to less than 100000 Baht ...... C<br>100000 up to less than 200000 Baht .... D<br>200000 up to less than 300000 Baht ..... E<br>more than 300000 Baht ..................... F | | |

| | | | |
|---|---|---|---|
| 19-3 | **Are you worried about your debts?** | Yes .................. 01<br>No .................. 02 | |
| 20-1 | *INT.: Please fill in without inquiry*<br>**Sex of the respondent:** | male ............... 01<br>female ............. 02 | |
| 20-2 | **Were you born in Thailand?** | Yes .................. 01<br>No .................... 02 | <br>20-4 |
| 20-3 | **In which province?** | ................................................<br>*(INT.: please write down)* | |
| 20-4 | **When were you born? Please state the year of your birth as Buddhist year.** | ☐☐☐☐ | |
| 20-5 | **What marital status do you have? What applies to you from this list?**<br>*INT.: Please present the list.* | I am married and live together with my spouse ................. 01<br>I am married and live separated from my spouse ................ 02<br>I am not married ................ 03<br>I am divorced .................... 04<br>I am widowed .................... 05 | |
| 20-6 | **Do you have children or even grandchildren?** | Yes ................................. 01<br>No .................................. 02 | |
| 20-7 | **How many persons are permanently and factually living in your household, including yourself? Please consider all the children in the household.** | ☐☐ Person(s) | |
| 20-8 | *INT.: ask only households with at least 2 persons.*<br>**How many persons living in your household contribute to your household income?** | ☐☐ Person(s) | |

| | | | |
|---|---|---|---|
| 20-9 | **Which is your highest level of education? Please give your answers according to the list.**<br>*INT.: Please present the list.* | I left the school without certificate .............. 01<br>I have finished $4^{th}$ year of elementary school .. 02<br>I have finished $6^{th}$ year of elementary school .. 03<br>I have finished $3^{rd}$ year of secondary school ... 04<br>I have finished 6th year of secondary school ... 05<br>I have obtained the Technical Education Certificate ........ 06<br>I have obtained the Higher Technical Education Certificate ........ 07<br>I have completed the bachelor degree ........... 08<br>I have completed the master degree ............. 09<br>I have obtained a PhD ................................ 10<br>I have a different certificate: ....................... 11<br>*(INT.: Please write down)* | |
| 20-10 | **What kind of job do you do at present?**<br>*INT.: Please present list.* | Worker / employee ..................................... 01 | |
| | | Official ..................................................... 02 | |
| | | Owner or renter of a farm............................. 03 | |
| | | Self-employed.............................................. 04 | |
| | | Trainee, student, pupil ................................. 05 | 20-12 |
| | | Housewife, househusband ........................... 06 | 20-12 |
| | | Retiree, early retirement .............................. 07 | 20-12 |
| | | Unemployed ............................................... 08 | 20-12 |
| 20-11 | **Are you employed full-time or part-time?** | Full-time................. 01<br>Part-time ................ 02 | |

| | | | |
|---|---|---|---|
| 20-12 | **What is the average net monthly income of your household altogether?**<br><br>**Please state the sum of wages, incomes from self-employment and pensions minus tax payments and social security insurance. Please also add the income from public subsidies, rents, housing subsidies, child benefits, and other sources of income.**<br><br>**If you are responsible for the support of a part of your family not living in your household, please deduct this amount. Your statement will be treated confidentially.**<br><br>*INT.: Please present the list.* | less than 6000 Baht .............................. A<br><br>6000 up to less than 10000 Baht ........... B<br><br>10000 up to less than 20000 Baht ........ C<br><br>20000 up to less than 30000 Baht ........ D<br><br>30000 up to less than 50000 Baht ......... E<br><br>more than 50000 Baht .......................... F | |

**Thank you very much for answering these questions!**

## 7.2 Correlations of socio-economic and attitudinal variables with TIF and TDF

### 7.2.1 Task independent factors

| Question | | TIF1<br>coeff.<br>(p-value) | TIF2<br>coeff.<br>(p-value) | TIF3<br>coeff.<br>(p-value) | TIF4<br>coeff.<br>(p-value) |
|---|---|---|---|---|---|
| **4-4a** | Worry about taste of the water | .057<br>(.105) | .001<br>(.971) | -.078<br>(.026) | .007<br>(.839) |
| **4-4b** | Worry about the color | .080<br>(.023) | -.046<br>(.196) | -.009<br>(.791) | .000<br>(.989) |
| **4-4c** | Worry about the odor | .083<br>(.019) | -.014<br>(.682) | -.007<br>(.837) | .054<br>(.127) |
| **4-5a** | Worry about diarrhea | .041<br>(.249) | -.015<br>(.679) | -.041<br>(.242) | .041<br>(.240) |
| **4-5b** | Worry about kidney stones | .032<br>(.358) | .026<br>(.469) | .006<br>(.870) | .058<br>(.098) |
| **4-5c** | Worry about cancer | .031<br>(.386) | .015<br>(.677) | -.049<br>(.161) | .059<br>(.094) |
| **5a** | Importance: no interruption of water service | -.047<br>(.190) | -.080<br>(.024) | .094<br>(.008) | .023<br>(.523) |
| **5b** | Importance: no biological pollutants in the water | .009<br>(.801) | -.024<br>(.500) | .148<br>(.000) | -.099<br>(.005) |
| **5c** | Importance: no pesticides in the water | .001<br>(.969) | -.008<br>(.815) | .157<br>(.000) | -202<br>(.000) |
| **5d** | Importance: clear color of the water | -.076<br>(.032) | -.059<br>(.098) | .162<br>(.000) | -.082<br>(.020) |
| **5e** | Importance: less soil degradation in the uplands | -.027<br>(.453) | -.014<br>(.698) | .076<br>(.032) | -.049<br>(.168) |
| **5f** | Importance: no accumulation of pesticides in ecosystems | -.070<br>(.048) | .002<br>(.966) | .074<br>(.036) | -.100<br>(.005) |
| **5g** | Importance: less pesticides in fruit and vegetables | -.019<br>(583) | .013<br>(.711) | .102<br>(.004) | -.092<br>(.010) |
| **5h** | Importance: reduced health threats for future generations | .017<br>(.637) | .028<br>(.431) | .091<br>(.011) | -.091<br>(.010) |
| 7 | Difficulty of response | -117<br>(.001) | -.023<br>(.510) | -.055<br>(.121) | -.012<br>(.736) |
| **8a** | Reason: save money | .034<br>(.330) | .059<br>(.094) | -.032<br>(.369) | .017<br>(.623) |
| **8b** | Reason: more convenient | .014<br>(.699) | .070<br>(.048) | -.012<br>(.741) | -.084<br>(.016) |
| **8c** | Reason: not become ill | -.002<br>(.947) | .063<br>(.074) | .096<br>(.006) | -.117<br>(.001) |
| **8d** | Reason: increased health of the population | .020<br>(.575) | .139<br>(.000) | .021<br>(.549) | -.102<br>(.004) |
| **8e** | Reason: color of the water | -.027<br>(.448) | -.079<br>(.025) | .104<br>(.003) | -.073<br>(.037) |
| **8f** | Reason: future generations | -.007<br>(.848) | .059<br>(.094) | .098<br>(.005) | -.146<br>(.000) |

| Question | | TIF1 coeff. (p-value) | TIF2 coeff. (p-value) | TIF3 coeff. (p-value) | TIF4 coeff. (p-value) |
|---|---|---|---|---|---|
| **8g** | Reason: I cannot afford to pay more | .117 (.001) | -.033 (.345) | -.024 (.499) | .041 (.242) |
| **8h** | Reason: I have severe doubts concerning the program | .087 (.014) | -.054 (.126) | .059 (.092) | -.018 (.602) |
| **8i** | Reason: government is responsible | .058 (.098) | -.014 (.693) | .058 (.102) | -.001 (.971) |
| **8j** | Reason: costs are already high | .037 (.291) | .098 (.005) | .016 (.643) | .025 (.472) |
| **10a** | Libraries | .037 (.293) | .119 (.001) | -.019 (.588) | -.042 (.229) |
| **10b** | Discotheques | .040 (.256) | .050 (.156) | -.078 (.027) | -.046 (.196) |
| **10c** | State Railway of Thailand | .043 (.227) | -.011 (.762) | -.068 (.052) | -.063 (.073) |
| **10d** | Swimming-pools, gyms, sports fields | .011 (.751) | .092 (.009) | -.086 (.014) | -.047 (.180) |
| **10e** | Schools | .010 (.768) | .015 (.672) | .022 (.531) | .008 (.814) |
| **10f** | Provincial Electricity Authority | -.034 (.336) | -.065 (.066) | -.036 (.309) | .044 (.209) |
| **10g** | Theaters | .014 (.696) | .104 (.003) | -.016 (.644) | .045 (.201) |
| **10h** | Provincial Water Authority | -.041 (.242) | -.043 (.218) | -.086 (.015) | .099 (.005) |
| **10i** | Mass Transit Authority | .011 (.761) | .042 (.234) | -.032 (.362) | -.018 (.602) |
| **10j** | Thailand Post | .043 (.226) | .004 (.919) | -.031 (.373) | -.038 (.286) |
| **10k** | Telephone of Thailand | .011 (.759) | -.014 (.698) | -.104 (.003) | -.006 (.856) |
| **11a** | I find it difficult to say "no" if a friend asks me a favor. | .198 (.000) | -.014 (.689) | .025 (.486) | .050 (.156) |
| **11b** | It gives me a good feeling if I donate money for people I do not know personally. | .145 (.000) | .052 (.136) | .181 (.000) | -.044 (.207) |
| **11c** | The increase of my "boon" associated with the donation is very important to me. | .226 (.000) | -.068 (.053) | .026 (.466) | -.063 (.076) |
| **11d** | I help other people because they will help me when I am in need. | .187 (.000) | .038 (.284) | -.133 (.000) | .069 (.049) |
| **11e** | I donate money because "giving" is an established habit in our society. | .175 (.000) | -.086 (.014) | -.017 (.649) | -.122 (.001) |
| **11f** | I promise to do something although I do not want to do it. | .168 (.000) | -.008 (.820) | -.092 (.009) | .046 (.191) |
| **11g** | I give promises and then I do not keep them. | .113 (.001) | .063 (.074) | -.148 (.000) | -.004 (.904) |
| **11h** | I am concerned what other people might think of me. | .050 (.155) | .072 (.042) | -.018 (.601) | -.050 (.158) |

| Question | | TIF1 coeff. (p-value) | TIF2 coeff. (p-value) | TIF3 coeff. (p-value) | TIF4 coeff. (p-value) |
|---|---|---|---|---|---|
| **12a** | Taking care of environmental protection is an important task of government. | .081 (.021) | .041 (.242) | .086 (.015) | -.105 (.003) |
| **12b** | Law enforcement concerning environmental management is usually not effective. | .070 (.047) | .058 (.098) | .149 (.000) | -.074 (.035) |
| **12c** | Usually, government's action concerning environmental protection is 'too late'. | .123 (.000) | .048 (.170) | .157 (.000) | .011 (.757) |
| **12d** | Government should collect more taxes to increase the budget for environmental management. | .066 (.060) | .117 (.001) | -.130 (.000) | -.056 (.113) |
| **13** | Classify: household richer or poorer than average | -.017 (.628) | .135 (.000) | .044 (.211) | -.161 (.000) |
| **14** | Classify: economic situation better or worse than average | -.088 (.822) | .125 (.000) | .149 (.000) | -.113 (.001) |
| **15** | Classify: consider income fair or unfair | .027 (.450) | .073 (.038) | .040 (.216) | -.057 (.108) |
| **16a** | I need money to be happy. | .076 (.032) | -.054 (.129) | -.019 (.585) | .232 (.000) |
| **16b** | I usually spend all my income because buying things makes me happy. | .073 (.039) | .135 (.000) | -.064 (.068) | .158 (.000) |
| **16c** | I like to buy things on installment. | .044 (.209) | .008 (.820) | -.093 (.008) | .052 (.137) |
| **16d** | I build up savings because I want to have security for the future. | -.004 (.691) | -.016 (.651) | .123 (.000) | -.053 (.134) |
| **16e** | I build up savings because I want to leave something for my children. | .068 (.054) | -.078 (.021) | .002 (.951) | -.020 (.566) |
| **16f** | Even with more money for myself I would not be happier than now. | .040 (.257) | .148 (.000) | .004 (.911) | -.015 (.673) |
| **17a** | Worried about own economic situation | .140 (.000) | -.068 (.053) | -.050 (.152) | .174 (.000) |
| **17b** | Worried about health | .186 (.000) | -.022 (.528) | -.031 (.378) | .022 (.537) |
| **17c** | Worried about progressive degradation of environment | -.034 (.339) | .103 (.003) | .100 (.004) | .004 (.912) |
| **17d** | Worried about peace in the world | .040 (.262) | .146 (.000) | .105 (.003) | -.026 (.457) |
| **17e** | Worried about the political situation in Thailand | .002 (.951) | .099 (.005) | .096 (.006) | -.047 (.186) |
| **17f** | Worried about the security of income | .082 (.021) | -.091 (.010) | -.052 (.138) | .168 (.000) |
| **17g** | Worried about the moral values of young people | -.026 (.467) | -.052 (.142) | .151 (.000) | -.028 (.431) |
| **17h** | Worried about decrease in social justice in Thailand | .018 (.613) | .103 (.004) | .138 (.000) | -.009 (.791) |
| **17i** | Worried about corruption | .017 (.639) | .097 (.006) | .139 (.000) | -.026 (.461) |
| **17j** | Worried about foreigners | .041 (.244) | .077 (.028) | .097 (.006) | -.008 (.814) |

| Question | | TIF1 coeff. (p-value) | TIF2 coeff. (p-value) | TIF3 coeff. (p-value) | TIF4 coeff. (p-value) |
|---|---|---|---|---|---|
| **19-1a** | Debts: bank or BAAC | -.033 (.356) | .036 (.304) | -.067 (.057) | -.010 (.772) |
| **19-1b** | Debts: friends or family | -.072 (.042) | .009 (.810) | .043 (.227) | .064 (.071) |
| **19-1c** | Debts: money lender | .055 (.121) | -.043 (.227) | -.016 (.659) | .074 (.037) |
| **19-1d** | Debts: village fund | .014 (.687) | .065 (.067) | .017 (.635) | .034 (.332) |
| **19-1e** | Debts: installment payments | -.088 (.829) | .014 (.692) | .005 (.891) | .046 (.190) |
| **19-3** | Worried about debt level | -.077 (.055) | -.118 (-.003) | .122 (.002) | .130 (.001) |
| **20-1** | Sex | -.076 (.032) | .235 (.000) | -.007 (.851) | -.076 (.033) |
| **20-4** | Age | .070 (.051) | -.055 (.126) | .008 (.833) | -.011 (.754) |
| **20-5** | Marital status | .057 (.109) | -.080 (.023) | .084 (.016) | .045 (.204) |
| **20-6** | Children or grandchildren | .029 (.408) | -.085 (.015) | -.082 (.019) | .049 (.162) |
| **20-7** | Household size | .007 (.854) | -.022 (.541) | -.036 (.314) | .061 (.085) |
| **20-9** | Level of education | -.108 (.002) | .121 (.001) | .068 (.056) | -.088 (.013) |
| **20-12** | Income | -.001 (.971) | .079 (.025) | .059 (.096) | -.063 (.075) |

### 7.2.2 Task dependent factors

| | | Payment Card | | | | Dichotomous Choice | | |
|---|---|---|---|---|---|---|---|---|
| **Question** | | **TDF1** coeff. (p-value) | **TDF2** coeff. (p-value) | **TDF3** coeff. (p-value) | **TDF4** coeff. (p-value) | **TDF1** coeff. (p-value) | **TDF2** coeff. (p-value) | **TDF3** coeff. (p-value) |
| **4-4a** | Worry about taste of the water | .081 (.141) | .107 (.054) | -.030 (.583) | .010 (.852) | .054 (.252) | .036 (.451) | -.039 (.409) |
| **4-4b** | Worry about the color | .147 (.008) | .162 (.003) | .028 (.610) | .002 (.997) | .028 (.560) | .042 (.380) | -.019 (.696) |
| **4-4c** | Worry about the odor | .120 (.030) | .083 (.132) | .035 (.532) | -.022 (.686) | .116 (.014) | .023 (.625) | -.018 (.708) |
| **4-5a** | Worry about diarrhea | .120 (.029) | .055 (.323) | .025 (.654) | -.049 (.375) | .075 (.115) | .011 (.820) | .012 (.794) |
| **4-5b** | Worry about kidney stones | .163 (.003) | .085 (.122) | -.023 (.682) | -.029 (.607) | .071 (.135) | .028 (.554) | -.043 (.368) |
| **4-5c** | Worry about cancer | .106 (.055) | .044 (.429) | .014 (.794) | .049 (.376) | .025 (.600) | .048 (.313) | .046 (.331) |

| Question | | Payment Card | | | | Dichotomous Choice | | |
|---|---|---|---|---|---|---|---|---|
| | | TDF1 coeff. (p-value) | TDF2 coeff. (p-value) | TDF3 coeff. (p-value) | TDF4 coeff. (p-value) | TDF1 coeff. (p-value) | TDF2 coeff. (p-value) | TDF3 coeff. (p-value) |
| **5a** | Importance: no interruption of water service | -.032 (.562) | .069 (.212) | .072 (.194) | -.172 (.002) | -.152 (.001) | -.070 (.144) | -.038 (.435) |
| **5b** | Importance: no biological pollutants in the water | .062 (.265) | .009 (.874) | .105 (.058) | -.190 (.001) | -.092 (.056) | -.083 (.083) | -.031 (.524) |
| **5c** | Importance: no pesticides in the water | -.026 (.645) | .035 (.526) | .073 (.187) | -.175 (.002) | -.053 (.267) | -.103 (.032) | -.032 (.507) |
| **5d** | Importance: clear color of the water | -.029 (.595) | .058 (.299) | .125 (.024) | -.075 (.174) | -.051 (.292) | -.110 (.022) | -.076 (.115) |
| **5e** | Importance: less soil degradation in the uplands | .026 (.646) | -.087 (.117) | .110 (.049) | -.071 (.201) | .032 (.504) | -.067 (.164) | .054 (.261) |
| **5f** | Importance: no accumulation of pesticides in ecosystems | -.005 (.931) | -.130 (.019) | .040 (.472) | -.013 (.812) | -.022 (.642) | -.045 (.352) | .090 (.061) |
| **5g** | Importance: less pesticides in fruit and vegetables | .043 (.434) | -.117 (.035) | .103 (.064) | -.023 (.674) | -.052 (.276) | -.032 (.446) | .104 (.030) |
| **5h** | Importance: reduced health threats for future generations | .035 (.526) | -.020 (.714) | .073 (.188) | -.145 (.009) | .004 (.940) | -.019 (.693) | .055 (.254) |
| 7 | Difficulty of response | .259 (.000) | .194 (.000) | .051 (.359) | -.079 (.152) | .264 (.000) | .182 (.000) | -.058 (.224) |
| **8a** | Reason: save money | .012 (.823) | -.120 (.030) | .042 (.452) | -.077 (.163) | -.045 (.342) | -.009 (.949) | .017 (.726) |
| **8b** | Reason: more convenient | -.168 (.002) | -.088 (.113) | .091 (.100) | -.100 (.070) | .005 (.910) | -.135 (.004) | -.072 (.129) |
| **8c** | Reason: not become ill | -.089 (.108) | -.027 (.625) | .031 (.529) | -.127 (.022) | -.041 (.390) | .022 (.638) | -.102 (.032) |
| **8d** | Reason: increased health of the population | -.047 (.402) | -.015 (.789) | .071 (.204) | -.043 (.443) | -.063 (.186) | -.022 (.637) | -.103 (.029) |
| **8e** | Reason: color of the water | .010 (.859) | -.075 (.178) | .063 (.255) | -.101 (.070) | -.087 (.067) | -.059 (.216) | -.041 (.394) |
| **8f** | Reason: future generations | .034 (.547) | -.127 (.022) | .056 (.318) | -.032 (.560) | -.042 (.375) | -.073 (.123) | -.036 (.450) |
| **8g** | Reason: I cannot afford to pay more | .235 (.000) | -.121 (.028) | -.047 (.400) | .046 (.403) | .159 (.001) | .170 (.000) | .038 (.423) |
| **8h** | Reason: I have severe doubts concerning the program | .244 (.000) | .008 (.891) | -.045 (.419) | -.011 (.840) | .004 (.925) | .021 (.660) | -.060 (.208) |
| **8i** | Reason: government is responsible | .170 (.002) | -.096 (.084) | -.083 (.136) | .026 (.644) | -.069 (.044) | -.007 (.887) | .072 (.129) |
| **8j** | Reason: costs are already high | .109 (.049) | -.019 (.726) | -.055 (.324) | .012 (.827) | .007 (.883) | .129 (.006) | -.047 (.320) |

| | | Payment Card | | | | Dichotomous Choice | | |
|---|---|---|---|---|---|---|---|---|
| **Question** | | **TDF1** coeff. (p-value) | **TDF2** coeff. (p-value) | **TDF3** coeff. (p-value) | **TDF4** coeff. (p-value) | **TDF1** coeff. (p-value) | **TDF2** coeff. (p-value) | **TDF3** coeff. (p-value) |
| **10a** | Libraries | .051 (.360) | -.008 (.882) | .011 (.844) | .010 (.853) | .005 (.915) | .025 (.604) | -.119 (.012) |
| **10b** | Discotheques | .034 (.540) | .026 (.642) | -.030 (.589) | .041 (.465) | .000 (.994) | .087 (.066) | .028 (.552) |
| **10c** | State Railway of Thailand | -.016 (.767) | -.111 (.045) | .022 (.698) | -.037 (.506) | .010 (.835) | .090 (.058) | .027 (.573) |
| **10d** | Swimming-pools, gyms, sports fields | .064 (.250) | -.062 (.265) | .033 (.547) | .017 (.759) | .082 (.083) | -.051 (.288) | -.026 (.587) |
| **10e** | Schools | .036 (.511) | -.014 (.794) | .084 (.127) | .034 (.537) | .002 (.960) | -.079 (.094) | .119 (.685) |
| **10f** | Provincial Electricity Authority | .076 (.168) | -.134 (.015) | .045 (.412) | .053 (.337) | -.042 (.373) | .039 (.408) | .102 (.032) |
| **10g** | Theaters | -.065 (.237) | .055 (.323) | .047 (.399) | -.007 (.894) | -.046 (.331) | .087 (.067) | -.017 (.720) |
| **10h** | Provincial Water Authority | .049 (.377) | -.045 (.418) | .038 (.488) | .103 (.063) | -.013 (.777) | .026 (.578) | .096 (.043) |
| **10i** | Mass Transit Authority | .090 (.106) | -.145 (.009) | -.016 (.768) | .008 (.890) | .001 (.985) | -.039 (.408) | .067 (.158) |
| **10j** | Thailand Post | .065 (.238) | -.068 (.222) | .031 (.575) | .024 (.670) | -.003 (.944) | .001 (.980) | .096 (.044) |
| **10k** | Telephone of Thailand | .118 (.032) | -.082 (.140) | .030 (.583) | .073 (.190) | -.047 (.326) | .039 (.418) | .121 (.010) |
| **11a** | I find it difficult to say "no" if a friend asks me a favor. | .061 (.270) | -.074 (.179) | .054 (.331) | -.033 (.554) | .105 (.027) | -.171 (.000) | .014 (.761) |
| **11b** | It gives me a good feeling if I donate money for people I do not know personally. | .066 (.235) | -.023 (.679) | -.038 (.487) | -.079 (.151) | .108 (.022) | -.055 (.243) | -.110 (.020) |
| **11c** | The increase of my "boon" associated with the donation is very important to me. | .027 (.632) | -.019 (.727) | -.033 (.550) | -.172 (.002) | .099 (.038) | .044 (.353) | -.003 (.947) |
| **11d** | I help other people because they will help me when I am in need. | -.056 (.315) | .045 (.412) | -.019 (.737) | -.027 (.620) | .012 (.794) | .015 (.755) | .120 (.011) |
| **11e** | I donate money because "giving" is an established habit in our society. | -.007 (.896) | -.058 (.297) | -.057 (.307) | -.106 (.056) | .066 (.162) | -.019 (.692) | .090 (.057) |
| **11f** | I promise to do something although I do not want to do it. | .168 (.002) | -.059 (.286) | -.002 (.967) | .080 (.147) | .175 (.000) | .053 (.267) | .118 (.013) |
| **11g** | I give promises and then I do not keep them. | .053 (.339) | .039 (.484) | -.023 (.679) | .115 (.037) | .072 (.132) | .172 (.000) | .134 (.005) |
| **11h** | I am concerned what other people think of me. | .073 (.186) | .083 (.135) | .086 (.120) | .037 (.499) | .064 (.178) | -.063 (.185) | -.003 (.946) |

| Question | | Payment Card | | | | Dichotomous Choice | | |
|---|---|---|---|---|---|---|---|---|
| | | TDF1 coeff. (p-value) | TDF2 coeff. (p-value) | TDF3 coeff. (p-value) | TDF4 coeff. (p-value) | TDF1 coeff. (p-value) | TDF2 coeff. (p-value) | TDF3 coeff. (p-value) |
| **12a** | Taking care of environmental protection is an important task of government. | .108 (.051) | .025 (.646) | .051 (.360) | -.065 (.243) | -.070 (.138) | -.035 (.462) | -.102 (.031) |
| **12b** | Law enforcement concerning environmental management is usually not effective. | .086 (.120) | -.066 (.233) | -.019 (.732) | -.065 (.239) | .034 (.474) | -.057 (.229) | -.139 (.003) |
| **12c** | Usually, government's action concerning environmental protection is 'too late'. | .080 (.148) | -.057 (.306) | .040 (.471) | -.095 (.085) | -.019 (.687) | -.083 (.082) | -.066 (.165) |
| **12d** | Government should collect more taxes to increase the budget for environmental management. | -.012 (.833) | -.073 (.190) | -.044 (.423) | .010 (.855) | -.046 (.337) | -.004 (.926) | -.097 (.041) |
| **13** | Classify: household richer or poorer than average | .011 (.846) | .001 (.985) | .007 (.897) | .036 (.510) | .003 (.956) | -.024 (.613) | -.062 (.193) |
| **14** | Classify: economic situation better or worse than average | -.032 (.557) | -.089 (.106) | .46 (.403) | .053 (.340) | -.026 (.579) | -.087 (.066) | -.022 (.636) |
| **15** | Classify: consider income fair or unfair | .018 (.749) | -.027 (.621) | .104 (.059) | .002 (.965) | .026 (.587) | -.184 (.000) | .094 (.047) |
| **16a** | I need money to be happy. | .146 (.009) | .034 (.537) | -.012 (.831) | -.079 (.157) | -.093 (.050) | .013 (.790) | .162 (.001) |
| **16b** | I usually spend all my income because buying things makes me happy. | .121 (.029) | -.016 (.778) | .021 (.713) | -.019 (.734) | .053 (.262) | .024 (.615) | .174 (.000) |
| **16c** | I like to buy things on installment. | .160 (.004) | -.106 (.056) | .083 (.135) | .096 (.084) | .141 (.003) | .077 (.104) | .169 (.000) |
| **16d** | I build up savings because I want to have security for the future. | .099 (.074) | -.052 (.350) | .086 (.121) | -.132 (.017) | .012 (.807) | -.134 (.005) | .053 (.263) |
| **16e** | I build up savings because I want to leave something for my children. | .098 (.080) | .012 (.825) | .069 (.218) | -.179 (.001) | .003 (.957) | -.023 (.626) | -.024 (.611) |
| **16f** | Even with more money for myself I would not be happier than now. | .119 (.032) | -.012 (.832) | .002 (.976) | .092 (.099) | .185 (.000) | .013 (.785) | -.011 (.812) |
| **17a** | Worried about own economic situation | .157 (.004) | -.032 (.565) | .063 (.258) | .089 (.108) | -.009 (.852) | .122 (.010) | .076 (.107) |
| **17b** | Worried about health | .200 (.000) | -.078 (.161) | -.022 (.687) | .096 (.083) | -.008 (.871) | .069 (.147) | .048 (.317) |

| Question | | Payment Card | | | | Dichotomous Choice | | |
|---|---|---|---|---|---|---|---|---|
| | | TDF1 coeff. (p-value) | TDF2 coeff. (p-value) | TDF3 coeff. (p-value) | TDF4 coeff. (p-value) | TDF1 coeff. (p-value) | TDF2 coeff. (p-value) | TDF3 coeff. (p-value) |
| **17c** | Worried about progressive degradation of environment | .014 (.808) | -.165 (.003) | .095 (.086) | -.023 (.677) | -.065 (.170) | -.076 (.110) | .016 (.734) |
| **17d** | Worried about peace in the world | -.020 (.716) | -.118 (.033) | -.007 (.898) | .001 (.983) | -.037 (.434) | -.102 (.031) | -.012 (.798) |
| **17e** | Worried about the political situation in Thailand | .021 (.702) | -.131 (.018) | .048 (.386) | .050 (.362) | -.011 (.811) | -.004 (.931) | -.023 (.625) |
| **17f** | Worried about the security of income | .104 (.060) | -.052 (.353) | .001 (.989) | .081 (.145) | -.036 (.450) | .072 (.131) | .056 (.240) |
| **17g** | Worried about the moral values of young people | .084 (.130) | -.094 (.089) | .106 (.055) | -.123 (.027) | .008 (.870) | -.148 (.002) | -.044 (.349) |
| **17h** | Worried about decrease in social justice in Thailand | .096 (.083) | -.118 (.033) | -.001 (.989) | -.049 (.382) | -.028 (.552) | -.032 (.494) | .034 (.479) |
| **17i** | Worried about corruption | .201 (.000) | -.197 (.001) | .003 (.962) | -.048 (.386) | .067 (.159) | -.031 (.518) | .053 (.261) |
| **17j** | Worried about foreigners | .070 (.203) | -.147 (.008) | .097 (.079) | -.066 (.236) | -.003 (.944) | -.059 (.216) | .062 (.191) |
| **19-1a** | Debts: bank or BAAC | .062 (.265) | .033 (.554) | -.001 (.979) | .070 (.206) | -.001 (.979) | .092 (.052) | -.034 (.480) |
| **19-1b** | Debts: friends or family | .017 (.756) | .012 (.835) | .091 (.102) | .107 (.054) | -.001 (.989) | .047 (.321) | -.045 (.348) |
| **19-1c** | Debts: money lender | .010 (.860) | .123 (.027) | -.008 (.890) | .022 (.686) | .026 (.589) | .060 (.212) | -.034 (.480) |
| **19-1d** | Debts: village fund | .144 (.009) | .121 (.029) | .016 (.773) | .072 (.192) | .080 (.091) | .113 (.017) | -.044 (.351) |
| **19-1e** | Debts: installment payments | .000 (.999) | -.004 (.937) | .042 (.451) | -.023 (.675) | -.042 (.377) | .111 (.020) | .016 (.740) |
| **19-3** | Worried about debt level | .009 (.890) | .070 (.274) | .008 (.169) | .034 (.598) | .125 (.019) | .141 (.008) | .081 (.131) |
| **20-1** | Sex | -.018 (.748) | -.023 (.679) | .000 (.993) | .034 (.327) | -.013 (.778) | .003 (.951) | -.044 (.352) |
| **20-4** | Age | -.027 (.625) | .143 (.009) | -.015 (.787) | -.017 (.757) | .060 (.207) | -.029 (.543) | -.057 (.229) |
| **20-5** | Marital status | .031 (.575) | .083 (.134) | -.037 (.508) | -.016 (.779) | -.018 (.705) | -.030 (.534) | -.012 (.799) |
| **20-6** | Children or grandchildren | -.017 (.759) | .056 (.316) | -.034 (.536) | .006 (.908) | .027 (.567) | -.013 (.783) | .007 (.880) |
| **20-7** | Household size | -.114 (.039) | .001 (.981) | -.079 (.156) | -.109 (.049) | -.012 (.799) | .057 (.233) | .098 (.041) |
| **20-9** | Level of education | -.036 (.518) | -.126 (.023) | .065 (.238) | -.088 (.111) | -.036 (.443) | -.048 (.309) | -.004 (.939) |
| **20-12** | Income | -.080 (.150) | -.078 (.162) | -.021 (.708) | -.065 (.245) | -.089 (.064) | -.125 (.009) | .063 (.187) |

## HOHENHEIMER VOLKSWIRTSCHAFTLICHE SCHRIFTEN

Band 1 Walter Deffaa: Anonymisierte Befragungen mit zufallsverschlüsselten Antworten. Die Randomized-Response-Technik (RRT). Methodische Grundlagen, Modelle und Anwendungen. 1982.

Band 2 Thomas Michael Baum: Staatsverschuldung und Stabilisierungspolitik in der Demokratie. Zur neoinstitutionalistischen Kritik der keynesianischen Fiskalpolitik. 1982.

Band 3 Klaus Schröter: Die wettbewerbspolitische Behandlung der leitungsgebundenen Energiewirtschaft. Dargestellt am Beispiel der Fernwärmewirtschaft der Bundesrepublik Deutschland. 1986.

Band 4 Hugo Mann: Theorie und Politik der Steuerreform in der Demokratie. 1987.

Band 5 Max Christoph Wewel: Intervallarithmetische Dependenzanalyse in der Ökonometrie. Ein konjekturaler Ansatz. 1987.

Band 6 Heinrich Pascher: Die U.S.-amerikanische Deregulation Policy im Luftverkehrs- und Bankenbereich. 1987.

Band 7 Harald Lob: Die Entwicklung der französischen Wettbewerbspolitik bis zur Verordnung Nr. 86-1243 vom 01. Dezember 1986. Eine exemplarische Untersuchung der Erfassung der Behinderungsstrategie auf der Grundlage des Konzepts eines wirksamen Wettbewerbs. 1988.

Band 8 Ulrich Kirschner: Die Erfassung der Nachfragemacht von Handelsunternehmen. Eine Analyse der ökonomischen Beurteilungskriterien und der wettbewerbsrechtlichen Instrumente im Bereich der Verhaltenskontrolle.1988.

Band 9 Friedhelm Herb: Marktwirtschaftliche Innovationspolitik. 1988.

Band 10 Claus Schnabel: Zur ökonomischen Analyse der Gewerkschaften in der Bundesrepublik Deutschland. Theoretische und empirische Untersuchungen von Mitgliederentwicklung, Verhalten und Einfluß auf wirtschaftliche Größen. 1989.

Band 11 Jan B. Rittaler: Industrial Concentration and the Chicago School of Antitrust Analysis. A Critical Evaluation on the Basis of Effective Competition. 1989.

Band 12 Thomas Märtz: Interessengruppen und Gruppeninteressen in der Demokratie. Zur Theorie des Rent-Seeking. 1990.

Band 13 Andreas Maurer: Statistische Verfahren zur Ermittlung von oligopolistischen Strukturen. 1990.

Band 14 Peter Mendler: Zur ökonomischen und politisch-institutionellen Analyse öffentlicher Kredithilfen. 1992.

Band 15 Heinrich J. Engelke: Die Interpretation der Rundfunkfreiheit des Grundgesetzes: Eine Analyse aus ökonomischer Sicht. 1992.

Band 16 Thomas Fischer: Staat, Recht und Verfassung im Denken von Walter Eucken. Zu den staats- und rechtstheoretischen Grundlagen einer wirtschaftsordnungspolitischen Konzeption. 1993.

Band 17 Stefan Elßer: Innovationswettbewerb. Determinanten und Unternehmensverhalten. 1993.

Band 18 Reinhard Scharff: Regionalpolitik und regionale Entwicklungspotentiale. Eine kritische Analyse. 1993.

Band 19 Karin Beckmann: Probleme der Regionalpolitik im Zuge der Vollendung des Europäischen Binnenmarktes. Eine ökonomische Analyse. 1995.

Band 20 Bernd Nolte: Engpaßfaktoren der Innovation und Innovationsinfrastruktur. Eine theoretische und empirische Analyse für ländliche Wirtschaftsräume in Baden-Württemberg. 1996.

Band 21 Klaus-Rainer Brintzinger: Die Nationalökonomie an den Universitäten Freiburg, Heidelberg und Tübingen 1918 - 1945. Eine institutionenhistorische, vergleichende Studie der wirtschaftswissenschaftlichen Fakultäten und Abteilungen südwestdeutscher Universitäten. 1996.

Band 22 Steffen Binder: Die Idee der Konsumentensouveränität in der Wettbewerbstheorie. Teleokratische vs. nomokratische Auffassung. 1996.

Band 23 Alexander Burger: Deregulierungspotentiale in der Gesetzlichen Rentenversicherung. Reformnotwendigkeiten versus Reformmöglichkeiten. 1996.

Band 24 Burkhard Scherer: Regionale Entwicklungspolitik. Konzeption einer dezentralisierten und integrierten Regionalpolitik. 1997.

Band 25 Frauke Wolf: Lorenzkurvendisparität. Neuere Entwicklungen, Erweiterungen und Anwendungen. 1997.

Band 26 Hans Pitlik: Politische Ökonomie des Föderalismus. Föderative Kompetenzverteilung im Lichte der konstitutionellen Ökonomik. 1997.

Band 27 Stephan Seiter: Der Beitrag Nicholas Kaldors zur Neuen Wachstumstheorie. Eine vergleichende Studie vor dem Hintergrund der Debatte über den Verdoorn-Zusammenhang. 1997.

Band 28 André Schmidt: Ordnungspolitische Perspektiven der europäischen Integration im Spannungsfeld von Wettbewerbs- und Industriepolitik. 1998.

Band 29 Bernd Blessin: Innovations- und Umweltmanagement in kleinen und mittleren Unternehmen. Eine theoretische und empirische Analyse. 1998.

Band 30 Oliver Letzgus: Die Ökonomie internationalen Umweltschutzes. 1999.

Band 31 Claudia Hafner: Systemwettbewerb versus Harmonisierung in Europa. Am Beispiel des Arbeitsmarktes. 1999.

Band 32 Jürgen Kulle: Ökonomie der Musikindustrie. Eine Analyse der körperlichen und unkörperlichen Musikverwertung mit Hilfe von Tonträgern und Netzen. 1998.

Band 33 Michael Ganske: Intertemporale Aspekte von Staatsverschuldung und Außenhandel. 1999.

Band 34 Margit Ströbele: Die Deregulierungswirkungen der europäischen Integration. Das Beispiel der Sondermärkte. 1999.

Band 35 Marion Benesch: Devisenmarktinterventionen in Theorie und Praxis. Eine umfassende Analyse ihrer Zielsetzungen, Wirkungsweisen und wirtschaftspolitischen Bedeutung. 1999.

Band 36 Torsten Gruber: Unterschiedliche geldpolitische Transmissionsmechanismen und Stabilitätskulturen als mögliche Ursachen geldpolitischer Spannungen in der Europäischen Währungsunion. 2000.

Band 37 Bertram Melzig-Thiel: Arbeit in der Informationsgesellschaft. Chancen und Risiken neuer Informations- und Kommunikationstechnologien für die Beschäftigung. 2000.

Band 38 Annette Fritz: Die Entsorgungswirtschaft im Spannungsfeld zwischen Abfallpolitik und Kartellrecht. Eine industrieökonomische Branchenstudie. 2001.

Band 39 Harald Strotmann: Arbeitsplatzdynamik in der baden-württembergischen Industrie. Eine Analyse mit amtlichen Betriebspaneldaten. 2002.

Band 40 Dietrich Benner: Qualitätsungewißheit bei Gütern mit Vertrauenseigenschaften. Entwicklung und Anwendung eines entscheidungstheoretisch fundierten Analyserahmens. 2002.

Band 41 Jürgen M. Schechler: Sozialkapital und Netzwerkökonomik. 2002.

Band 42 Kay-Uwe May: Haushaltskonsolidierung durch Ausgabekürzungen. Restriktionen und Strategien. 2002.

Band 43 Peter Kühnl: Der Wechselkurs als Zwischenziel der Geldpolitik im Aufholprozess. Die monetärkeynesianische Entwicklungsstrategie der Berliner Schule vor dem Hintergrund der makroökonomischen Entwicklung ausgewählter Länder Mittel- und Osteuropas. 2003.

Band 44 Steffen Wirth: Nichtparametrische Analyse von Bildungsertragsraten. Neuere Entwicklungen und Anwendungen. 2003.

Band 45 Bernhard Holwegler: Innovation, Diffusion und Beschäftigung. Die ökonomische Theorie der Technologiediffusion und ihr Beitrag zur Erklärung technologischer Arbeitslosigkeit. 2003.

Band 46 Guntram R. M. Hepperle: Zukunftsorientierte Industriepolitik. Möglichkeiten und Grenzen. 2004.

Band 47 Udo Vullhorst: Stabilisierungspolitik bei supranationaler Geldpolitik und nationaler Fiskalpolitik. Eine spieltheoretische Betrachung. 2004.

Band 48 Matthias Rösch: Die Bedeutung von Investivlöhnen und Gewinnbeteiligungen für Einkommensverteilung und Beschäftigung. 2004.

Band 49 Michael Bubik: Erfolgskriterien für Unternehmenszusammenschlüsse. Eine theoretische und exemplarische Analyse. 2005.

Band 50 Jörg Weltin: Internationale Unternehmensbesteuerung. Allokation der Besteuerungsrechte unter veränderten Rahmenbedingungen. 2005.

Band 51 Susanne Reichart: Zum Konvergenzprozess der mittel- und osteuropäischen EU-Beitrittsländer. 2005.

Band 52 Daniel Hartmann: Geldpolitik und Beschäftigung. Die geldpolitische Strategie der Federal Reserve: Vorbild oder Auslaufmodell? 2005.

Band 53 Marc Peter Radke: Explaining Financial Crises. A Cyclical Approach. 2005.

Band 54 Katja Hölsch: Umverteilungseffekte in Europa. Eine Analyse für ausgewählte Länder. 2006.

Band 55 Ulrike Lehr: Contingent Valuation Daten und Bayes'sche Verfahren. Ein Vorschlag zur Verbesserung von Umweltbewertung und Nutzentransfer. 2006.

Band 56 Jutta Maute: Hyperinflation, Currency Board, and Bust. The Case of Argentina. 2006.

Band 57 liegt noch nicht vor!

Band 58 Oliver Frör: Rationality Concepts in Environmental Valuation. 2007.

www.peterlang.de

Michael B. Hinner

# Intercultural Application Guide for Work and Studies in the USA

Frankfurt am Main, Berlin, Bern, Bruxelles, New York, Oxford, Wien, 2005.
158 pp.
ISBN 978-3-631-53121-1 · pb. € 17.50*

This application guide explains how one applies for work and studies in the USA, and why typical German application documents and behavior could result in a rejection. While this guide is primarily directed at students, anyone seeking employment in the USA might find useful information and tips in this work. In addition to describing all phases of the entire application process, this guide also presents examples of all application documents – including letters of recommendation, acceptance, and rejection.

*Contents*: The Application Process – The Preliminary Phase – The Application Phase – The Post-Application Phase · The Application Documents – The Resume and the Curriculum Vitae – Letters – Concluding Remarks

www.ingramcontent.com/pod-product-compliance
Ingram Content Group UK Ltd.
Pitfield, Milton Keynes, MK11 3LW, UK
UKHW021842100926
8556IPUK00019B/1011

9 783631 573365